Dark Corner of the Mind

Other books by Anthony Anonimo:

Lord of the Wind

Dark Corner of the Mind

Anthony Anonimo

HenschelHAUS Publishing, Inc.
Milwaukee, Wisconsin

Published by
HenschelHAUS Publishing, Inc.
www.henschelhausbooks.com

ISBN: 978159598-472-2
E-ISBN: 978159598-473-9
Library of Congress Number: 2016939787

Printed in the United States.

*To all of those who are still suffering and the ones
who have passed from this deadly disease,
especially Bobby P. and Jesse Mechanic Bern*

*And a special thanks to my three children,
Gina, Tony Jr. and Nick,
who woke me up to the fact that I wasn't only hurting myself.*

And to family who never gave up on me.

Prologue

In this story, you'll learn the pitfalls that came with what looked to be a short jaunt into the beautiful poppy fields. A onetime experience of what many will say is the ultimate pleasure. But what came with my pursuit of pleasure and excitement was a WAR ZONE and the mother of all battles.

For me, my drug addiction was a battle that ensued in a dark corner of my mind. This was a part of my mind that was my secret corner and my sanctuary from the outside world, the place in my head where my committee, which I refer to as the insane voices of reason in my head, would convene and decipher my thoughts. It also decided my self-worth. The dark corner of my mind, as I see it, was a battle zone.

The committee seemed to make the decisions about who I really was, what I wanted, and what I needed. And it always seemed to seek pleasure and drown out rational thoughts and feelings. It was like a black hole, where one taste of pleasure was always too much, opening a floodgate, and after that a thousand was never enough. It's just that simple. Or in my case, it was just that complex.

CHAPTER ONE

From the Beginning

As I write this story, I sit and wonder who may even comprehend the degree of insanity this story conveys. I will do my best to explain the story from the beginning, with my first recognition and awakening. This is the true account of my life through my childhood, years of hell and complete insanity, to points just short of death.

I was the fifth of seven children. My father was a first generation Italian American, born and raised in Kenosha, Wisconsin. He grew up working at a very young age. As he would tell us, "I was shoveling horse shit while I was still in diapers." Well, I knew he was old, but horses and buggies? He was the kind of a guy who always had an old joke to tell, and he repeated them over and over. "Any man a hundred pounds or less, I'll tear him apart." And: "I'm so mad I'm ready to jump out the basement window."

My mother was first-generation Canadian, born and raised in Medicine Hat, Alberta, Canada. She was a typical hardworking mother and an ex-army nurse. She claimed that in her younger days she had walked seven miles to and from school every day. She said there were mountain lions waiting to pounce on her and her brother. After her beating me with a wooden spoon I would think to myself, "Where the hell is that mountain lion when I need it? I wish he had eaten her!" OK, now I really did not wish that. But, maybe a good bite in the ass would have been sufficient.

My mother and father were probably very unlikely to meet under normal circumstances After finishing high school, my father moved to Phoenix, Arizona for a period of time. Doctors had advised him that a warm, dry climate would be good for some ongoing sinus issues he had.

He worked for the Arizona Biltmore Hotel, and we were regaled with stories of how hard he worked there. (One thing my parents did instill in us was a good work ethic.) And he probably worked just as hard as he said. The guy was a dynamo with a very strong type 'A' personality. After his Arizona years, my father joined the United States Army. He made Second Lieutenant.

After moving from Canada to Seattle, my mother went to nursing school. From there, she joined the United States Army. She eventually became a First Lieutenant. It was in California, at an Officers' dance on the base, that Alex and Catherine met. But the communion of the two didn't go far at that time because of the Japanese invasion in the Philippine Islands. Alex was a heavy artillery specialist and a Judo instructor, which made him useful in the Philippines, so he was shipped there shortly after he and Catherine met.

Alex and Catherine stayed in touch via the US Army mail. Eventually Catherine was shipped off to the Philippines where there was a need for nurses and other medical staff as the fighting on the island escalated. It was in Manila that my mother and father hooked back up. And so commenced the story of Alex and Catherine. At the end of World War II, they wedded in Manila on October 31, 1945 and returned to the states. Our family and friends knew it as 'The Thriller in Manila,' not to be confused with the Joe Frazier vs. Mohammed Ali fight. My father said they stole his thunder.

My mother was the first to bring her mate home to Seattle to meet her family. Here she was bringing home an Army officer, a dark-skinned Italian. It was accepted but left her family scratching their heads.

Then it was off to my father's hometown of Kenosha, Wisconsin. I understand this was not as welcoming a reception. My father brought home a white woman, with very light skin. And she didn't speak Italian. Now you need to understand that my Nonu and Nona (grandpa and grandma) didn't speak English. And Alex's brothers and sister just didn't date outside of the Italian heritage. He had brought home a *persona Americano* (an American person).

My father's family, 'The Kenosha Sicilian Clan' as our relatives were known, was not well accepted in those days. There were many areas of Kenosha where Italian Americans were not allowed. Those were interesting times in our wonderful country, for sure! However, as Alex and Catherine's history would have it, they endured, and all seemed good.

That is, on the surface. A happy couple, a good Catholic family, having children one after the other, life was pleasant. My mother kept up her nursing license, and my father got a job in the Pabst Brewery in Milwaukee. Alex also attended Marquette University, studying dentistry; he subsequently had a change of heart and switched to business administration. Alex was all business anyway, so this made sense. For some reason, my father began to drink a bit more. This was a man who never really drank through his teen years, or into his twenties, and not even during World War II. As an Italian child he had been served wine at dinner, but that is their custom.

The Early Days

My life began on a warm day in the middle of June in 1955, at Milwaukee's St. Mary's Hospital located at the lakefront on the Hill. I was the fifth child born to Alex and Catherine, and the second boy. From what I understand, I was named Michael at the time of birth, but my name was changed to Anthony at the suggestion of a Catholic nun. She felt it would be appropriate as my birth date was the day of the feast of St. Anthony of Padua, from Italy. St. Anthony is the patron saint of miracles and of lost things.

My welcome home began with my older brother who was extremely excited to have a little brother. He wanted a new playmate as he was the sole boy at the time, with three sisters. I heard of the day my parents brought me home from the hospital. My brother, who had been anxiously awaiting my arrival, looked at me and said, "Take him back! He's too small!" A hell of a welcome. This guy wanted to play, and he wanted to play now. But I just wasn't going to cut it for him! Looking back, I think we all may have all benefited if they had taken me back and dropped me at the nun's house.

Some of my first memories were of my mother pushing me in a stroller. She took me for walks around our neighborhood and down a path by a place called Lincoln Creek Parkway. My mother pointed out birds to me. I remember the sun shining, birds chirping, and the sound of the water flowing over the rocks down the creek. It was peaceful, yet exciting. My mother was, and still is, something of a bird watcher. She bought me a book about birds at a young age, probably because of the look on my face when I'd see one. I was fascinated by these colorful things just spreading their wings and flying freely while making music.

Back at home my brother and I would play with plastic army soldiers. His lineup always had a few standing at the end of our wars, with him being the winner, of course. I learned at an early age that the only way to beat this guy was to get mad and knock all his soldiers down with a swoop of my hand. But then I'd pay the price! He would hold me down and tease me. It's just what brothers do, I guess. Our sisters were playing with cut out dolls and coloring with our mother, while my brother and I were waging war! Our afternoons ended with our father making his grand appearance from work. Dinner was coming soon.

When my father came home from work in those days, after stopping for drinks, he was an absolute showman. He would sing Italian songs and hand out money. Now what kid wouldn't enjoy a dad like this? But my mother didn't always find it so amusing. Apparently he had been hitting telephone poles and garages, and driving into storefront windows with the company car. I thought, "What's the problem? They can all be fixed, and he wasn't hurt." To my mother he would say, "Don't worry, Cath, in ninety-nine years, you'll never know the difference." I thought—what a freaking genius!

The Boss

As time passed, there was a lot of debris left behind: cracked and broken boards on our garage, tilted telephone poles with my father's car paint on them, tire marks on lawns. There were calls from the police, asking if someone in our household could stop up to the local bar and drive Alex's car home. Alex knew a lot of people, being the active, outgoing man that he was. And quite a few police officers also knew Alex, whether it was through one of their friends, relatives, or some bar owner. This man was 'personality plus,' and people just loved him.

I remember the summer days, while I was playing out in front of our house with my friend Stevie. I would see my father's company car pull up to the front curb. I would look up and see this man, who stood about six feet tall, broad shoulders, and dressed to kill. He could very well have been mistaken for a Mafia boss. My father wore the best looking suits with Allen Edmonds wingtip shoes and his black hair slicked back this guy looked sharp, always. As my father walked toward Stevie and me, all we could do was stare. His every step was impressive, crunching the small pebbles that lay on the sidewalk. I will never forget the feeling of thinking he was God himself. What an entrance! The guy had a knack of making his presence known, and he wasn't even trying. That was just who he was.

When he entered the house, he would kiss my mother and ask how her day was. There were many nice things that man did, and he taught us by example. But then again, there were those other things that probably were not so admirable.

After his grand appearance and the kind greeting to my mother, he would go to his room. Ten or fifteen minutes later, he came out in his boxer shorts, knee-high black silk socks, slippers, and a T-shirt. He then grabbed a big cigar, lay on the couch with the afternoon newspaper, placed his ashtray on the floor, and asked who wanted to light his cigar. I thought it was so cool. I wasn't crazy about the cigar smell, though it sure beat the hell out the cigarette smell that flooded some of our neighbors' houses. But what an honor, lighting a match for the boss. He would puff that big old cigar like it was his reward for a hard day's work.

Dinner Time

My father's next move was from the couch to the kitchen when my mother told us it was time to eat. She cooked day in, day out—happy, sad, sick, or well, she cooked. It was just what she did, every day, for the boss and seven crazy Italian kids.

The dinner menu was set in stone. For Monday, dinner was round steak, which my mother pounded with a tenderizing hammer for what seemed like hours. Tuesday was pot roast. Wednesday was meatloaf. Each of these meals came with some canned vegetable shit I had to force down unless I could get our dog, Peppy, to come under the table for the handoff. But there was always someone watching and wanting to make sure I didn't succeed. Of course my rat sisters had my health in mind when they said "Peppy is under the table," while looking directly at me. WTF? I was willing to share Peppy. But I think they just loved seeing me get pinched. And by 'pinched' I don't mean getting caught. When I got pinched, it was a literal pinch from my father, who always sat at the head of the table, directly next to me.

Now Thursday was fantastic because my mother made spaghetti. She used my Nona's recipe, old-school Calabrese style. The sauce was out of this world—spicy, sweet, and tangy. There was always some weird meat cooked in with it, usually ox tail—the Southern Italian peasant way. Whatever it was she used, each week seemed to be better than the next. And none of that damned canned vegetable shit—just the pasta, Italian bread, and a salad, which we ate after the main dish.

On Friday, it was fish sticks and Kool-Aid. They were both new on the market. Saturday meals were leftover spaghetti or homemade pizza. On Fridays and Saturdays, it was just usually my mother and the seven kids. I believe my father was working those nights. He had a part-time job bar tending at the Blue Dahlia, located near Milwaukee County Stadium. With him being gone, I didn't have to worry about getting pinched.

Sunday's were always a special day. My parents and all of us seven kids would cram in my father's company station wagon and go to church. As good Catholics, that is what you do. After church let out, we all climbed back into the station wagon and waited for my father to light a cigar. I remember watching the smoke bellow throughout the car. Sometimes he would blow us some smoke rings. What a guy. Then we went to Capital Court shopping center, the only shopping mall in Milwaukee in those days. Those trips were my mother's idea; she wanted to window shop. We stayed until my mother was done looking—that was the deal.

Next we stopped at the A&P grocery store, and my father bought hot sliced ham and fresh rolls. There was the occasional stop at the produce department, where my father would purchase a watermelon when they were in season. Then we headed for the meat department, where my father would search through the sirloin steaks. If there was a butcher on duty, he was summoned. My father would ask for a fresh piece of sirloin cut, and if the guy said "It's all out on the floor," he'd receive a few cuss words in Italian, and we'd be on our way.

Finally, we'd get back to the house, and eat our ham and rolls. Then it would be time for some whiffle ball. What a waste of time, this church thing, the window shopping, and the store. After all, it was about me. These people had no clue of what was important in life. Perhaps they should have played a couple innings of whiffle ball. Then they'd see.

Sunday evenings were scheduled for my father to cook. He'd put on an apron, get the broiler heated up, and throw on the sirloin steak. Every six weeks or so, he would make lamb chops. Whether it was sirloin or lamb chops, it was always good. Sunday was my mother's day of rest. Not real sure why she needed it; there were only seven kids. Our neighbors had twelve kids, so what the hell? OK . . . I am kidding!

Rocks in His Head

I do remember some of my mother's sayings, things like "Hell's bells" and "You are so ungrateful." And we were. Looking back, all seven of us were ungrateful brats. My mother never swore. Not a swear word in this woman's vocabulary, ever. But she did wield a mean-ass wooden spoon. Shit, when she went to the drawer, and her hand was on the spoon, it menat one thing—run! It was like a horror movie, and she was the monster. But, if it was one of the other kids she pulled it on, I ran to watch. That was great!

As Michael Corleone would say, "Keep your friends close, but your enemies closer." I think I lived that creed as a kid. With seven Italian kids in the same household, you knew there was going to be some trouble. And you also knew there were going to be rats. We all had to have dirt on as many siblings as we could. It's called leverage. If one of the other kids tried to rat on you, you dropped the atomic bomb on them. Spilled your guts. It diffused the dirt they had or at least lessened the blow.

Back in those days, my brother had a longing for collecting rocks. He was always surveying for different type of rocks, whether we were walking our dog by Lincoln Creek, on the way to our paper route, or just digging around in our backyard. When he saved up his allowance, or gathered our paper route earnings, he'd ask our mom if he and I could go to the museum. He wanted to look at and buy some rocks.

With permission to take the bus downtown, we would walk up to the bus stop for the twenty-minute bus ride. These bus rides were a highlight of my day. There was a man named Michael who lived in Parklawn, and we knew him fairly well. We knew there was something different about him, not at all dangerous, just odd. A very pleasant guy, from a very nice family, we knew.

Michael was a tall black gentleman, about 6foot 3 and around 170 pounds soaking wet. Michael would almost always greet us at the bus stop. He'd tell my brother he was going to race us downtown. This guy would wait for the bus to come by. And, as soon as we left, he'd begin to run alongside the bus. Michael would run past the bus, waving all along the way, for almost six miles. Now the bus would make regular stops, but I was amazed at the speed this guy could run. In his high school years, Michael had broken many track records in practice. However, he apparently was kept out of track meets due to his mental health. What a shame!

Always Smarter

My brother used his head. He wouldn't blow a gasket in front of our parents, as I would, instead playing very meek and mild. When they weren't in the room, the gloves were off. This prick would tease the shit out of me. Knowing my predictable disposition, he would taunt me until I blew. When I attacked, he not only had probable cause, he had dirt on me! How freaking genius! When I came at him he'd throw me to the ground, pin me with his knees on my arms, and say, "Kiss my muscle" (his bicep). It was humiliating. My only counterattack in the pinned position was to spit at him. I learned quickly that would only aggravate things.

If my mother or father walked into the room while this was going on, guess who the culprit was—me. They knew my explosiveness, and my brother would say, "He came after me." I would have to sit on the couch without moving as punishment. There was a lot of planning going on in my head because my brother needed to pay, and that was the bottom line. And of course, my brother didn't sit idle. He was always smarter. He seemed to anticipate my planning, and always had a comeback to every move I made. I realized any attempt to get him in trouble was futile.

I always had to be on guard. We had bunk beds. At bedtime, we both retired to our spots, Alex on the top bunk, and me on the bottom. Alex would say, "Tony, you know what? Grandpa Sicilia is under your bed, and he's going to grab your feet. As soon as you're almost asleep, he'll reach out and grab them!" I tried to ignore this but I'd look up at the big, bronze crucifix on our bedroom wall and imagine that it might happen. The crucifix had been on our Grandpa Sicilia's coffin. He had died a few years earlier. I always did feel strange seeing that thing on our bedroom wall. I tucked my bedsheets under my feet and slept in a fetal position, just in case I felt a hand come from under the bed.

My First Recollection of Mortality

July 10, 1961, was a wonderful summer morning in Milwaukee, Wisconsin, with the sun shining brightly, about eighty degrees, and very low humidity. I had just turned six years old a few weeks before, and on my birthday, I received a load of baseball card packages, each with five cards and a delicious piece of bubble gum. Though I loved the gum, my ultimate desire was to get some of the Braves players' cards. In particular, I was determined to get Hank Aaron. I would do anything I could in order to earn money to buy those cards.

My brother Alex and I did chores like sweeping the shed and the garage, picking up dog crap, and the worst job of all, picking up gum wrappers. Our father used to stand at the kitchen picture window, supervising our every move. He would point out every gum wrapper with his finger, motioning with the nodding of his head. He could see every damn one, even if it was an inch underground. I despised him for his thoroughness. But at the end of all the chores, we received a dime (worth two packs of baseball cards) or, if it was a great day of work, a whole quarter (five packs of baseball cards!).

Now, my brother Alex was always smarter than me and wise beyond his years when it came to money. He saved his. What a concept. Four years older than me, he may have had the edge due to his age. But shit, I never saw the point in saving money! "For what?" I thought, "There are freaking baseball cards left in Eddie's truck!" And I would be damned to see someone else get Hammering Hank Aaron. I knew he was in one of those packs, and if I wasted one damn nickel on anything else, my odds of getting Hank would be hindered. There was no room for moderation; that seemed to be a theme throughout my life.

Stevie, my best friend growing up, told me he got an Eddie Matthews card on that day. I remember being excited and a bit anxious, knowing that Hank Aaron may still be in one of those boxes of baseball cards in Eddie's truck. Eddie came once or twice a day. His usual stop was on North 47th Street in front of Parklawn, a housing development for returning World War II veterans and lower-income families. Eddie pulled up in his produce truck with fruit, vegetables, other food, and those all-important baseball cards. It was a very convenient thing for so many people. And it worked very well for Eddie, too.

Hell, I could have walked into the truck blindfolded, and told you exactly where the baseball cards were. The truck smelled like fruit and vegetables, but it was those damned baseball card packs, with the smell of the bubblegum, that I homed in on. After Stevie informed me of his Eddie Matthews jackpot hit, I was determined to make this the day that

Hammering Hank entered my possession. There was no tomorrow. This was it.

That day, July 10, 1961, is a day that went down in history for me. It was the day to get Hank. When I look back, I think I may have been a bit excessive, a bit impulsive, or just plain possessed. Yes, maybe all of the above. I was one f***ed up kid, but had no clue then. Shit, my parents had no clue of what went on inside that treacherous head of mine. There were seven of us to keep track of.

So, after Stevie's visit to tell me about Eddie Matthews, I was bound and determined to get the hell out there and get Hank. I remember digging in my pocket for at least a nickel, which I knew damned well I didn't have. Why would I have anything? Yesterday was the day I was going to acquire Hank. Why would I have a nickel today?

Well, here was the matter of my needing some coin. And as I thought about my needing at least a nickel, there was my solution, right in front of me! It was my brother's coin collection. He always collected coins, as well as rocks. He had a threefold blue book with round slots for each year minted according to the type of coin. There was his Mercury Head dime collection book. I remember thinking, "Shit, one of those is two packs of baseball cards, and I could double my chances of getting Hank Aaron."

OK, now I saw that he had doubles on some of the dimes. So I took the plunge. I stole one. Holy shit, I did it. There were so many thoughts going through my mind. First was Catholic guilt. Well, that was bad, but it didn't make me put it back. Second, this is Alex, the prick who had tortured me from the time I came home from the maternity ward.

With that shiny Mercury Head dime in my pocket, off I went. As I ran across the back yard and the alley to cut through Steve's yard, all I had was about fifty yards to Eddie's truck. When I got through the yard, I looked up the block, and there it was, Eddie's truck, with people lined up to buy stuff. I ran in between two parked cars to cross the street, and there was a loud screech of car tires. Suddenly there I was, lying under a car. Looking up, all I could see was the underside of a big car.

In the early sixties, cars were still pretty big, and from the underside, this one looked huge. My elbow was bleeding, and it hurt. My initial thought was, "Where is the dime?" What else would somebody think about after being hit by a car? I realize I may have had some screwed-up priorities. I was probably wired a bit differently than the normal human being. When I saw the dime a foot or so away, I grabbed it. Coming somewhat to my senses, I had a horrible feeling of guilt and embarrassment.

I crawled out from under the car and ran about twenty feet, then collapsed to the ground. My breathing was very shallow. It felt as if there was a lead weight on my chest, and I gasped for air. My heart was pounding. My body was crying for oxygen, but I couldn't get any. I felt cold and light headed. Even though it was probably eighty to eighty-five degrees that day, I remember feeling as though I had been put in a freezer. Soon, a crowd of people surrounded me and someone yelled to call an ambulance. One woman called for someone to get a blanket. The next thing I knew, I was being loaded into an ambulance. As the ambulance was leaving the scene, I looked out the window and saw Stevie. All I did was shrug my shoulders, as if to say, "I'm sorry."

I was burdenbed by a dark and heavy cloud of guilt. I felt regret with absolutely no way of rectifying it; there was no way to justify or rationalize what I had done. What played through my head as I lay there gasping for life was my mother's voice. She was crying profusely. I don't know that there is any way of numbing out the sound of a mother's weeping over a child who may die. At the time of the accident, I believe my mother was eight months pregnant. She had learned of my accident from a neighbor's child running to our house and screaming that Tony had been run over by a car.

I know I didn't feel so good, to put it lightly. But, I cannot even imagine what my poor mother went through. I thought to myself, "Look what I have done." All over Hank Aaron. But, in reality, it wasn't about Hank Aaron. It was about Tony—an obsessive, impulsive, and messed-up kid.

I remember the ride to the hospital, though I think I went in and out of consciousness. We were headed to Milwaukee County Hospital. The ride down Wisconsin Avenue looked so sunny. It seemed so very long, like I was on a gravel road to heaven. Or, in my case, probably headed for purgatory.

I thought that this was the end. I was going to die. But there was a feeling of peace also. My mother sat beside the stretcher I was lying on, her hand holding mine. She felt so warm and caring. I had her alone. Her gaze was one of love and compassion toward me. I felt that there could not be a better way to go—unless, of course, I had that damned Hank Aaron card in my pocket.

As we pulled into the hospital's emergency room, I remember a doctor approaching us. A man was yelling for help. I learned later that he had been shot in the arm. The doctor told the man he wasn't going to die and that he was going to have to wait.

The doctor took me, along with my mother, to a room. I remember him pulling out a huge syringe with a very long needle. As he stood over me, he said, "I want you to be very brave. Can you do that?" He said, "OK, now I want you to hold your mom's hand." Then I saw him take a huge syringe, which he plunged into my stomach. He drew back the plunger of the syringe, and nothing happened. He then pierced me again, and I remember seeing dark red blood flowing into the tube. He did it a third time, and again, blood flowed up into the large tube. The doctor said, "He's bleeding internally." Then a nurse approached with a small syringe and injected my arm.

My next memory was a unique experience. My mother said she wanted a priest with me. She wanted me blessed. As I lay on the hospital bed, I had the strangest experience of my life. It was as if I were floating at the ceiling, looking down. I remember seeing the top of an old man's head. His hair was gray and partially balding. He was standing over a little boy, blessing him, and anointing his head with the sign of the cross. The boy was me. Holy shit, this must be some type of out-of-body experience.

The next thing I remember was waking up just off the operating table. I was very groggy, but I remembered the shiny metal table. I woke up again and I was in a bed. I heard my father's voice, in a gentle tone. I looked up, and there he was, all dressed up in a dark blue suit, holding an entire box of baseball cards. I think it was a carton that held about twenty-five packs of cards. There I was, some twelve hours after I thought for sure I was on my way out of this world. At the time this happened, I honestly did not feel so terribly frightened. In fact, I felt at peace. I may have been too young to fear the loss of my life. Or maybe I just didn't know how very close I had come.

As I came to, I noticed that both my arms were tied to the bars on the hospital bed. Apparently, it was to deter me from pulling at the bandage, which was approximately twelve-by-twelve inches and covered my stomach. My spleen had been removed. It had been forced into my rib cage and damaged, causing the internal bleeding.

With my father standing there in front of me, I asked if I could hold the box of baseball cards. I had to promise the nurse that I wouldn't remove the bandage or touch the scar area. So, she kindly untied my arms, and I immediately reached for the cards. My father, with a big smile on his face, handed the box over to me. I couldn't wait to open each and every pack of cards as fast as I could.

As I opened the first few packs, I stuffed the bubble gum sticks into my mouth. My father softly advised me to slow down and that they were not going to go anywhere.

"They're yours to keep," he said with a gentle grin, and reminded me I would have plenty of time to open them all. I made sure that I opened each pack of cards, frantically searching each pack for Hank Aaron. Well, no Hammering Hank in any of those boxes. I went from being elated to thinking, "Oh, what the heck."

My Operation

About two weeks later, I was released from the hospital. The directions from my doctor upon my release were no lifting, no running, no fighting, and not to touch the bandage or stitches in my stomach area. Of course not! The first thing I did when I got home was to get reacquainted with my baseball cards—and tear off the top part of the bandage. I had no idea what stitches were. They said they were made with cat guts? WTF? I was very curious what the stitches looked like. I fiddled with a few of them, but no real damage was done.

Then I had to test how strong they were. I saw my mother rearranging the living room, and I insisted on helping. She told me to stop, but I proceeded to help her push our big couch. I felt the stitches tear into my skin a bit. To this day, I can see where I stretched it pretty good. All the whiffle ball and fighting with my brother didn't help those scars either. Whenever my brother messed with me around that time, all I had to do was say that he hurt my wound. Finally, I had some good ammo to use against him.

The fallout from this incident had not yet completely manifested itself. On July 23, thirteen days after my accident, my mother gave birth to my sister. Elizabeth Ann was stillborn. My mother had just returned home from the hospital, and I was sitting in my room, taking it easy for a change. All the other kids were out with friends, playing around the neighborhood. My mother was in a somber mood. She and my father were in their bedroom, across the hall. I heard their conversation, and my father saying, "Do they know what caused the complications?" My mother responded with, "It could have been from the shock of the accident."

Apparently, upon finding me lying on the ground with a crowd over me, my mother went into shock. My vision of a person in shock was that of someone incapacitated: eyes wide open, hair standing on end, frozen—a kid's impression from watching cartoons. The reality is, I believe, that there are probably degrees of human emotional shock. I can only imagine a mother's initial reaction to her six-year-old being run over. Outside, looking in, the thought sickens me.

The series of events that had transpired over a two- or three-week period was devastating to say the least. I had violated my morals, and God, by stealing from my brother, which was bad enough. Then, through the chain reaction of travesties caused by my poor decision making, here was my poor innocent little sister, lying in a morgue. Some poor man would have to live the rest of his life with the memory of hitting a six-year-old kid while driving down the road. And my mother, mourning the loss of her baby. Not to mention the thought of almost losing her youngest son.

Did my mother have feelings of guilt? She may have been thinking of what she should have done differently in the way of teaching me not to cross the street without an adult, or at least, to use a crosswalk. I had never been told not to cross streets between cars, seeing that I was not even tall enough to see over the hood of a car.

So, there was a lot of guilt flying around back then. But I knew who actually owned that guilt, and it was me. Yes, I was six years old. And yes, my errors might have been excused due to youth. Nevertheless, the fault was mine, and I was living with a big, dark secret.

My parents had my sister blessed, and there was a small funeral service with my sister laid out in a baby-sized white casket. I remember wanting to attend the service. Looking back, I am not sure what my motivation was in wanting to go. Guilt, compassion, pity, or just plain curiosity? But, I was not allowed to go. Would I make the same decision for my own child today, given similar circumstances? There is plenty of time to go to funerals as we age—this I learned as the years went gone by.

Life After Death

Time passes and life goes on, no matter who leaves this world. Our family life continued, much in the way I described earlier. The dinners, whiffle ball with Stevie, fighting with my siblings. However, the runs to Eddie's truck for baseball cards were very different. I was extremely hesitant to even walk near the scene of my accident. I had to cross with my brother or older sister at the corner instead of the middle of the block. One day, my brother escorted me to buy some more baseball cards, and he said he would pay for my two packs. The poor SOB didn't miss that dime I stole. He never said a word, and I sure as shit wasn't going to admit it. It was all part of my big secret. And that was the way it needed to remain.

Through the years following the accident, I had recurring nightmares. I would see some sort of huge wave of something I still cannot identify. It wasn't a car, it wasn't water, it was just a thing. A thing that was ready to consume me by rolling over me, like a huge swell of mud. And each time the dream came, a physical feeling came with it. I heard what I can only describe as constant buzzing. It was similar to a mild, pulsating electrical shock. Whatever the hell these dreams were, they were very scary to me at the time. I would wake up with a horrible feeling of suffocation. They went on for years, though they gradually diminished over time.

Brotherhood

Meanwhile, in my waking life, my constant battles with my brother continued, business as usual. The battle in my mind continued to haunt me, and I now seemed to feel I deserved his punishment. Yet, I was still out for revenge on this prick. Whenever we fought, he would still win. But I was getting closer to getting back at him. I would make sure we were in closer range to my mother or father when I fought back. And then I could say that I was going to tell Mom or Dad, and hope they'd hear it. My brother was about ten or eleven years old, and I was about seven when I remember us playing army in our basement. He said to me, "Tony, if you tell Mom or Dad, I'm going to have to tell them about the pictures of the naked ladies."

I was shocked. I remember thinking to myself, "Where the hell did this come from? What the hell was he talking about?" I had never, ever, had any pictures of naked ladies. In fact, the best I could ever get were the Sears or JC Penney's catalogs, in the pages with bras and panties. Then I thought to myself, "How the hell did he know I had even thought of naked ladies?" Was the asshole listening to me talking in my sleep? Well, either way, there was no way I could rat on him now. To risk him even saying something like that to my mother would be devastating to me. Especially with the Catholic guilt thing added to my plate. Instead, I had to just walk away.

But then I realized he probably had some of those naked pictures he was talking about. I never knew that pictures of naked ladies, not just images in my mind, even existed! I kind of wanted to see them. I investigated, digging through his drawers, under his bed, in the garage, and any place I could think of, to no avail. I was stuck with the Sears and JC Penney's bra pages.

Let the Good Times Roll

Well, it was at about the time I turned nine years old that something literally sobering happened in our household. My father's drinking over the previous years had escalated. He did a lot of the same old hitting the telephone poles, scraping the garage, and parking cockeyed. To be honest, I enjoyed much of the entertainment. Some of the events surrounding his drinking were absolutely fantastic, I thought. But then again, I was a naive nine-year-old, blind to the path of destruction that his actions were leaving behind.

One of the most vivid stories I recall was when my father had called to notify my mother he may be home late from work. My mother's response did not sound very kind. I remember her telling him, "Alex, don't forget that we need milk! The kids need milk for cereal in the morning."

This was a weeknight in the middle of November. A blizzard had already laid down about eight to ten inches of snow. All seven kids, from ages five to sixteen, were in the house with Mom. Most of us were in the front room, keeping a lookout for my father. It was about 7:30 pm when he pulled up. His car was halfway up the curb, with the front end of the car facing toward the middle of the road. Out of the car came my father, staggering. He stumbled to the back of the station wagon, swung open the door, gathered his groceries, and attempted to make his way to the house. We watched in amazement. He was carrying several big boxes, staggering and falling in the snow. There were fifteen boxes in all. Fifteen boxes of cereal, and no milk.

My brother and I thought it was hilarious! She asks for milk, and he brings fifteen boxes of cereal! Our mom was furious, yelling out the door at my father. "Alex, Hell's bells, what is the matter with you?! I said milk. We needed milk!"

And my father responded with his classic remark, "Don't worry, Cath. In ninety-nine years, nobody will know the difference."

My mother yelled for my brother to go outside and help him in. At the time, I didn't understand why my mother was snuffing out the fun. The next morning, my brother and I found at least seven boxes of cereal strewn across the yard, in the snow. We had enough cereal for a while.

My next memory is another story for the ages. My father was a district sales manager for a Wisconsin brewery. Part of his job involved meeting with bar owners, and that usually meant drinking with them. While he was out working late one evening, making his rounds, he met a patron at one of the local pubs. This guy was giving away a spider monkey, cage and all. Apparently my father thought it would be great to have this monkey. He bought it and brought it home. All of us kids were sleeping, from what I understand. My mother insisted that he take it back.

The next morning, it was a topic of discussion. We had heard about the incident through our parents' discussion about his drinking. The monkey business came to light, and my brother and I were intrigued to say the least. We wanted to know why we were not able to have the monkey. Our mother just gave us an emphatic denial. "We are not going to have a monkey in this house." She said they were dirty and carried diseases. "Forget about the diseases," I thought, "I want that monkey!" But, it was not to be.

About a month later, my father came home late from working his rounds. He came in carrying a big box. Inside the box was a little white puppy. It was cute as hell, as are most puppies. That is how we got our dog, Peppy. Peppy become our family pet and consumed our family's attention for some time. It was not a monkey, but it was the next best thing, and probably a better option. Our mother, who did not like the idea of having an animal living in a house, accepted Peppy just the same.

Looking back, it's easy to see the wreckage my father's drinking was leaving. We had been receiving calls from bar owners, asking that someone come to the bar and get him. At these times, he was so drunk he couldn't even walk. I remember my mother asking my brother to drive my father's car home from a neighborhood bar. He wasn't old enough to drive legally, but he handled it well.

You see, my brother always had a paper route, and I was his permanent helper. When we did our Sunday morning route, our father assisted by loading the newspapers in the back of his station wagon. My brother and I would take as many as we could handle, deliver them, and come back for more. When we completed the route, about three or four o'clock in the morning, our father would take us to the Capitol Court shopping center parking lot. The lot was empty at that time of the morning, perfect for driving lessons. My brother was always very teachable.

With my father spending more and more time working late and drinking, my mother's temper grew more ominous. I remember her mood changing over time. It was as though she was lost. I could tell she seemed to have something in the back of her mind all of the time, and she flew off the handle much more quickly.

One night, my father had been out very late, later than his normal late nights. The following day, he was up at his usual 6:00 or 6:30 am and off to work. At about ten in the morning, there was a knock at the front door. Two police officers stood there with my father between them, each one holding an arm. My father was slouching forward, his face and nice white, starched shirt was covered with blood. His nose looked broken, and his hands were bloody. My mother and I reached out to help the police officers bring him into the house.

We guided the police officers to my parents' room, where they laid my father down, resting his head on a pillow my mother had covered with a towel. The policemen guided me out of the bedroom, and I clearly remember my mother's anguish. Before the officers left, they took her aside and spoke with her in confidence. Apparently, my father had gone to a local bar as soon as he got up. Upon leaving the bar, he had been so drunk that he fell flat on his face. His normal reflex just didn't work to brace his fall. One of the police officers had apparently known my father for many years, through his own dad. I remember being almost in shock and sick to my stomach, I thought for sure my father was either dead or was going to die.

In retrospect, there were quite a few times that I recall my father's drinking had been getting way out of hand, and our family dynamic had slowly but surely turned into a train wreck. And I don't think anyone even realized it.

My God

After much pressure from my mother and my father's boss, my father realized his drinking was a problem. He was admitted into a hospital to dry out. I remember going with my mother to visit him. Here was this indestructible dynamo, my entertainer, my hero, and my rock, lying in a hospital gown with a somber look on his face. I felt lost.

My father was a changed man. Life was very different now. It seemed so quiet around our house compared to the old days. I really missed the way it used to be. My mother seemed to be less agitated. She appeared to be very empathetic and kind with my father. Over the previous couple years, it seemed as though she had slowly become cold and depressed. And now, she was different. Our house was more subdued, but it seemed as though our family's internal dysfunction had not changed. There was still fighting between my sisters. And my brother and I still had our occasional scuffles. The dynamics seemed more evident when the house was without our star actor, Alex.

My father returned to work, though his evening hours were shorter than they had been. And when he came home, we were back to our same old dinners. Only now, my father attended them pretty consistently. For a couple of years prior to that, he had been missing dinner two or three nights a week.

The thing that was different now was that my father would leave for an hour or two after dinner each night. When we asked our mom where he was going, she simply said he was at a meeting. My brother and I figured that these were not your everyday work meetings. We knew what was going on. He was mobbed up. He was going to meetings, and wouldn't talk about them, saying only that he had to go see a friend. We knew what the heck was going on!

My sobering experience came one Saturday morning. It was just after breakfast. I was going to find my father to see if I could make a quarter doing chores. As I walked into my parent's room, I saw something that shocked me and put butterflies in my stomach. It was my father, kneeling at the end of his bed. He was praying! The guy I looked at as my god was on his knees praying. It really caught me off guard. Even though I was feeling let down toward my father, it reinforced my own faith.

CHAPTER TWO

Moving On With Life

As time went on, friends came and went. After Stevie N. left St. Stephen's to attend a different school, we drifted apart. So, I began to spend more time with my friend Billy Biggie, who lived across the street from our house. Billy was the youngest of three children. His parents were a funny couple. They were laid back and kind people.

And, there was my other friend, Barry Jones, a very tall, large-framed black kid. He had the makings of a lineman for about any football team. He lived on the other side of the block in the Parklawn Housing Project with his mother and his grandmother. He and I were very close at one time, and I slept over at his house once. It was the first time I ever slept over at a black person's house. In fact, I had never slept over at anyone's house, other than Stevie Newman's.

I recall the first time I ever called a black person the "N" word. Barry and I got into a fight, and the altercation evolved from play fighting to a mean-spirited brawl. Barry was twice my size, and he eventually had me on the ground, hitting me. It was then, as in fights with my brother, the devil came out. Defeat seemingly brought out deep emotions in me—either homicidal or suicidal. In this case, I just blurted out the "N" word.

Barry stopped hitting me and gave me a stare. He was really hurt. I felt terrible! He was a guy I liked and admired. He simply got up off me and said, "Let's go, Tony." I felt as if I had to apologize, but I believe Barry knew without my saying a word. If my father had heard of the incident, he would have surely come down hard on me. The fallout seemed to diminish pretty quickly. Barry and I went on to play marbles and laugh together.

I believe Barry's mother and grandmother were originally from Mississippi. They spoke with a strong Southern that I found difficult to understand. Barry's grandmother, "Grandma Maxim," wore a flowered dress with a scarf on her head. Everything she did was accompanied by humming. Whenever she'd call Barry for anything, he was there in a split second. That guy had more respect for his Grandma Maxim, as well as his mother, than I had ever seen in a man.

That night we ran outside for a while, teasing some neighborhood girls. At dinnertime, we made our way back to his house. This was also my first dinner at Barry's house. I was a pretty picky eater. Before I left home, my mother had admonished me to eat what I was given, like it or not.

Dinner was on the table: cauliflower, biscuits and gravy, and fried chicken. Barry's mother dished out the food. Grandma Maxim, still at the stove humming, glanced over at the table every once in a while. I wasn't quite sure what the look meant, but I sure as hell wasn't going to question it. I'd just look at Barry, and from the expression on his face, I could tell he wondered about my reaction to the food. Of course, he was looking for approval. And perhaps he was self-conscious because he knew his family was very different from mine.

Despite the strict atmosphere, there was a feeling of love and nurturing. But I wondered if I was really welcome. I really didn't know what to expect, and I'm not sure they did either. But I can tell you that Grandma Maxim made the best fried chicken I have ever had in my entire life. As I accepted another piece of chicken from his mother, I noticed that she and Grandma Maxim exchanged a big smile. Shit— maybe these ladies did like me.

After dinner, Barry and I went back out to play football. When we came in the house to go to bed, I remember seeing some religious plaques on the wall. There were two pictures on another wall, one of Martin Luther King Jr. and one of John F. Kennedy. I remember thinking, "Shit, they have a white guy on their wall." I hadn't ever seen a picture of a black guy hanging in a white home.

My Unforgettable Camping Trip

Later in the summer, Barry and I, and my old neighbor, Billy B., decided to take a camping trip. It was 1968, and this would be a trip for my history book! We packed a tent, some cooking utensils, food, and (hidden from our parents) cigarettes into Billy's mother's car. Off we went to a camp ground near a lake, about forty miles north of Milwaukee.

When we arrived, we set up our tent with Mrs. Biggie's assistance. She told us to find a local ranger if we had any problems, and she headed home. We planned a lot of fishing, hiking, and smoking our cigarettes. The campground was pretty full, but there was plenty of room between camps so that we had our space. And we made good use of that space, laughing as loud as we wanted.

In the morning, we made bacon and eggs on the campfire. We then gathered our fishing gear and headed out to the lake. We rented a rowboat, which turned out to be a fun time in itself. Here was big Barry Jones directing us on which way to row. It would be Barry yelling, "Tony, to the left! Billy, to the right!" We were sweating our asses off. And there sat Barry at the front of the boat, all two hundred-plus pounds on his thirteen-year-old frame!

When we returned from fishing, we cooked up a few of the bluegills we had caught and settled in for the night. We roasted marshmallows and smoked cigarettes. On the second day, we repeated our fishing jaunts. I was addicted already. I loved it!

That night, while sitting around the campfire, two girls walked up to our camp. They asked how we were doing and insinuated that they wished to join us. They were pretty girls in their late teens. They had a bottle of wine, and they shared it with us. We passed the bottle around for a while.

The prettier of the two asked me if I would like to kiss her. This embarrassed me, but I agreed that I wanted to. We were kissing by the campfire when Barry escalated this situation. He said, "Tony, go in the tent and show her the sleeping bags." We laughed, but I complied. Next thing I knew, the girl and I had our clothes off, going at it. I was a virgin. I was nervous as shit, but also very excited. The whole time, Barry was outside the tent laughing and egging me on.

It didn't last long, as you may expect. I realized I liked it, and I liked it a lot. But, of course, being the good Catholic boy I was, it came to mind that I was going to have to go to confession. But an additional twenty Hail Mary's wasn't going to stop me from wanting to repeat that experience! It brought me to another world of pleasure. I had now graduated from looking at the Sears or JC Penney's bra and panty sections to the real thing. It was a very unexpected thing, but I wasn't complaining.

Changing Times

I had a history of living life against life's terms, full steam ahead. I had graduated from baseball cards, but I still loved Hammering Hank! Even though the Milwaukee Braves had decided to move to Atlanta, Hank Aaron was still my guy. Losing the Braves to Atlanta was a very depressing thing for me, as it seemed to be for most of Milwaukee.

At this time of my life, about twelve years old, I had a number of options, all very appealing—sports, girls, booze, and drugs. There were so many things going on, both in my personal life and in the outside world. In the evenings, my father would be in his place on the couch, my mother would be cooking dinner. But on TV, something began to change me. It changed my neighborhood makeup. And possibly it changed my father as well. It was Vietnam. Every day after school as I did homework, the news on TV showed the body count. That part always grabbed my attention, especially since a few of our neighbors were being drafted and sent over.

Locally, at that same time, there were the riots in Milwaukee, as well as many other parts of the country. I didn't understand the riots. Why did some of the people riot and some did not? The Parklawn Housing Project had about a 50/50 ratio of black to white folks. No one was rioting here. I remember asking my father what the reason was for the rioting. Did they need free stuff, or what? My father just shrugged, and said some of them might.

He reminded me of the time he cussed out one of our neighbors. Our cousins had come to visit from Kenosha. Some of them were pretty dark-skinned. The neighbor opened his mouth too loud, saying that the Sicilians had niggers at their house. My father confronted him, saying that people are people, some good and some bad. Regardless of color, he said, we all put our pants on one leg at a time. I thought shit, sometimes, when I am in a hurry, I jam both feet into my pant legs simultaneously. But my father's point was well taken.

He had a lot of knowledge, that father of mine—still an asshole when he pinched me, but OK most of the time. Yes, my father knew a lot, but one thing he didn't know was that I was stealing some of his beer and experimenting with marijuana.

Johnny Be Bad

My brother had started earlier down the path of smoking pot and drinking. The attention was on him because he wasn't real good at hiding the fact he was using and drinking. He would come in the house staggering. I then began to be the smarter brother, but smarter at the wrong things. I had tapped the wisdom of Johnny, one of our neighbors. Johnny was wise beyond his years. He prided himself on being a drug dealer and a self-proclaimed gangster. He taught me a protocol to follow after smoking a ton of pot at his house. I needed to air out my clothes, use Visine eye drops, and avoid eye contact. He would say, "Tony! Handle it! Now what are you going to do when you get home? You go in your room! You stay there until you come down, got it?"

At age twelve, I thought this guy was pretty smart. One day I returned home from across the alley, and I heard my father arguing with my brother. The argument was about smoking pot and drinking. I went right to my room, nervous as shit, naturally. I lay on my bed, listening. My brother was slurring and very docile. Then my father took him into the bathroom, right across the hall from my room, and put him in a cold shower, clothes and all. My brother yelled in protest. Of course, I thought this was hilarious. But then I thought, "Shit, am I next?"

Still, apparently my father had no clue I was doing anything other than playing baseball and collecting cards. As for my brother Alex, I guess that shower did the trick. He seemed to have quit that day. He graduated from high school with good grades and then went on to the University of Wisconsin Milwaukee to study geology, making the Dean's list. "What a dick," I thought. He couldn't handle it, is all. He went on to play with his rocks, just like he did as a kid.

As for me, I decided to take a different route. I continued to be Johnny's lackey. He would give me bags of pot and ounces of hash to sell for him. He had me go out to Parklawn Housing Project to find customers. How freaking stupid was I? Yes, that stupid. When I returned with his money, I got to take some of his hash. I remember knowing I was being used. And deep down, I felt it wasn't right. I hated it. But, I had a very hard time saying no to him. By age thirteen I was selling mescaline for him. I didn't even know what the f*** it was. He told me it was something like LSD, but milder.

Apparently, he had other people selling for him. One day, the police picked up an old friend of my brother who was working for Johnny. He had been carrying some mescaline. While he was in the precinct holding cell, he panicked and swallowed all of what he had and died. I remember my father swearing in Italian. He declared that he hoped they caught the people selling it and hung them by their toes outside.

After that, I didn't want to even look at Johnny anymore. I avoided him, despite the guilt trips he laid on me and his bullying tactics. I felt so relieved freeing myself from this guy's grasp. Johnny remained in the neighborhood, but his influence on me and my brother was not the same.

High School Days

My high school career began at John Marshall. I went from a small neighborhood Catholic grade school to the largest public high school in Milwaukee. My five sisters went to Catholic high schools, while my brother and I went to public schools. I guess it was our parents' way of protecting the girls and saving some money at the same time.

In high school, I still had a few friends from St. Stephen's grade school. So, in the beginning, we hung out. We all smoked pot and drank, but I gravitated to pot and hash rather than alcohol. Alcohol always took a toll on me, and I really didn't like the after-effects. It made me feel sick most of the time. We skipped classes occasionally and would hang out in a back alley. It beat the hell out of the classroom. When the absentee slips got handed out for parental signatures, I had that covered. I was always pretty good at forging my mother's signature.

It was around this time that I began to look for jobs. I didn't see being a paperboy as cool anymore. My brother worked at a restaurant, so my search began with area restaurants. In those days, the minimum age for such jobs was fifteen. I went to a place on the east side of Milwaukee called the Brothers Two Steakhouse and Lounge. On the application I wrote that I was fifteen though I wasn't quite fourteen at the time. I wanted this job bad, and it sounded as though the tips could be good.

They had me interview with the hostess. Then she took me into the manager's office. His name was Russ, a middle-aged Sicilian guy, with a raspy voice. He seemed like a no nonsense kind of guy. He looked a lot like Joe Pesci. Russ asked me if I was Irish, and I told him I was Italian. He laughed and said, "With that name, yes, I know you are. I like the name." He proceeded to tell me to show up for work at 4:00 pm on Tuesday of next week.

I had the job! Elated, I went home to tell my father about it. He said that it was great, but asked me how I planned to get there as it was about thirty minutes away by bus. Plus, he insisted that I would need finish my homework before going to work. What homework I did do, I usually did in study halls and not at home, so I was OK with that.

On my first day I filled out paperwork, and the hostess introduced me to the entire restaurant staff one at a time. She was a tall blonde, very classy, intelligent, and professional. I felt comfortable with her, which made it so much easier to learn what I needed to learn. As I worked with the waitresses, I learned what each one wanted done with her customers, and what they needed from me in the way of assistance. I also quickly learned which ones shared their tips with the bus boys— some were cheap, and some were quite generous. I loved the job, and especially the money. I remember going to pick up my check on payday. It felt so rewarding, and since I enjoyed what I was doing, it was that much better.

Toward the end of my first month there, I picked up my paycheck and Ted, a cook, asked if I wanted to buy some pot. At break time he and I would sit out back, smoke cigarettes, and joke around, so he knew that I smoked pot. He saw I was not the innocent young kid I appeared to be.

I had heard a story about this cook from the dishwasher. Ted, the cook, had worked at a Greek restaurant prior to Brothers Two. He had been arrested for possession of a nickel bag of pot about six months before getting the job at the Greek place. He went to sentencing before a big-name Greek judge at the time. I heard the judge was a very nasty guy. He sentenced the cook to five days in jail and five years' probation, just for a nickel bag of pot.

Ted was working at the Greek restaurant one night when the judge came by for dinner after court, as he did almost daily. He always ordered the fried squid. The manager of the restaurant would always go back to the kitchen to inform the staff that the dinner was for the judge, so as to be sure it was top notch. Hearing this, Ted prepared the dish with extra special care. He pissed in the pan, fried up the squid, and personally delivered the meal to the judge. He even returned twenty minutes later to ask how the judge had enjoyed his dinner. Every time I thought about this I had to laugh. How sick was that? This guy was quite a hero in the kitchen, but I always watched when he'd cook my burger for break time.

I did end up buying a nickel bag from him, and it became a weekly thing that we'd smoke after work before heading home. After a few months went by, I learned that the cook also had some acid, better known as LSD. I bought some and found a safe weekend to try it when I wasn't working and didn't have to be home early. It was weird stuff, but I liked it, and I felt that I had to try it again.

This opened a new world for me. It was like visiting a different planet, almost a cartoon world where everything was my own personal cartoon. I really can't describe it any better than that. It made me laugh, and it also altered my thought processes, sending me to very deep places way different than I'd ever experienced. This would be my secret little escape for a while.

Back at school, I was spending more and more time in the alley smoking pot each morning. And the afternoons were mainly spent at a nearby park. There were a few girls who joined us, which always made things more fun. During lunch hours, we frequented a couple of restaurants where there were always a few people who had an array of different drugs, in addition to pot and hash. These included speed (amphetamines), Quaaludes, acid, and, very rarely, someone had cocaine. In all honesty, I did not enjoy marijuana. I think it was just a social lubricant and a way to fit in. The first few times I smoked pot, back when it was introduced to me by Johnny, I remember laughing my ass off. After that, I became bound and determined to find the ultimate bag of weed, the best.

It seemed like I was pursuing the same goal with marijuana that I had with the damn baseball cards. I needed more. I needed the best. I had to complete the cycle. It was almost like searching for Hank. I never did get Hank, but if I had, would it have been enough? Looking back now, I'm not sure that anything I enjoyed was ever enough. I always had to have more. I didn't have the appetites of a normal person. A 'normal' person seemed to enjoy something, and then they were full and satisfied. How the hell could they not want more? More and more, and only the best stuff, was my motto. I never seemed to be satiated.

So, with my disappointment in the marijuana, I wondered if there may be a better option to feel good or to feel normal. But I never did know what 'normal' was. To have your fill, call it a day, and go on, finally just lying down to a restful sleep? How the f*** did normal people do that? For me, that was so foreign, yet so desirable. But, I felt I would recognize it if I had the chance to feel it. To me, if there was something I liked, I obsessed about it, with little satisfaction. I wanted so bad to be 'normal' but I had no clue what that even felt like.

When I explored the options in front of me, there was acid, mescaline, hash oil, Quaaludes, speed, or cocaine. I confided in one of the 'experts,' a nerdy but gentle and kind Jewish kid I knew, and he suggested White Cross, an amphetamine. I took his suggestion.

I took one White Cross. It felt great, and then I took another. In history, with Mr. Spicuzza, I found myself actually enjoying the class. What a concept—going to a class and liking it! Now my parents would be off my back about absenteeism and grades. What a relief! But, what about my friends? Would they disown me? Well, I could still smoke pot with them, while taking the White Cross. But it was different then, because I didn't get as tired after smoking.

I remember seeing my new (self-proclaimed) 'doctor,' whom I will call Mr. Goldstein. Crossing in the hallway in school, we just smirked at each other and did the head nod thing. At lunch hour that day, I had to seek his guidance. I bought more, took more, and went to classes. I seemed to be getting involved in classes, going to the gym, and liking sports once again. Football, basketball, baseball, you name it, I enjoyed it. I think Mr. Goldstein was on the right track. I just needed some focus. It wasn't long before I wondered, could this get better? Could I feel better while I did what I did?

So, of course, I had to up my dose. And Dr. Goldstein wasn't going to argue with me about that. Then he had another suggestion. He had obtained some Black Cadillacs, a stronger amphetamine, which not only gave focus but a feeling of euphoria. What more could you ask?

I was doing great in school. My teachers liked me, and I was making friends that were normal. There was Mike P., who wasn't the brightest guy in the world, but fun. He was a Golden Gloves boxer. He would come to our history class with Mr. Spicuzza and Mike would take over the class. He would bring a reel to reel tape of his last fight. I remember laughing my freaking ass off, and I hadn't even smoked pot. Mike was showing his fight while animating what he did to his opponent. He'd jump out of his seat, swinging at air, giving a blow by blow interpretation. He was knocked down in the fight but won anyway. He explained how he had slipped on perspiration. He kept rewinding the tape to show it was not really a knockdown. Mr.

Spicuzza just had a look as if to say, "Can I have my class back?" It was hilarious.

I received a 'B' in that class, my first grade above a 'D' that I could remember. I received an 'A' in my math class that same quarter. Things seemed to be looking up. I even went to study hall. That was unheard of then. None of the cool kids went to study hall, especially if it ran right before or after lunch hour. If you skipped it, you could have a double lunch hour.

Then one day, during my fourth hour study hall, I looked out the door. There was Johnny, our neighbor. He was motioning for me to come out, to skip and do the double lunch hour thing. He had some beer, which he flashed out of his pocket, along with a bag of Columbian Gold weed. I shook my head no—to be honest, with a lot of angst. I was refusing a bully. They're the kind of kid that you have to be nice to just to keep them off your back. The kind you dislike deep down but need to please, because you can't avoid them. If you try, they either punish you with brute force or do it through emotional warfare by embarrassing the shit out of you. Johnny gave me a look of disgust and left.

When I left study hall to go for lunch across the way at Barnaby's restaurant, there was a crowd of people gathered. A girl I knew came over to give me the news. Johnny had been racing around in his car about two blocks from school. Apparently he violated someone's right of way and struck another car. A young man about seventeen or eighteen years old in the other car was killed. Johnny fled the scene on foot. We found out Johnny had run two miles all the way home. When he later turned himself in to the police, he was charged with vehicular homicide.

I was sick to my stomach. Sick about the guy that was killed and sick for Johnny. I wouldn't wish either side of the situation on anyone. And what if I had skipped school and accompanied him? It was a horrible day. I remember it was a cold, damp, and windy fall day in Wisconsin. I always felt weird on the cloudy, windy days. They seemed so ominous to me, almost as if the day was giving way to something bad.

When this event was brought up at our dinner table, I was terrified to even discuss it. My parents had asked my brother if he had been hanging around Johnny anymore. He just said no, and didn't look my way. I feared he might disclose that Johnny had been around me.

On Johnny's court date, friends at school learned of the verdict. He was found guilty of manslaughter (unlawful killing without malice). He was actually extremely fortunate. He received six months of probation and no jail time. But there was the matter of some guy who would never breathe again and a family that lost a son, a brother. It was a horrible misfortune. Another life had just been ended due to alcohol and drugs.

Parklawn

Feeling somewhat relieved by the disappearance of Johnny, I began my new adventure. It seems I was never content in the everyday process of a normal life. I'm still not exactly sure what my problem was. All I knew was that the boring life I saw so many people leading just wasn't going to cut it with me. There had to be more to this life, a lot more, from my view. How screwed up I was, no one knew. I remember someone talking about people having that dark corner of their mind. I'll be damned if mine wasn't a whole suite in my mind, the biggest room in the house. When I look back at my decision making, I can't believe how messed up I was!

I gravitated back to Parklawn, the housing project our family started out living in. It was only a block away from home and many of my friends were still there. There was always something going on. It was a hang out after school many times for football, basketball, or just to smoke pot, especially during the summer. Our spot was the 'horse shoe,' a road that looped around the middle park area of the project. It was always a good time.

There were a number of characters I could never forget. Guys such as 'Ace,' Johnny L., Randy, Barry, Gerald, two crazy twin brothers, and Paddlehead, to name a few. One of my favorites was Ace. He was a thin black guy, who walked with crutches. He was a character! He would make an occasional cameo appearance, dragging himself up the steps where everyone would congregate to smoke and drink. Someone in our crowd of misfits would yell out, "If it ain't old cripp kick. What's up, Ace?" In his high-pitched voice, he'd drawl, "Who got the weed for me today?" And, of course, someone would answer, "Take your monkey ass home, Ace, ain't nobody got nothin' for you!"

Such a kind and gentle group we had! Ace would head on up to join the smoke out by getting a few tokes of weed. He always had some funny response to anything that was thrown his way. It must have been a defense mechanism, a reaction to his condition and the cruel remarks made to him all his life. One of his best lines was, "You f*** with me, God bless you, Gaudalebene and Amato will dress you!" Guadalebene and Amato was an Italian funeral home in Milwaukee. He always enjoyed the Mafia style remarks. There was always a lot of life in that frail body of his.

There was many a time when boredom struck us. And what we turned to then was stealing cars. Now, the two crazy twin brothers were notorious for being in and out of Wales School for Boys, a juvenile prison in Wisconsin. They were always into stealing cars, holding up stores—you name it, they probably did it. They seemed to have the answer to our boredom. Whoever would go out of the neighborhood to steal cars would always make their way back to the horse shoe to show off whatever they had stolen. Of course, it had to be fast, and it had to be a chick magnet.

I remember an evening sitting at the park, about ten o'clock at night. Johnny L, a classic hardheaded Dego (or Italian, if you will), drove up in a Dodge Charger with a Hemi engine. He was screaming the car around the horse shoe, showing off. He stopped to talk about his new ride. About ten minutes into his discussion about how fast this car was, we heard a woman's loud voice. "Johnny! Get home!" It was his mother, and you could tell by the tone in her voice that she meant business. He parked that car in the parking lot and ran home so quick, it was funny! Here's a guy that had the balls to go out and steal a car, afraid of his mother.

Well, about thirty minutes later Johnny reappeared to get his car. He must have climbed out of his bedroom window. He pulled up to us, gave us this bold, proud look, and tore off. After he did this a couple times, we saw him try to make a turn too fast. He spun the car off the road, down a hill, and smashed into the basketball court fence. He jumped out and ran home.

About thirty minutes later, the police came. They checked the car and the damage, while a couple officers asked us what we knew. We had no information for them, of course. About ten minutes into appraising the damage and searching the car, one of the officers lifted his head out of the stolen car. He said in a sarcastic voice, "Here's Johnny!"

As it turned out, Johnny had hit his head and his glasses had come off. Johnny's mother, as the loving mother she was, had his name engraved on the inside of his glasses. I think Johnny ended up with a short stay in Wales Juvenile Center and probation. Poor Johnny.

A few years later Johnny ended up being arrested again, this time for armed robbery. He was sentenced to four years in the Green Bay Reformatory, a Wisconsin State Prison, since he was an adult at the time of this offense. But later Johnny seemed to straighten out his life, and he became a pretty upstanding guy, running a painting business. He hooked up with a great woman, and the last I heard, life was good for Johnny.

And then there was Gerald. He was a character in a class of his own. Hanging around Gerald was more than an adventure—it was a learning experience. He carried himself well, always dressed sharp, and took pride in looking good. The women loved him! Gerald always had his guys with him too, like Mickey A., his right hand man. Mickey too was always sharp. And he was there for Gerald through thick and thin. They were called "The Brothers"—the neighborhood guys who happened to be black. Being around them, I learned a whole new language. It was a cross between a southern drawl and Italian. The word "mother f***er" was tossed around incessantly. It was mother f***er this, mother f***er that, and just plain mother f***er.

Gerald and I were pretty close for a while. We connected well and did good business together. At that time of my life, when I was just 16, I was moving pounds of pot for my neighbor Dennis, who had just gotten back from Vietnam. It seems he picked up a trade there and passed it on to a few of us whom he trusted. Gerald would come to my bedroom window, tap three times, and I would give him a big bag of weed to sell. Gerald and I played ball, had an occasional joint together, and always had a good laugh.

Our lucrative business went on for quite a while. But, it came to an abrupt end one day. Dennis was part of a sting run by the Milwaukee Police Department, and was arrested in a roundup of about eighty-five people.

Gerald and I remained buddies until gradually drifting apart, as he had his group of friends, and I had mine. Gerald's mother eventually decided to send him to California to live with his uncle. Apparently, she thought this would be the best thing for him. From what I understand, Gerald got a good job and pursued Golden Gloves boxing. I guess he was very successful at it, which wasn't surprising since he had a lot of physical talent. Later, I heard from Gerald's sister in California that he had died at age forty. I remember thinking what a shame it was. He was a good man with a good heart. Despite his pot dealing days, Gerald had the most admirable qualities of class, wit, and respect for his elders.

Barry, with whom I had remained friends for years after our childhood, was still around, and we did our usual thing at the park. He was the friend who had gotten me laid for the first time. The last thing I heard about Barry was that he attended college under a scholarship to play football, and then he began to coach the sport as well.

Paddlehead, whose real name was David, was another real character. He grew up in a very dysfunctional family. I think he was also very much bullied at some point. He was always very uptight. And he was the cheapest guy I had ever met, always pinching pennies. Money was at the forefront of his mind.

Last but not least, there was Randy. Randy was one crazy son of a gun. He was very young at heart but lived much older than his years. He was built like a bull! When we played football, there was no one that wanted to be in his way. He was punishing with his brute strength. I can remember waking up the day after tackling him, or even trying, with bruises and sore muscles.

As we sat around Parklawn one summer day, we decided to shake things up a little bit. A few of us friends had old cars. Paddlehead had an old 1963 Chevy Impala, and Randy had a 1955 Cadillac. Randy's Cadillac was a bit beat up, and he planned to fix it up eventually. But for now, it was a means to get around and have some fun. On this day, after smoking a bowl of black Afghanistan hash, we came up with a new game similar to demolition derby.

Randy and I drove the Cadillac to my parents' house. My parents always liked Randy. My father would always insist that we sit down at the kitchen table while he made us a sandwich. My mother and father loved to sit and laugh with Randy, so we had to make our visit a bit longer than I wanted, but it was fun just the same.

When our sandwiches were done and our laughs with my parents out of the way, we went to the basement. Our mission was to get a couple of football helmets. The helmets would be crucial for our new game of demolition derby. We grabbed a Philadelphia Eagles helmet and, of course, a Green Bay Packers helmet. As we were walking out of the house, my father laughed and said, "Don't hurt anyone playing football."

Randy and I jumped in the 1955 Caddy and headed out to begin the games. The first order of business was to smoke another bowl of hash. We then began to drive the neighborhood looking for our first target— Paddlehead. After another bowl of hash and about fifteen minutes of cruising around, we spotted Paddlehead in his 1963 Chevy. Right as we saw his car, Randy blurted out, "Get your helmet on—this mother f***er is going down!"

Randy turned down an alley and sped up to try to cut Paddlehead off at the middle of the block. As we got to the street, sure enough Paddlehead was just coming up to cross in front of us. It was perfect timing. Randy stepped on the gas and I remember seeing Paddlehead looking our way with his eyes and mouth open like he'd seen a ghost. Right then Randy's big Caddy hit the rear panel of the Chevy with a loud crunch. Paddlehead's Chevy almost hit a curb.

Honestly, I don't think Randy had really meant to hit Paddlehead's car as hard as we did. But the damage was done. Paddlehead jumped out of his car, looked at the damage, and said, "OK you guys, this is war!" He jumped back in his car and sped off. Randy again began to chase. It wasn't long after that we caught up to Paddlehead again. Randy caught him from behind and rammed the Chevy. Paddlehead then put his car in reverse and gunned it. The Caddy barely moved, and Randy and I were laughing hysterically. Paddlehead was not as amused, as his car was pretty battle worn. As he drove off, the Chevy was driving almost sideways down the street because the sway bar in the back of his car had been broken from the impact.

This insane game went on for most of that summer. There were a few other guys in the neighborhood that had old junker cars, and they also joined in the derby we had going. As for me, I stuck with Randy and his big old Caddy.

It was all something we did to fulfill our craving for excitement. Personally, it was that taste of euphoria that always made me want more. I remember waking up during that period of time thinking of ways to make that crazy demolition derby more exciting. I even dug out old football shoulder pads to have the advantage. It seemed that whenever I liked something I liked it too much.

Randy and I got very close in those days. We had graduated from playing football to smoking pot and then to the crazy days of LSD. We did our first LSD trip at the lakefront of Milwaukee and spent the entire summer pursuing our experience with LSD. Along the way, Randy must have done at least five different women a week. He was one wild dude! I was amazed at his success in that realm. I sure as hell couldn't match it.

Through our crazy days that summer, he took me to eat at his father's house on the east side of Milwaukee. Since we were frequenting the lakefront, it was very convenient. The thought of meeting his father, however, made me a bit uneasy. From what I had heard, he was a connected guy. I didn't know much about the Mafia in those days, but I did understand that it probably could be dangerous.

When we stopped to see his father, he made us some bombers (Italian sausage sandwiches with sauce and green peppers). The sandwiches were great! But the whole time he gave me a menacing look. He looked every bit the part of a gangster. As we finished our lunch, he called me into his living room. He had asked Randy to wait in the kitchen. I was nervous as shit. I followed him into the living room, and we sat down. He said, "Sicilian. I've heard your name connected with drugs. And if I ever hear of you giving drugs to my son, I will have you shot." He was plain and simple, to the point. No anger in his voice, no expression on his face, just a monotone statement accompanied with a very dark stare.

Randy came into the room, scolding his father. I was almost in shock. Randy was motioning for us to leave. As we exited, he apologized and said, "Don't worry about that. He has a temper." Well OK . . . nothing to worry about there. WTF?! I ruminated on that for quite some time. We were both involved in drugs, but I was the supposed culprit.

Randy and I continued to be lifelong friends after our crazy days of demo derbies and getting our feet wet in recreational drugs. At one point, we began a business of driving around Milwaukee buying old junk cars, stripping them for parts, and taking them to salvage yards for cash. It was extremely profitable. Randy ended up finding his niche by following in his father's footsteps and opening a couple of large salvage yards in the Milwaukee area.

Family Affairs

As life went on for me, I continued to do better in school for a couple more quarters, provided I had my amphetamines. I never did care for the way amphetamines made me feel, for the most part. However, they did make a huge difference in my focus on schoolwork and completing things I never thought I could. Remarkably, my attention gravitated away from my complete obsession with drugs, to girls and sports. That school year, my Junior year, was consumed by basketball and football.

With basketball, we would simply shovel the snow in the area of play. We played until dark or until someone yelled for one of us to get home. As for football, there was no need to shovel anything. We would just make an outline in the snow for the goal line and the out of bounds line. Football got crazy. When I was taking Mr. Goldstein's White Cross or Black Cadillac's, I played like a champ. I loved it either way, but my reflexes where so fine-tuned when I was on the pills.

I met my first real love, whom I will call Jackie. She was North American Indian. Her family came from the towns of Keshena and Neopit, in Northern Wisconsin. She had three younger brothers and one older sister. Her family, from what she described to me, was every bit as f***ed up as mine.

Now when I say this, I do not intend to say that we were bad families. I just mean to say that we were probably somewhat colorful. I believe we had quite a bit to laugh about. Laughing was always a plus in any relationship I ever had. Our teenage romance involved a lot of it.

Jackie and I spent almost every free moment together for months and months. I was obsessed with this relationship, as I was with anything that I liked. I could never get enough. The first year of the relationship was very nice and very fun. We laughed about our families' idiosyncrasies.

There was my father—a typical Dago. He would walk around in the yard, cutting the grass in his boxer shorts, knee-high black silk socks, and a T-shirt, a cigar hanging out of his mouth. There was my brother, who had gone from a long haired pothead to a sober and peace loving guy planting sunflowers all over the neighborhood. And my five sisters, who shared two small bedrooms and had brawls every other day. And my poor mother, who had to endure a husband who was always on the go, whether it was back in his drinking days or his twelve-step period. Either way, he was always on the move and very colorful.

As for Jackie, her family was also of the very colorful variety. Her father, who had grown up on the reservation, was famously known as the toughest guy in town. And her mother, also raised on the reservation but across the way, was the big catch of the women on the reservation.

I would have to describe her father as one tough son of a bitch! But, Henry had a heart of gold. Though he was normally a quiet and reserved man, he was not a man you would want on your bad side. Though I never ever heard Henry say a bad thing about anyone, there was this feeling that I picked up about him. When Henry drank, he drank. He would work out of town for a few weeks straight. During that time, he stayed completely sober. He would also sometimes spend a week straight at home, reading books. No talking, no nothing. He read.

On the reservation, I guess he was known as the best boxer of his time, and I do not doubt that to this day. But when Henry went on his drinking binges, he drank. Kat and I knew exactly where to find him. During binges, he was absolutely hilarious. He would give me what he thought was a pat on the back, nearly knocking the wind out of me, though he had no intention of harming me. He was just a bull, with a bull's physical strength. He would call me his "God Damn Guinea," or "You damn Italian."

Her mother was a small quiet woman. She was very kind. Kat always had a sad and concerned look when talking about her mother. I believe she suffered with some mental health issues. She would pace for hours and hours through the family room at their house. There was actually a path worn out on the carpet where she would pace. But, I must say, this woman always treated me with care and respect.

Her brothers were somewhat quiet, but all very kind souls, and all three very good looking young men. Her sister, the oldest child, was an absolute GEM! She was a very kind person and a protective sister, always looking out for family. She was an extremely intelligent person and did quite a few homework assignments for others. Jackie and I were almost inseparable for the first couple of years. This would gradually change due to my drinking and drugging. With Kat came her neighborhood friends. I loved hanging out with my newfound friends in her neighborhood. But, with it came a lot of drinking, and a lot of drugs.

CHAPTER THREE

Bad Decisions

My drinking, along with the best pot money could buy, took a pretty big commitment on my part. I was dedicated to this stuff. It was one of the things that defined who you were, I thought. I sure didn't want to end up like my brother. He was a quitter. And he had lost all of his friends. At least what I deemed as friends, in those days. You had to be cool. That's all there was to it. I think I learned that at a very early age from Johnny.

It was Christmas Eve in 1972, and I was at my parent's house with our entire family. We all got gifts, and I only asked for cash. Around that time, the only money I was making was for shoveling the snow at some neighbors' houses. So, I asked for cash. And, cash I received. I left our house immediately after getting my money. I met Johnny to buy some pot and then headed over to Parklawn. I figured I would have a warm welcome since I had some good weed.

There were a few old friends sitting by the park drinking. I joined them and pulled out my bag of Columbian Gold weed. We all smoked and drank a bit. Then, a friend of a friend, whom I'd just met for the first time, had an idea. He knew of an area of some suburb of Milwaukee where everyone was rich. He said he had a foolproof way to break into the houses. Of course he did—they always do. He had just gotten out of the juvenile facility after doing nine months for stealing a car. Do you think he had a foolproof plan for auto theft too?

Well, after about an hour, he persuaded us to go along with his get rich quick scheme. I honestly felt sick to my stomach. I knew this was messed up, even while I was messed up. It was an extremely bad decision on my part, and I felt it in every fiber of my being. But, if you want to be cool and you want to be accepted by the cool guys, you do as cool does. Looking back, it was one of the all-time worst decisions of my teen years.

We drove down to the suburbs, and my friend's acquaintance showed us a house. He jumped out and told us to wait for him to get inside and let us in. He was in the house within minutes, opened the front door, and told us to grab only stereo equipment, cash, and jewelry. As we rummaged through, I felt nervous not only about the idea of the crime of burglary, but also of violating someone's home. This was sick shit!

Sure enough, within about ten minutes of being in the house, we saw flashlights. It was the police. We ran into the attached garage and lay down. We were f***ed. In an instant, they opened the garage with their guns pointed dead at us. Since I was still a minor of seventeen years, they called my parents. They told my father I would be at the Milwaukee Juvenile Center. I was shipped there to stay for about a week or two until my court date. The other two guys were sent to different facilities. The acquaintance of my friend was immediately sent back to his old jail facility to face his parole revocation. He went away for quite a while. Our other accomplice ended up with a sort jail term.

My father came to visit me while I was in lockup. He just said, "You got cash for Christmas. You had all you could want and every-thing else, so what the hell were you thinking?" I had no answer for that. He was absolutely correct.

At court I faced a new judge in Milwaukee Juvenile Court, Vel Phillips. She was the first female and first black judge in Milwaukee. She had a way about her that seemed to me she was determined to do right by the law. At the same time, she took into consideration the humanity of the perpetrator and the family unit of the young person. She asked me questions about my future plans and about my thought process when committing the crime. I simply told her as I did my father: I just hadn't been thinking. I said I knew it was wrong before I even entered the home and violated the lives of these strangers.

She ultimately handed down a sentence of six months of strict probation whereby I was to meet with a probation officer weekly to report every detail of my daily activities. I complied with it totally and completely. I took jobs shoveling snow for the City of Milwaukee. I helped my disabled neighbor lady with some chores around her house and shoveled her snow. And I saved money. There was no drinking or smoking pot.

The only thing I did outside of work was to visit with my girlfriend Jackie. We would meet almost daily at a secluded spot by Lincoln Creek, which was halfway between the two of us. This was another type of obsession for me, but one that didn't seem to get me into trouble. But those meetings with Jackie didn't appear on my weekly reports to my probation officer.

Certificate of Completion

My probation proceeded well. Once my six-month term was completed I received a certificate. That was both a good and a bad thing. Since I was off the hook for going to jail or having to check in weekly, I began to spend more time with Jackie and also my friend Brian, whom I'd known from high school. He was interested in dating my younger sister.

Brian and I were hanging out pretty often by then. With summer just starting, we went swimming at the local pools and quarries. Of course we had pot, and a novel thing for us was this new wine that had come out called Boone's Farm Strawberry Hill. It was a sweet, fruity, and inexpensive wine. We drank and smoked more and more daily. We spent that whole summer drinking that stuff and smoking the best weed we could find. During this summer, my sister began to date Brian. My drinking in those days was just way out of control. It was one big party.

Animal Farm

One morning, my sister and Brian came by the house. He had been quite occupied with her. He was a great guy and a great friend to our entire family. We all got so drunk that evening. As the hours went by, we came up with a great idea to visit the Capital Court shopping center, where there was an animal farm. I think they always had it around Easter. There were baby ducks, roosters, goats, and pigs. We went to the animal farm at about three o'clock in the morning. I was with my best friend at the time, Brian, and a friend from Jackie's neighborhood by the name of Todd.

In the animal farm display we laughed at the animals for a while and interacted with them. We talked with the baby goats. They would let out a big "maaaaahhh." And sure enough, here came the momma goats. They would let out the bigger "baaaahhhhh" as if to protect the baby goats. Several times, Todd grabbed hold of a goat's horns. He looked them directly in the face, with about six inches between his face and theirs, and imitated them. Finally a bigger one rammed him in the side of the head, knocking him to the ground. He was so damn drunk, as we all were, that it took both Brian and me to help him up. I hadn't laughed that hard in years.

I decided it would be a good idea to adopt a piglet. The plan was to grab one and carry it about thirty yards to Brian's Chevy Corvair, simple as that—but it was a bit more work than I anticipated. With the bigger pigs making rushes at me, I finally caught a little prick! It squealed all the way to the car where I settled it into the trunk.

I had a destination for the pig. At about four o'clock in the morning I asked Brian to stop at Jackie's house. As we pulled up, I told him to open the trunk. He asked, "What the hell are you going to do?" I simply told him to wait there and I would be right back. I needed to bring this pig to its rightful owner.

I pounded on the front door. Jackie's father, Henry, answered. He gave me a look of bewilderment, staring at the present. I just blurted out in a drunken slur, "I brought your daughter home, Henry!" Now, if calling his daughter a pig wasn't bad enough, this was Henry! He could have broken me in half. He said, "You dumb, crazy Dego, you probably want to go take a cold shower." Somehow, within a matter of about ten seconds after the words left Henry's lips, I felt sober. All I can remember thinking was, "What the f*** am I doing?"

I returned to Brian's car, where he and Todd were almost crying from laughter. I didn't even take the time to put the pig back in the trunk. The poor animal was just making little grunts by now. I think he may have taken a liking to me. I was petting his head and stroking his snout. I kind of wanted to keep it, but I didn't even know what it ate. Pig feed? OK, WTF is pig feed? So, back to the animal farm he went. He made little sound until I put him back in the pen. As soon as his feet hit the ground he squealed—probably ratting on me.

Taking a Toll

Needless to say, I didn't visit Jackie at her parents' house anytime soon. She and I laughed about it, but I was truly embarrassed. Without alcohol, I was actually a quiet kid, self-conscious, very respectful to people, and especially deferent to adults. The pig incident was out of character for me. (Damn father corrupted me at a young age with the f***ing monkey!)

Regardless of my dislike of the taste of alcohol and my boredom with pot, I now resumed my usage with a vengeance.

Oh, how the drinking took its toll on me. I was kicked out of high school three months before graduation, because I was accused of hitting the assistant principal in the head with a twelve-ounce can of Pabst Blue Ribbon. It could have been Old Milwaukee, so I guess I felt he was special. In all seriousness, I was one f***ed up young man. There was no one who had control over me at that time in my life. Even Jackie had lost faith in me.

I had become so inundated with drinking and smoking pot, I don't think I knew half of what I was doing. The few incidents that I did remember scared the shit out of me once I sobered up. I would then drink to get rid of the memories. But I didn't have a drinking problem. I was just in a bad situation and alcohol cured that, I thought.

One night I was at a place on the east side of Milwaukee called Humpin' Hanna's. They had a band, girls frequenting the bar, and penny beer nights. I don't really remember much of being there. I do remember the last part of my ride home. Suddenly there were flashing lights. My next memory was pulling over on to the curb, stepping out of the car, and saying, "Your Honor, I wasn't speeding."

It was a Milwaukee cop. The officer asked me where I lived. I told him I was only a few blocks from home. He then told me to get in my car and that he would follow me home. He told me that I needed go sleep it off and that the next time he saw my car after 10:00 pm, he was going to stop me and ticket me. He went on to say that nothing good goes on after 10:00 pm. I think I remember my father saying that, too.

He followed me home, I parked my car in front. It was a bad night for me but probably a very fortunate night. Lucky in the way that no one got hurt and that I ended up with a big break from a caring cop. Back then, there weren't a lot of drunken driving tickets given out. I think they were only given if there was an accident or you landed on someone's lawn.

Around that same time period, I was at a bar on the northwest side of Milwaukee called Beneath the Street. They had a drink special. I recall walking into the bar but nothing further till I heard a tap at my car window. There was a flashlight in my face. The officer said, "Can I ask what you're doing?" I responded that I was trying to start my car. He looked at me with a blank stare and silence.

He then said, "You're going to need to get out of the car, young man." I thought WTF? As I got out of the car, it was like a light went on. I had regained a bit of consciousness, and I saw that I had been in the passenger's seat. My keys were stuck in the glove compartment lock. Asked where I had planned to drive, I told him I was headed home, only about a mile away. He told me to walk home and went on to say that he would be expecting my car to be there before his shift ended at 7:00 am. While walking home, I fumed about how that guy had a lot of nerve—it was about forty degrees out!

Still, I believed that I didn't have a drinking problem. It was just this damn boredom shit going on in my life. And if only these cops would let me just get home in my own time, I'd be fine. Every time there was a band playing at Humpin' Hannah's, of course, it was penny beer night. I might have no idea who the band was, but I'm telling you, they were probably great! I always guzzled the first couple of beers.

In another incident, I wasn't so fortunate. I woke up with a cop outside of my car yelling at me. I stepped out of the car, and the next thing I knew, he cracked me on the top of my head with his flashlight. In a stern voice, he said, "I don't get paid enough to chase punks like you!" I thought, "What a f***ing prick!" He then told me he had clocked me at seventy miles per hour in a thirty mile an hour zone. He asked me how much I'd had to drink. I admitted to a couple of beers. In a sarcastic tone he responded, "Or do you mean a couple of pitchers? Now be happy I'm not taking you to the drunk tank!" He ended up giving me a ticket for 'Imprudent Speeding' and told me to take my butt home.

The very next evening, I went to some bar way out on the south end of Milwaukee County. There was a disco floor, and I wasn't crazy about dancing, but I think I did. I know that I woke up feeling like shit. My mouth was as dry as the desert, and the taste in my mouth told me I had drunk wine, and a lot of it. The weird thing was, I was lying next to some girl I'd never seen before. The room was hot and stuffy, and I could hear flies stuck between the shade and the window.

I slowly got up, peeked out the window, and saw my car outside. I was on some farm. I quietly grabbed my clothes and shoes and made a break for my car in my underwear. I ran out of the house, passing some couple lying in the living room, and I jumped in my car. I stopped on a side road to get dressed. I thought I had probably been a rude guest, so not visiting any south side bars was the plan for a bit. Even after a rough week or so of heavy drinking, I never once thought of it as a real problem. It was just what we did in those days.

Time for a Job

My father, I believe, was dismayed that he couldn't get me to straighten out. He had been sober for a few years. He was getting back to the old Alex—more laughter, more jokes, and just overall a happier man—without the alcohol. I guess those AA meetings were making some inroads to peace and serenity for both him and my mother. She seemed much more content. My father casually mentioned to me that I should try a meeting myself. I rejected the idea immediately. I didn't want to hear about any of the shit for quitters.

During those days I spent a lot of time with my friend Brian. He was dating my sister, and I had Jackie, so it worked well. When we were not with the girls, we spent a lot of time smoking and drinking. We both had some pressure from our parents to find jobs. After all, they had been putting up with having us in their homes.

One day Brian's father mentioned that Brian and I should go to visit Brian's uncle. His three uncles owned a fairly large factory, which is now a very large company traded on NASDAQ. With Brian's father, it was usually a given that you would listen to him. He was a very big, tough-looking sergeant at a police department in a suburb of Milwaukee. You could usually find him in his kitchen cooking his famous matzo ball soup or cleaning his guns. He would look through the scope, glancing every once in a while at us. That menacing look kept me feeling that I should probably watch my step.

We went to meet with his uncle, and we both had jobs starting the following week! The pay was good, the factory was very clean, and the job offered us some training. Our work had to do with making institutional-sized ovens. We both loved the job and the work environment. We also met a few people there who would become friends. And we obviously made friends with people who liked smoking pot and doing other drugs.

As we got to know the other guys on our lunch break, we learned some of their recreational drug habits. Percodan was a standout. Brian and I found these to be a nice buzz. One guy that worked with us just happened to be someone I knew from my girlfriend's neighborhood. His name was Terry. He was a very quiet, gentle, soft-spoken guy.

The insanity of drinking and drugging became a big part of my personal and work life. We got very buzzed one day before work smoking some Thai Sticks, a strong form of pot. Brian and I could barely keep our eyes open. They puffed us up so much that when I looked in the mirror, it reminded me of someone with a horrible allergic reaction. Still, I felt pretty good.

When we went to work, I avoided looking at anyone. Then my boss called me over to show me something. Our boss was a pretty good guy, a middle-aged, hard-working family man, and he wasn't stupid. He asked me to take a load of sheet metal and spot weld it. As he was talking, he noticed my appearance and wondered if I was ascertaining his directions. He started laughing and said, "My God, son, what the hell were you doing?! Are you even going to be able to work?" Holy shit! I guess I wasn't as slick as I had thought. And there was Brian in the corner laughing his ass off. But, the job went on, business as usual. We continued our crazy lifestyle and made it to work every day.

The Treasure Chest

Brian and I got into some crazy shit in those days. We lived hard and fast. We spent some of our free time with our girlfriends, but that was curtailed by our other activities. I had all but moved in with Brian, upstairs at his parents' house. My house was just too busy and constrictive.

While we were in his room one night, Brian mentioned that his brother had some bottles of pills in the cubby room upstairs. He told me that his brother was a head pharmacist at a large local hospital. We entered the small room, and Oh My God, it was like walking into heaven! We were astounded. There were shelves and shelves, boxes upon boxes of almost every drug imaginable.

We sorted through the bottles, and I discovered one that said 'Casey Jones Riding That Train.' We looked at each other baffled. We both hummed "riding that train...high on cocaine." Could this be what we thought? Sure enough, we dug deeper into the boxes and found a dark brown bottle labeled 'MERCK Pharmaceutical Cocaine.' The label said 'Old School.' It was like one of those museum displays with the old brown bottles sitting on the shelves.

While sifting through the boxes, we found a number of interesting and appealing treasures—Demerol, tinctured opium, Dilaudid sulfate. After researching the PDR (Physicians' Desk Reference), we found we had hit the jackpot! With any reference to opiate or morphine, and the words "may be habit forming," we knew that we were on the right track.

Brian and I each grabbed bottles of the available drugs. We knew that there had to be a way to cook these up in a spoon and inject them in our veins. Ingesting them and waiting for results wasn't for us. Patience is never an addict's strongest trait. We wanted what we wanted, and we wanted it NOW! We started out by injecting some of the magic flakes, the pharmaceutical cocaine. It was real, it was pure, and IT WAS GOOD!

Now that we were pretty sure of what we had at our disposal, we tried some of the morphine derivatives. Dilaudid was a quick relief for any aches or pains. It gave a very similar feeling to the heroin we had tried before. Demerol was next. We soaked the pills with warm water in a spoon, and when we drew it up in the syringe, it was white as snow. When we punctured our veins and slowly drew the plunger back to ensure a clear passageway, the blood from our veins made it look like a strawberry sundae. I understand that this is a very graphic description. Even to me, IT IS SICK SHIT! But it depicts the insanity of our lifestyle.

The train Brian and I were on was absolutely crazy, experimenting with all these different drugs. We mixed them up, attempting to numb ourselves to the cruel world of up and down withdrawals. We didn't need to be at the mercy of these drug dealers and their schedules, according to when they felt like getting out of bed or their family obligations or when they ran out of product. F*** them, we thought.

Brian gave me a bunch of Demerol to take with me. (He was generous to a fault with his supply. Since he wasn't paying for it, he didn't hoard.) I remember going to my parents' house to get some clothes. They were both working. I went down in my old room and decided to do some more Demerol. It hit me instantaneously, and I heaved my guts out all over the laundry room floor. I felt good, but I was also sick to my stomach. I cleaned up the room and got out quickly before someone came home.

Brian called before I left and said he would meet me at our friend Scott's house. There we did more Demerol. Then, Brian pulled out a bottle of tinctured opium. We all did some of that and became numb to the world. It was a winter day, but I felt like I was floating on a cloud. This insanity went on for months. My lifestyle was once again taking a toll on me. Both physically and mentally, I was exhausted, as we all were.

The Train Ride

We looked at it as just another chapter in our lives. I had no clue what life was all about. I couldn't see past the present day. As the old saying goes, 'Live like there is no tomorrow.' And I honestly felt that tomorrow wouldn't arrive.

One evening Brian and I were back to digging through the cubbyhole for some drugs to cure our ills. A short while later Brian's brother, the pharmacist, noticed his nest of medicine had been invaded. Brian was called into a confidential discussion. I heard raised voices and Brian's loud denial, "I didn't take shit." Hell, I knew this was going to be a problem sooner than later. But, then again, neither of us gave a shit. We took care of the immediate, which is what it's all about for an addict. Cross the bridge when you get there. We just did what the monkeys on our backs taught us to do—lie. We didn't see any other option before us.

Nick was not one that any rational person would want to cross. He was a well-built man who carried a .45 caliber gun in a shoulder holster. He was also known in the organized crime world as a tough and crazy son of a bitch. Brian and I may have been sickly insane, but we were not stupid. And we found that our lies got us off the hook for another day by seemingly pulling the wool over Nick's eyes.

Brian and I had plans for bigger and better things. What we discovered in that treasure chest was a proverbial map leading to the other end of the rainbow. Without going into ugly details, Brian and I used our cunning and deceitful imaginations to pull off what was probably one of the biggest pharmaceutical cocaine heists in the history of Milwaukee.

We knew we needed to get rid of the stuff as fast as we could. That way we figured we'd also have money to buy some heroin to feed our habits. We both knew we had to somehow wean ourselves off our heroin habits. It felt fantastic when we had it, but the price we paid when we were out of it was horrible and depressing. It damaged every single relationship we had left in our lives—with the exception of the heroin dealers, of course. They loved us!

Heroin takes a toll on every fiber of your physical, mental, and spiritual well-being. It will rip apart any relationships you have, regardless of the strength of those relationships. It will come to rule your life. It will dictate how, when, and where your life will navigate. Heroin carries the devil through your veins. No matter who you are, big or small, strong or weak, this shit will own you. It may not happen upon your first try, but it has the patience of a saltwater crocodile. And its moment does come. Don't be fooled by the beast.

As Brian and I discussed our goal of freedom from this beast, we knew it wouldn't be easy. We also knew that having money from our new venture, if it materialized as we planned, would probably make it even more difficult. Thus we began to get feelers out to find an interested party for our rare find. This type of cocaine was almost unheard of on the streets. Yet, there did happen to be someone we knew of who could manage it. I'll call him Guy. He was a regular at a neighborhood bar near Jackie's house. My friend Mike seemed to know anyone and everyone that had to do with drugs or any other criminal activity. This bar seemed to clone that type of person.

We gave a gram of this stuff to Mike, and he shopped it around. Less than an hour later, he called me. He said he had someone that would buy all we had. His contact, Guy, had been hounding him to get more as soon as possible, after trying some that Mike had left with him. However, there was one condition he demanded of Mike—a guarantee the future stuff would be exactly the same as the small amount he originally sampled. He made it very clear if the future stuff was stepped on in any way that, in his words, the 'Outlaws' would cut off our hands.

Brian and I came up with a price we thought was appropriate, given the going price of the best street stuff. I went to meet Mike and told him that whatever he sold it for over our price was his. The bottle we had was obviously short a couple grams or so, and I told Mike to keep that in mind. We discounted it accordingly. Now, I will be the first to tell you that neither Brian nor I were then, nor ever were, the savviest drug dealers. Neither of us could usually hold on to something long enough to sell it. If we did sell drugs, the money we made went for heroin, usually faster than the money came in.

What we didn't expect, nor had we ever given thought to, was the possibility of being accused of cutting the dope. Just by looking at it you could tell this stuff was pure. Doing it, we thought, would tell the story. Of course, with drug users, skepticism runs rampant. The fact that the bottle wasn't sealed became a bone of contention with the buyer. He apparently had a partner, or buyer, to whom he had to answer. And they were very skeptical. They were especially suspicious because this type of cocaine was pretty rare, at least in our area.

I just told Mike that the story was what it was. And if they didn't want it, we had other buyers available to us. If they wanted a sealed bottle, the pricing would be higher. The initial deal went through, and they said they wanted the sealed bottle without even balking at the new price.

Now that spiked suspicion with me. Brian and I discussed the possibility that these people might be cops. It was odd that a buyer wouldn't try to negotiate a lower price. Later in the week I spoke to Mike about our concerns. He assured me that the players in the buying scenario were surely not connected to any law enforcement. In fact, he told me that the buyer was a high profile person who was paranoid about anyone knowing of his connection to this stuff. I had known Mike for years as very cautious in any of his dealings. He was a very good judge of people in the arenas where he worked, and his instincts were sharp.

So the deal went through. Immediately after they bought the first batch, they requested more. Mike told me they were interested in all they could get. I gave Brian the whole story of my findings, and he told me he would talk to his dude.

Brian and I still had to contend with the monkeys on our backs. We talked about a number of options available to us. Brian told me he couldn't go ahead with selling anything until we both got things under control. We talked about going on the methadone program out at the county clinic or to a treatment program. We decided to revisit the options in another week or so. With some cash in our pockets, it was pointless. Any active junkie with cash on hand is almost destined to fail in an attempt to quit.

While I was out tracking down some heroin, I ran into Mike. He told me that his person had been calling him daily and was anxiously waiting on the possibility of getting more coke. I told him that I was basically a middleman at the mercy of time and destiny. When I returned to Brian's house, he informed me that we had been given an ultimatum by his brother—get off of the shit. This came with an offer of some assistance.

You see, this dude truly did care about seeing Brian and I get straightened out. Beneath his tough exterior, he was really a teddy bear, the kind of guy that would give the shirt off his back for anyone he cared about and who found it very difficult to say no. But there was also the fact that if we didn't get off the shit, we may be flirting with what I was told would be an old-fashioned Italian Style Ass Whooping, followed by, "I'm just saying."

At this time Brian obtained a few sealed bottles of Dilaudid He was told that was it—these pills were for the purpose of weaning off of heroin. We had been getting these occasionally and cooking them up to inject them for the heroin-like effect. On the street, these pills were going for $30 to $40 apiece.

Brian now had such a habit built up that he would cook up five or six at once. It barely seemed to touch his Jones (withdrawals). He would give me a couple here and there. I appreciated any little scrap of dope. Junkies are pretty possessive of their dope. To give anything away was being more than generous. At this time, we were feeling like kings, almost like hitting the top tier of a slot machine. With a seemingly endless supply of Dilaudid the idea of weaning was off the agenda. After all, this wasn't heroin; this was a prescription drug. Pure, measured, and free.

I was meeting up with Mike quite often in those days. We began to run the flakes a couple times a week. And, the bottles continued to come at a heavy clip, three or four weekly. With the money coming in, I splurged dangerously on heroin. Brian was still doing his Dilaudid in massive proportions. In all of this insanity, my only fear was that my heroin dealer would be out of stuff. Asking Brian for his Dilaudid felt like a violation of our relationship. After all, I was living in his house, making money at his expense, and using his house as a shooting gallery. The possibilities of going to jail or overdosing didn't scare me; my fear was just the possibility of crossing the line with Brian. He was my consigliore, my paisano, the younger brother I never had.

We went on for months with this crazy lifestyle, and I grew more and more tired. My physical and mental health was deteriorating. Daily socialization became a blur. My spirit was taxed to the point of exhaustion. I was in for the long haul with no intention of turning back. I felt I deserved nothing but to fulfill the covenant of the dark corner of my mind—to destroy the little boy who had dishonored his god and the young man who had violated society.

Brian and I went through the motions of selling our bottles of cocaine, supplying our habits, and satisfying our monkeys. For me, it was a maze I had been building over time while doing my best not to look back at the entanglement. By then, I doubted there was a way out, short of death.

Life on Life's Terms

It seemed that one thing I always did when I was feeling completely lost or defeated in life was to seek my mother's advice. So, whenever those feelings came on, I'd call or stop by to see her. We'd sit down to talk at our old kitchen table. While we talked, she'd make some of her buckwheat pancakes. They always seemed to hit the spot and make me feel grounded and ready to listen to her words of wisdom. This woman had a lot of wisdom stored in her soul.

I guess after the life her generation went through—the Depression, World War II, and seeing death on a daily basis while in the Philippines—she seemed to look past some of the shit I had been into. She looked at what she could use to guide me in a different and better direction. Not that I'd follow her advice, but those conversations did stick in my head, somewhere. If I had just followed the path she tried to lay out, things may have turned out differently.

I talked with my mother about the fact that I needed to find another job. Neither she nor my father knew to what extent I was into drugs. I think they just figured I was smoking pot occasionally and drinking booze. My mother told me about some new program for the City of Milwaukee that was taking applications for available positions. The jobs would be temporary at first, but there was a good possibility of being hired on permanently.

I went to the Milwaukee Public Schools administrative building where they were accepting the applications. The job was working for the Milwaukee Public Schools Recreation Department. The pay and benefits were double what I had been making. Only a week later I was called to come in for an interview. I went the following week and was hired a week later. However, I had to go in for a blood test and a drug screen. I delayed it for four days to ensure a clean test.

But, I also had to find a way to cover my needle tracks from the heroin use. My blood test was the next day, and I knew I had to find a way around it. Then it came to me—makeup. I needed some makeup. I called Jackie and asked for her help. She told me to stop by her house later in the evening. Her sister was there, too. Her sister, always one to help out anyone she could, suggested that she could apply makeup to my arm.

On my way to the clinic, I was extremely nervous. I had my makeup carefully blended over the needle marks, and my shirt sleeve carefully separated from my skin to avoid the chance of rubbing it off. After I checked in at the clinic, a very pleasant woman in her mid-thirties came out from the back room and called my name. We proceeded to the room, and she asked me to first give a urine sample. I went to the restroom and did my thing, placing it in the sealed bag. She then asked me to roll up my sleeve. Both arms were riddled with tracks, but they were well made up. So either arm was ready for the task at hand.

As the nurse tied the rubber noose around my arm, I attempted to distract her as much as I could to avoid too much attention to my tracks. "Pay no attention to that arm behind the curtain," I thought. She took an alcohol swab and wiped the area. The swab turned f***ing orange! She continued her blood draw, not without difficulty. Given my collapsed veins from intravenous drug use, it was apparent that it wasn't going to be a cinch, but she eventually got it.

I am not sure if she didn't see the swab turn orange. It was quite obvious that my arm had been covered with makeup. Was she that naive? Or was she just a very caring person who knew that this young man in front of her needed a job? I tend to believe that she was extremely caring and just very suave about the whole thing.

Three days later I received a letter telling me that I got the job, and my start date was one week away. Thank God! He got me through it! (But it would have been His fault if I was exposed. That was a given. I was the victim here, you know.) "I will never do drugs again," I thought to myself. If I could just keep it to drinking and smoking pot, I would be fine.

The Other Hank

When I was re-introduced to heroin, I absolutely fell in love. At that time it wasn't an everyday thing. I honestly didn't even know what it was, other than something used by the guys coming back from Vietnam. They called it 'Junk.' It was the ultimate escape from reality. Heroin took away all your emotional pain and made you feel, as one of my old friends used to say, "Like Jesus' Son." He overdosed at age twenty-four. Fifteen to twenty acquaintances of mine have met the same fate.

Heroin was also commonly called 'Hank.' Well, as I loved Hank Aaron, this Hank had come to catch my attention too. It definitely hit a home run with me! In the beginning of my heroin use, it was a weekend thing. Brian and I would do it, celebrating our new jobs. We had graduated from pot, Quaaludes, and other items from his treasure chest. Things were escalating. From time to time I would attempt to dry out. I felt that if I spread out my usage, I could control it better, and that way I might be able to have my weekends with my new lover, Hank. Inevitably, we began to miss work. Promises to free ourselves from this lifestyle were laid aside.

One day, while trying to track down some heroin, I called Mike, and he mentioned my old friend Paddlehead as an option. This guy had not changed much since our childhood days. The only real change was that he too had graduated to heroin, and he had been selling the stuff. Paddlehead usually had some very good heroin. And he lived fairly close by. He had rented an apartment on Thirty-Eighth and North Ave. Our visits to buy heroin were weekly or monthly, depending on our finances.

After a nearly wordless phone conversation, we were both there in a matter of minutes! When we arrived at Thirty-Eighth Street, we knocked relentlessly until he answered. He was living there with his girlfriend Judy. Judy acted like his boss. After we badgered him to let us in to buy some junk, he made it very clear that he needed the money first. We always responded by saying he shouldn't freaking worry about it, we had the money.

His second demand, which was a 'Judy rule,' was that we couldn't shoot up in his house. He would say, "Hey, just don't shoot up in there." "OK, sure," we responded. The we ask to use the bathroom. As soon as that bathroom door closed, the needles were out, and the dope was cooked up. We were getting off in a matter of seconds. One of the reasons for Judy's rule was that as soon as we shot the junk, we would always puke. Just the mere smell of cooking it in the spoon made us gag. Now I know this sounds gross and sick. As hard as it may be to imagine this as a pleasurable activity, it was like no other pleasure on this earth.

This activity went on for months. Mike would call me or I would call Mike. And the conversation didn't change. It was always the same fight with Paddlehead and Judy. I wasn't quite sure why he would want to deny us making him money. Or why Judy would get mad about someone puking in their toilet. Shit, we wiped the freaking thing down every time before leaving. I failed to see a problem.

The Sandwich

As months went by, we became pretty strung out. The withdrawals came faster and harder. The amounts we used got larger, and cost was going up. The toll it took on my sleep and my job performance was intolerable.

I really began to slip at the job. What an idiot I was. This was a real chance to right the ship. I had a very good job from which I could eventually retire at about the age of forty-eight. And, as I hadn't finished high school, I was very blessed to even have the job.

Mike and I were really getting on with this stuff. It completely ruled our lives. Mike handled things much better than I ever did. He showed up for work every night, second shift at Evinrude Motors. Evinrude made boat motors. This guy had a lot of willpower!

One evening Mike couldn't make it to Paddlehead. He called and said he was getting sick but couldn't leave work. I could hear it in his voice. He sounded weak, and I could hear him sniffling, which was always one of the first signs of withdrawals. I wasn't going to miss the hookup, because I was already feeling sick from withdrawal. I had the chills, a slight fever, and diarrhea. I told him I would get an extra quarter-gram for him and bring it by his work. He warned me that the security people at Evinrude were very tight, and they would not let him come out to get it. Being in a hurry to catch Paddlehead, I agreed to get it in somehow and hung up.

After going through my begging routine, and lying that this time was different, and agreeing not to use the bathroom as a shooting gallery, I was let in. I felt sick, and this prick made money off me, so the hell if I was going to feel guilty using the bathroom. I made it my shooting gallery anyway. As for Mike, shit, here I had an extra quarter-gram of heroin. And it was pretty damn good. Hmmm, decisions. . . .

I decided to head out to Evinrude. How the hell would I get this past security? It was about a twenty-minute drive, and being the junkie I was, that was plenty of time to get creative. Heroin addicts can be the most creative and deceitful people on the face of this earth.

When I arrived, security immediately asked what my business was. It was about midnight, and I wasn't sure they'd believe I was a vendor. So, I just said that I needed Mike to come and pick up his lunch, delivered from his mother. They said they would get it to him. I had thought that they would let him come to the gate to get it, but that wasn't going to happen. Son of a bitch! Now what?

I went back to my car and then back to the gate. I said, "Can you believe this shit? I came all this way and forgot it!" I told them I would go to his mother's place and come right back. Well, now I thought that this shit just wasn't going to work. But, while on my drive there earlier, there was one crazy ass idea I had.

I ran to a gas station/mini-mart nearby. I grabbed the key to the bathroom and cooked up the heroin. I drew it up in the syringe and went out into the store with the full syringe in my sock. I bought a loaf of bread and some bologna and proceeded to my car. Yes, I made a sandwich with the syringe in between the bologna. The bologna was layered on pretty good, and I wrapped it in Saran wrap.

When I returned to Evinrude I stopped at the gate. The same security guy was there. So I made some funny conversation about the sandwich, anything to divert his attention. He just said, "OK, I will get it to him." I said that I knew he was pretty hungry, because he had called his mom three times. He just laughed.

The next hour or so was somewhat nerve-racking. The phone rang about an hour later. It was Mike, and he was laughing his ass off. He said, "What the f*** is wrong with you?" I knew Mike was just being facetious and was actually elated that our scam worked. He'd made it through another night without being sick.

CHAPTER FOUR

Geographic Escape

Mike and I had gotten pretty crazy. Around this time, my job was becoming more and more of a pain in the ass. But I needed the money, and actually I needed more than I was making. My job performance had increasingly become an issue. I was arriving late and nodding off at work. And it became evident to my boss that I was having problems. He called me into his office and asked if there was something I needed help with. I think he may have suspected a drinking problem, or something to do with pot. I wish to hell I would have spilled my guts.

This went on for another couple of months. My attempts to withdraw from the junk were feeble, and my will power was absolutely absent from every fiber of my heart and soul. Then, I lost my job. To be honest, I really didn't feel anything. Not good, not bad, just numb. I knew why they fired me. I knew I deserved it, and I knew that my life was spinning way out of control. I couldn't walk the line anymore.I felt as weak as I could ever imagine a man could feel.

I called Mike to tell him what happened. It was a cold February in Milwaukee, and I was thinking of an escape. We agreed that we needed to find a way out of this maze we were in. Mike said we should go see Paddlehead for another spin. We went through the Paddlehead routine once more, laughing the whole time doing it. David (Paddlehead) and Judy would always argue in front of us. I know watching people argue should not be entertaining but, I have to say, this was one of the highlights of going to Paddlehead's house.

We felt that this was going to be the last time there because we had decided to go to Key West, Florida. We had no specific destination. We were just heading for a place where it was warm and there was an ocean to look at—a place to dry out, go through the physical withdrawals, find some peace of mind, and get healthy again.

I'd had a run of bad luck or, in all honesty, a run of absolutely horrible decision making. Mike and I loaded up his American Motors Gremlin with clothes and a twin mattress, and headed out. I drained my bank account of every last dime. As always, I wasn't thinking about the future.

We headed out on our new adventure, with thoughts of the sun, warm weather, and a day without physical withdrawals! The usual recovery time from heroin withdrawal is three days, but it always seemed longer. Even after some normalcy returns, the psychological withdrawals seems to stay forever. How could they not? Heroin was like nothing I'd ever experienced. It was an escape from the everyday shit in life. It surpassed any expectations. If only I could have kept it to a daily maintenance dose. . . .

Well, we didn't have to worry about that anymore, at last! We were on our way to freedom from addiction, and all the shit that came with it. We drove off, feeling physically sick, but with hopes of paradise. We took turns driving, the twin mattress flopped over the lowered passenger seat. Yes, the new Gremlin had reclining seats! The drive was great. We talked and laughed about Paddlehead and Judy, battling with both of them, puking in their bathroom. I wasn't unhappy about leaving the cold and snow of Milwaukee behind. I wasn't going to miss that shit! We did smoke some pot every once in a while to lessen the anxiety, but it didn't seem to help me. It made me feel nauseated.

At Last

Well, that was all behind me now. And my new world was just ahead! Mike and I meshed very well. We both felt life was f***ed up. This trip gave us some hope of finding a better way. We agreed that just enjoying the weather, women, and pot was probably the route to happiness. As we reached Florida, dawn was approaching. We could see the sun and feel the warmth. It was great! We hadn't felt warmth for months in Milwaukee.

We stopped at a rest area to change into shorts. A deputy sheriff was walking the area, apparently looking for someone or something. We had pot hidden in the car, and Mike had long hair, down to the middle of his back. When the deputy approached us, we were both nervous as shit. He said, "Fellas, did you happen to see a tall thin guy in the men's room?" We replied in the negative. He said, "If you see someone like that, you tell me. I'm parked right over there. There's a guy named Pete, and he's a queer. And there ain't nothing I hate more than a f***in' queer."

We were still nervous, with Mike's long hair and all. And we weren't quite sure if he didn't think we may be 'queers.' As we headed back to our car, Mike said to me quietly, "Hey Tony, we're not in Kansas anymore." We both realized that 'down South' was a different world. But, we were in the clear. It took our minds off of our withdrawals for a while.

Heading through the Orlando area I remember the smell of the orange orchards. It was like nothing I had ever experienced! It beat the smell of the foundries in downtown Milwaukee! This was going to do the trick, I knew it. We drove through the morning and arrived at the Seven Mile Bridge which was absolutely beautiful, extending over a part of the Atlantic Ocean. Mike mentioned that he wanted to buy a big bunch of Key limes to bring back for his mother so she could make Key lime pie, one of his favorite desserts.

It was warm and sunny when we finally reached Key West. We checked into a cheap motel with palm trees blowing in the wind outside our patio and a view of the Atlantic Ocean.

After settling in, we headed out to the beach. The sun seemed to be just waiting, to bake the last of the heroin out of us. We set up with our towels on the sand and a couple bottles of beer, but the beer didn't settle with me. Alcohol didn't help me through withdrawals. It seemed to push out the heroin faster than it needed to go. And it aggravated the sick feeling I had. But, it was a buzz—I couldn't argue with that.

After about four or five hours of sun, we started to look like lobsters, so we headed back to the room to rest some more. That evening, we found a nice little bar called the Parrot Lounge. I had never seen a bar with no windows. It was pretty inviting. We sat and drank Heineken beer, which was new to me. All I had known was Pabst, Blatz, Schlitz, and Old Milwaukee. By this time the withdrawals were gradually leaving. The Heineken went down well.

After a week in Key West, we had our fill of sun and the Parrot Lounge. We headed out, with a plan to make a layover in Orlando. Mike had heard they had some discos there, and with my new outlook on life, I guessed the disco scene may not be a bad idea.

We arrived in Orlando and found a hotel and a disco. It seemed strange that only ten days ago we were in frigid Milwaukee shooting heroin. Maybe this was the ticket? The disco seemed like a nice change of scenery to me. The girls looked better too. While into my heroin lifestyle, women just seemed to be in the way. But here I was, starting to feel somewhat normal again.

The second night at the disco, we met a couple of girls who were fun to be around, so we had a good time. They invited Mike and me to stop by their place for a couple of beers. Of course we accepted the invitation, and they laughed about us accepting so quickly. Now, why the hell wouldn't we, two guys in our twenties, and 1,400 miles from home? Before we left the bar, they had decided who was going to get which of us. The one that was going to take me was a pretty dominant Jewish girl named Elise, from New York City. The other was a thin, pretty girl from Brooklyn.

We soon found that there was a catch. When we pulled up in front of what looked to be a park area, they informed us that they were going to have to sneak us into their room. It turned out to be a woman's dorm at what I think was Winter College, just outside of Orlando. We weren't opposed to that at all. But at the same time, we didn't want problems, especially in a part of the country we didn't know well. Somehow they got us in without any problems.

The next morning, they woke us up early and frantically told us they needed to get us out of the room quickly. Half dressed, we gathered our stuff and they ran us to a back exit. We heard a woman shouting, "What is going on in here! Get back here!" Half asleep and half dressed, running down a girl's dorm hallway, we were laughing the whole way. I had been thinking we might go back for another round that night, but . . . probably not a great idea. Mike and I stayed around the Orlando area for another few days longer, and then we knew that we needed to head back to the freezer, Milwaukee.

A Slap in the Face

We were all sun-tanned and a few pounds heavier, feeling good on our drive back. We had finally kicked this shit out of our systems, for the most part. We were still using some pot and beer to assist with our cleansing.

When we got as far as Chicago, there was at least ten inches of fresh snow—certainly different from Florida. Shortly after crossing the Wisconsin border, I said I felt like the withdrawals were gone, and Mike replied that he felt the same. There was complete silence for about fifteen minutes. Suddenly one of us said, "Shit, I bet I'd get off good now." This meant that our tolerance was most likely way down and we'd get high much more easily with a lot less money. This is the way an addict thinks.

That was all it took. Mike pulled off the expressway to a phone booth. We called Paddlehead. He said, "Well, well, look who's back. I knew I'd see you guys again." As much as we hated the thought of seeing him, or his dope, we asked to stop over. Mike had two more days of vacation. Paddlehead told us we would have to meet him at the 'Indian's house.' We knew the place because we had shot dope there before. We hightailed our asses there so fast, we ended up arriving at the same time Paddlehead did. There he was, looking like Satan himself. (Actually, he looked like Oil Can Harry from the old cartoons.)

I was feeling healthy, looking for a new way of life without heroin. Right in front of me was the path to a normal life, free of the chain. But, the dark room in my mind seemed to say to me, "What the f***, you're a loser anyway. You don't have a job to go back to. You have alienated your family, any good friends, and your girlfriend, so who the f*** cares about doing right. It's the pleasure that's minutes away that's important! And it will remove all your fears and pains."

For a junkie like me, if there is any feeling at all that you don't like, your disease will make it a major problem. There is no negative feeling that is minor in the brain of a junkie. There doesn't seem to be any solution at all for a junkie unless they have some heroin in front of them, or they know it's on the way. Here I was about ninety feet away from having a place to shoot some Hank. Mike and I followed Paddle-head into the house on Arlington Street.

At the front door were Steve and Ronny, both very big weight-lifters. These were the kind of guys you'd probably want to be on the good side of. They told us to have a seat in the kitchen. Mike sat on my left, Paddlehead (Dave) sat directly across from me, and Ronny and Steve sat to my right.

"Ok Dave," I said, "Let's see what you have." He pulled out a bag of heroin, which was about a half ounce. He mentioned that it was very strong stuff, so he had to charge more. I bit my tongue over the price. He knew how bad we wanted this shit. At this moment in time, we were more concerned with getting him to dish it out than with the cost.

As soon as he dished it out and collected his money, we were ready with the spoons. We had agreed while driving in that this was going to be a onetime thing, a treat for being clean of heroin for over fourteen days and not to be continued. Wasting no time, I cooked up the little rock of heroin. I quickly drew it up in the syringe, all the while gagging from the smell. It was fairly easy to find a good vein, since we'd had a short break from poking our arms like pin cushions.

As I pushed in the plunger and watched the cylinder empty into my vein, I was already feeling how strong it really was. Before the needle was out of my arm, I was calling Paddlehead out. I began to tell him that he ripped us off, and we wanted more. But that was the last thing I remembered. As I spoke, darkness began to come over me. That was it. A dead black out.

My next recollection was of having no feeling or sound or sight. I heard yelling in the background. I couldn't make out words. I felt something scraping on my face and on the front of my pants, down to my crotch. I then began to feel a cold sensation. As the yelling in the background continued, I could distinctly hear Mike frantically saying, "He freaking went out man! We got to do something, the f***er's dead!"

My physical senses started to come back. At first it seemed like a huge hand being slapped across my face back and forth. I can only describe it as being numbed up in a dental office. The slapping of my face continued, and shortly after, I felt the cold sensation again, as if snow was being stuffed down the front of my pants and pushed across my face. It was like a piece of cold sandpaper.

Then I was gagging, and as my sight came back, here was big old Ronny. He had apparently been stuffing snow down my shirt, down my pants, and in my face. I was lying on my back, in a big snow bank, with Ronny shaking me. He was saying, "Thought we lost your ass, man! We aren't out of the woods, Tony!" Then he told me that I needed to get up and move around. As he walked me around the backyard awhile, he told me I needed to drink tea. He took me inside Steve's house, made me some tea, and continued to watch me.

Mike was visibly shaken up, and he looked like he was sick to his stomach. As for Paddlehead, he was shaking his head in disgust, saying, "Hey man, you can't do this shit to me." All I thought was, "Go f*** yourself, and your dope, you freaking devil man." But, then again, whose decision was it to follow the so called devil? I had no clue how close I had been to not coming back. And if it weren't for Ronny, I would not have come back.

After finally leaving the east side, Mike was speechless all the way home. He dropped me at my parents' house, at about one o'clock in the morning. I faintly remember him walking me up to the house and helping me in the door. At the time, my brother and I were sharing the basement as our bedroom. I managed to stumble downstairs, and my brother asked me what I had been doing. He helped me into my bed. He never mentioned it again and never said anything to my parents.

Lost Love

The sad part of this whole thing is that it didn't seem to faze me. It seemed to affect Mike more than it did me. I just didn't feel. I was empty. Maybe, in some strange way, I felt I deserved to die. I had no fear of death—just concern for the hurt and loss it would cause for the people who love me.

Shortly after this flirtation with death, life went on, as it always does. There was our dog, Peppy. My father had brought her home from a bar one day, and now she was about twelve years old. Whenever I was home, she would crawl next to me, or next to my bed. Peppy had been sick for about a year. She had one tumor removed, but another had developed. I was sure that her time in this world was coming to an end.

While I continued to live in a state of doom and gloom, using small amounts of heroin here and there, life was pretty f***ed up. I really wasn't sure where I was heading. I did know that I wasn't real happy about being here in this world. Nor did I deserve it. I had more and more thoughts of suicide, though I didn't have the testicles to carry out a gunshot to the head, to hang myself, or even to do a hot shot of heroin I felt completely useless to those around me, as well as to myself. But, Peppy still seemed to care. My dog was there for me with unconditional love.

Then one day, I woke up and heard Peppy under my bed. She was curled around one of the legs of my bed, squirming in a circle around it, obviously in pain. I got sick to my stomach. It seemed all that was wrong in my life jumped to the forefront. Watching the pain and suffering Peppy was going through brought my fears and emotional pain to the surface. Here was this innocent animal with her uncondi-tional love, who had stood by us through every childhood sickness, every bump and scratch we endured through life, and all of our times of laughter. And she was leaving. I had such a bad feeling in the pit of my stomach. I cared, but I wanted the pain to go away! Poor Peppy, our little emotional sponge, was dead. That one really hurt.

I was dealing with the shit I had carried through this life—the hurt, the deceit, the regrets, and now, the memories of Peppy. They all accumulated in that dark corner of my mind, and that dark corner that was becoming the biggest room in that housing called my head. It was so full, yet I always made room for more. The bad decisions were taking their toll.

No Show

Shortly after Peppy left us, my brother announced he was getting married, and he asked me to be there for him. As the time approached, I had been working at a new job at a plastics factory. The pay was OK, and the hours weren't too bad either. I worked twelve hour shifts, three days on and three days off. I had also found a way to alleviate the heroin withdrawals.

Some of my friends had found a doctor nearby who was handing out prescriptions for Percodan and Dilaudid. These were semi-synthetic morphine, and they worked great. This doctor, 'Dr. G, would hand out a prescription for $20 cash. Every single time I went to his office there were fifteen to twenty others in the waiting room, many of whom I knew from the streets. When he came in the examining room, he'd ask what the problem was. You would point to your back, and just say that you once had some yellow pain pills that worked great. You'd say the pills said "ENDO 122" on them and that they were the only thing that worked. The next words out of his mouth would be, "You going to pay me?" And that's when you'd pull out a $20 bill. His pen would come out of his pocket so fast your head would spin. It was the same every time.

The only difference from one patient to the next was how many he would prescribe. The norm for most of us was ninety. But I would always say I really needed 120 because my back was hurting. (I was going through withdrawals.) I saw nothing wrong with this. 'You have money, I will write,' seemed to be his motto. Word went around the street pretty quickly.

When I had my three or four days off, depending on the week, I would make time for some heroin. At that time, there was word that some China White had come in. It was a class of heroin that I had heard about for years, but never saw around Milwaukee.

I had just completed my last shift of a four day forty-eight hour work week. It was about 7:30 am and I had just gotten paid. I ran to the local tavern to cash my check. After two quick beers, I made a call to the dealer who supposedly had the China White. He answered half asleep and reluctantly agreed to see me. I was out of that bar and in my car in about ten seconds flat. It took me all of about ten minutes to get to his house. He showed me the dope and explained the dangers of doing too much. He said a few people had overdosed on the shit, and he didn't want me on the list of obituaries. He showed me the amount to do—the size of a couple of small grains of salt—and sat there while I cooked it up in a spoon. I tied up my arm and proceeded to shoot. As soon as I had untied the arm, I was feeling a strong rush, with that taste in my mouth, a taste unlike anything else on this earth.

I was so f***ed up that I was nodding out at his kitchen table. He nudged me a few times to be sure I was OK and breathing. I remember hearing him say, "I told you mother f***er! I told you it'd be the best shit you ever had!" When I left his house, I still had enough dope for about three more hits, which would be about two or three days of relief.

The morning of my brother's wedding, my mother yelled downstairs to remind me of the time. I replied that I knew the time, and that I would meet them there. My parents knew I was having issues. But they had no clue of the extent about my drug use. I believe they thought I was smoking pot with some of the neighbor kids who had returned from Vietnam. Beyond that, I think they were oblivious.

As I got ready for the wedding, I took a quick shower, got dressed, and decided I should do one quick bump of the China White just to calm my nerves. I waited for everyone to leave the house. Then I did my thing. Well, it felt so freaking good that I just had to sit and nod out for a bit. I lit up a cigarette, and that was the last thing I remembered. I woke up to the phone ringing. As I heard it ring, I looked up, and I saw that my cigarette had burned all the way down through my index and middle fingers. It had welded the two fingers together. I never felt a thing. Now I knew why this stuff was used for cancer patients. Holy shit!

The phone rang again and again. When I finally answered, it was my brother. He asked if I was still coming. I said I had fallen asleep, apologized, and said I'd be on my way. Then I nodded off again! I never did make it to my only brother's wedding.

This is my big brother. Now who the f*** does that?

CHAPTER FIVE

The White House

Well, that selfish act remained lodged in the dark room in my head. There was a lot of shit in that room. It was like a black hole—always room for more. And it always seemed to cloud my decision making. I kept a small stash with me at all times, even at work. I was on second and third shifts, so it was pretty much a skeleton crew at the factory during those hours. On my breaks, I would go into a stall in the men's room to shoot up.

Around that time there was a new buzz in the neighborhood about some good heroin going around from a guy named Chuck. He lived with his mother, over on Hopkins Avenue. Chuck was one crazy son of a bitch. He had claimed this area to be his territory.

The house they lived in was a big, white, three story home. According to Chuck this was 'the White House.' "F***ing Pennsylvania Avenue," he'd say, or Hitler's or Napoleon's estate. This guy wanted to be 'The King.' And for a while, he was. We all helped him to be exactly that. We needed him. He had top grade heroin.

At this time, I was somewhat back with Jackie, my first love. I was stuck on her, and for good reason. She was a sweetheart, and we had great physical chemistry. Until of course, 'Hank' got in the way. At this point, I think she was just feeling sorry for me. Maybe she still cared for me, but this seemed to be pity love. She knew she couldn't compete with my relationship with 'Hank.'

Mike and I had been hanging with our other friend, Terry, from his neighborhood, known as the Glendale Park area. This was where Jackie, Mike, and Terry all grew up. It was very convenient, seeing that it was only about a block from the White House. Terry and Mike had just met two women at Glendale Park. They were seeing the girls every night, dropping them off, and then going to the White House. Where the hell was all that money coming from? Apparently one of the girls had inherited a large sum of money in the range of a hundred thousand dollars. Back then, a hundred grand was big money! They started kicking some dope up to me, as friends would. It got very crazy.

We were all still visiting Dr. G., who continued handing out prescriptions for Percodan like candy. The joke around the neighborhood was his line, "You going to pay me?" Anytime you went in for a prescription, he'd hold the prescription pad in his left hand and his pen in his right, exercising the power of his signature. Of course, he had room in his right hand for your $20. Eventually, we were sending anyone we could find and trust to go in to see him. We would give a girl $20, and tell her to say her back hurt. She gave him the $20, and asked for Percodan. It worked every time.

Before long there was a big stir in Glendale Park. Chuck got busted, and the White House was shut down. It was a huge deal. Apparently, someone had snitched on him. He had his day in court, and it turned into a circus. A guy we knew named Mackie was on the witness stand, set to testify against Chuck. As he testified, Chuck jumped out of his chair and yelled, "You a dead mother f***er, Mackie!" Just as the judge pounded his gavel, Chuck shouted out, "And f*** you too, Judge!" Chuck went away for a few years.

Drastic Measures

Because we were now somewhat cut off of our heroin supply, we had to look elsewhere. We gravitated back to Paddlehead. Yeah, he was still around!

I had just lost my factory job. They said I was absent too often, and my production was slipping drastically. I didn't see that coming. Nothing mattered, and why should it? The monkey on my back had become a full grown gorilla. He was one hungry SOB! I had to resort to whatever I needed to do to feed that beast each day.

By this time, my arms were riddled with needle marks, and my hands were swollen beyond recognition from constantly shooting Percodan. With Percodan, I would throw about ten in a shot glass and melt them down to a soup with hot water. The aspirin would separate, and the Oxycodone would be liquefied. I would tear off a corner of a cigarette filter, put it on the needle point, and draw the liquefied Oxycodone up into the syringe. It was a quick buzz, and a total relief from withdrawals, as well a temporary escape from everyday boring freaking life. But I warn you: Don't try this at home. Finished with that, I would throw in ten more, again and again, until they were all gone.

When the Percodan were gone, it was back to heroin. But now, Paddlehead wouldn't front us anymore heroin until we paid our debt first. The next step was to get some money. I didn't have a job, and there wasn't anyone to borrow from. I couldn't go to my parents. My mother, as a nurse, would certainly have known what the story was. And I knew it would break her heart if she saw me this way. I just locked it up in the dark corner of my mind. Holy shit—that thing was full.

I decided to make a visit to Steve and Ronnie. They had saved my life once. Now maybe they could help save my ass from being broke.Mike and I went to visit them over on the east side, but they, too, were broke. However, they had an idea. "Rip off some dope dealers. Do you know any?" one of them asked. I thought about it . . . Paddlehead? No, I've known Paddlehead my whole life. Plus, he was probably the kind of guy that would have his money booby trapped. If he couldn't have it, nobody could.

Well, Mike and I knew a guy that knew some guys. We called him. And sure enough, he said he knew of a big pot dealer. He said that he wanted fifty percent of any haul we pulled. Well, after talking to Steve and Ronny, who were some pretty menacing guys, settled for an even cut. Five guys go in, five guys split. When we checked out the situation, Steve had it down to a 'T' how it was going to happen. They had fake guns. Guns always scared the shit out of me. I never wanted a gun near me even if it was fake.

The plan was cut and dried. I'm not quite sure why I went along with this. I guess I didn't have the balls to back out. We headed out to the west side home of the targeted drug dealer. He was supposed to have about a hundred pounds of pot, along with cash. When we arrived, we planned our entrance, our escape, and our backup plans in case things got ugly.

It was about ten o'clock on a hot summer night. As we approached the house, I could hear the crickets chirping and my heart pounding. We carefully walked up the steps. Through our face masks we all looked each other in the eyes, seeking assurance that we'd make it back out. Standing on the big open porch, we could hear voices.

When Ronny waved his gun and clenched the doorknob, that was it—no turning back. We rushed the house. Ronny said in a stern voice, "Everyone on the floor! Face down. Now!" There were at least ten guys sitting in the living room who appeared to be smoking pot and drinking. At Ronnie's order, they all dropped to the floor. He told them to reach in their pockets and remove all wallets, money, and weapons, "Right f***ing now!"

Ronny kept his fake gun pointed at the ten men on the floor while the rest of us stepped over them and headed for the back part of the house. It felt like walking through an alligator pit. Here I was, all of about 5'11" and weighing in at about 150 pounds, dominating a house full of drug addicts. We stormed the bedrooms and kitchen, ransacking every cupboard, every drawer, the refrigerator. We dug for any signs of cash or drugs.

One of the guys kicked open a door to a bedroom, and there was a couple in the bed, completely naked. The woman screamed, and I heard one of our guys shout, "Shut the f*** up, and give us the money!" All the while, I could hear Ronny still holding up the group of men in the living room, ordering, "Everything out of those pockets!

I had no feeling in my body, just the impetus of kinetic motion. It was as if I was operating on an electric current. The only sensation I had was hearing. No sense of touch, smell, or even sight. It seemed as though my hearing and instinct were running the show.

After grabbing everything we could, we made our way down the stairs to the living room. There was Ronny, still holding the guys at bay! We were out of that house, down the block, and in the car, in what seemed like under a minute. The whole thing was crazy. On the way back to the east side, we checked all the bags, wallets, and cash. I was still numb, but I knew there was some good heroin at the end of the rainbow. If it wasn't as good as China White, I would just do more of it.

After the count, I think we ended up with about $850 and a couple pounds or so of weed for each of us. It wasn't the haul we'd hoped for, but it was enough for the immediate future. And to a junkie, today is the future. Tomorrow is the day you're going to quit anyway.

It wasn't long before we needed money again. The guy who led us to the last bust apparently felt like everything worked OK for him, because he called again, this time to point us toward a woman he knew who was selling heroin. He showed us the house and told us the room she kept it in. After driving by a few times, one of the guys said he saw her leave the house. So, now was the time. I parked the car and told them to go at it. I said I was just too f***ed up to do it. I'd be the getaway driver. In all honesty, I was just plain sick and scared.

So, off they went. They broke in, dug through the room, and sure enough they found about a quarter-ounce of brown heroin. That's a pretty good score considering the time it took them. Could have been more, but how could I complain? I thought I had enough for a couple of days . . . or did I? My share of almost two grams lasted till the end of the night. It was cut pretty badly. Still, I nodded into a deep dream state a long time! After a few more of these scenarios, I felt physically, mentally, emotionally, and spiritually bankrupt. I had felt sick and tired in the past, but never to this extent.

In Their Dreams

After those few weeks of this insanity, running with the big boys, I felt I was through. It was time to clean up and take a shot at a new beginning. I went back to my parents' house, for which I still had a key. I waited until two o'clock in the morning, figuring I could sneak in without questions. When I arrived, I looked at the old house from the street, the house with all of my memories. Walking up, I passed by my parents' bedroom window. I sat down in the grass. It was another warm summer evening. The only sounds were the chirping of crickets and a neighbor's window air conditioner.

It was so still. I was just trying to absorb the feeling of home, of my parents, who had worked so hard all their lives. They had been through the Depression, the wars, both of them completing college and landing good jobs, and then they had done their best to raise seven kids. I felt such deep regret. I found myself whispering apologies to both of them. I hoped that God would relay the message to them in their dreams. I eventually entered the house and went downstairs. I heard only the sound of the dehumidifier in the wash room. Nothing had changed here in the house. It was home.

I realized that I may not have it in me to change. I felt I had crossed a line to a point of no return. I wanted so badly to make all the insanity just disappear, to strike my past from the record. I wanted it to be cleared out of that dark corner of my mind. But I knew it wasn't possible. So, I decided to sit over at Parklawn until daylight and wait until I could call my old friend Brian. He'd always been there for me.

Stan the Man

The daylight finally came. I got in touch with Brian and told him I couldn't stay at my parents' house, as I didn't want them to see me going through this shit. He offered to let me stay at his parents' house for a while as his family was up north, in Upper Michigan. I took Brian up on this, grabbed some clothes, and we headed over. I wanted to get out of the house before my mother and father returned from work.

We stopped downtown by a guy's house on Thirty-First and Highland Avenue. He was known as 'Stan the Man.' Stan had recently been released from the federal prison in Terre Haute, Indiana. And apparently, he was the guy Paddlehead was getting his heroin from. We thought eliminating the middleman would be great! Stan was in his mid fifties. We thought of him as just some old fart, but an old fart with a lot of heroin. When we arrived, he was sitting in his third floor apartment window, staring out at the city and stroking his gray goatee. He buzzed us up, and we went in to speak with him. It turned out he had some new heroin that was supposed to be pretty strong. He told us to each take a $50 bag, and bring him the money the next day. We thought, WTF? This is something new. Usually we had to have the money up front and were told to wait. This was foreign to us.

So, we figured there was some catch that we might be overlooking. We thought about it, discussed, and analyzed what it could possibly be. Maybe he was just an old dumb f**t? We went to Brian's house and spent the rest of the day doing our bags of dope. The stuff was good. All we could figure out was that he was just a dumb old f**t. But no! That surely wasn't it. This guy had too much history. Was he the devil?

Whatever—we wanted to get what we could as long as he was being generous with his heroin.

The next day, Brian and I scraped up some money and headed back down to Stan the Man. We parked down the alley, walked up, and there he was, sitting in the window and stroking his goatee, pretending not to notice us. Abruptly, he invited us to come on up. We complied, got some more heroin, and were ready to go. He said he would be getting a new batch tomorrow for us to try.

We returned to Brian's place and went through the same routine. Do the dope, then nod off for hours. The next morning Brian had to go to see my sister. She was worried about him and me being together. She knew we were not good for each other. So, I decided to see Stan. When I arrived, he asked for the money. I told him that Brian and I would be getting some money in two days to pay him and then buy more. He said that was fine. He told me he'd gotten his new batch. He went to his counter and pulled out a bag of light brown heroin that looked like it was at least a quarter-pound. He took a matchbook cover, dug into the bag, put it in a spoon, and said, "Test it. It's on the house."

With the amount he gave me, and considering the strength he said it was, I wanted to put half away for later, or save it for Brian. Yet, I was due for a good buzz. After all, it had been almost twenty-four hours since I'd had a good hit. As I cooked it up in his bathroom, he sat by his window, stroking his goatee. I watched the stuff come to a boil and could see it cooked up very clear. I was so ready to put all that shit in the dark corner of my mind, to hold another day at bay. I could quit tomorrow.

For now, I was going to celebrate my last hit before quitting. As it turned out, it almost was my last. I tied off with my belt, drew back on the syringe, and hit a good vein. I began to push on the plunger, and felt it going in well. In less than five seconds, I could feel it was too much! All I remember was a sensation coming over me like a huge, warm wave of fresh water. I collapsed to the floor.

The next thing I remember was Stan pulling on my shirt and dousing me with cold water. He was saying, "Don't you go out on me! Don't do it, man!" I was on his kitchen floor with water dripping down my face and shirt. I felt so good, I remember thinking, "Just let me go." How sick I was! What human being could want this way out of the world? Once I was back on my feet and breathing again, Stan looked at me with a smirk on his face. He said, "I thought I lost you there! Good shit, huh?" Then I thought, "Wait till I bring Brian some of this shit!"

Stan gave me a whole gram wrapped up in a packet. He said, "Just sell some of it for me, and this is yours, on the house." Sure thing, I thought to myself. This was almost as good as the China White, with no Paddlehead to deal with. When I left Stan's apartment, I was buzzed as shit. I had to shake my head a few times to gather my bearings before starting the car, but I managed to make my way back to Brian's.

Champ

As I arrived back at Brian's house, he was pulling up in his Pontiac Firebird. He had that old grin his face. "So, did you cop?" he asked. I just said, "Let's go." I told him the story of how good the stuff was, and he was excited. He relayed my sister's message for me, saying she was worried about me. I thought, "No worries, sister. I got this under control."

When we got into his house, the first thing we did was cook up, and got off right away. After the initial rush, we nodded off for a while. About an hour or so later Brian went into the kitchen and pulled out his father's matzo ball soup, which we had been feasting on for the past week. Now, for a junkie, food wasn't always important. But this stuff was special. We lived on it, day and night.

His dog Champ, a big yellow Lab, would always get a taste too. This dog would sit by and guard us. I always felt safe with Champ around, especially given the fact that I was constantly paranoid about the police showing up. As the day progressed, we ate the matzo ball soup, smoked cigarettes, talked, and nodded off. Most of our conversations were probably meaningless.

But our last discussion before turning in for the night was important. We had planned how we were going to get dope. We agreed we would give Stan a visit. Brian headed to bed in his parents' bedroom and I lay down on the front room couch. There was the faint sound of the air conditioner behind the closed bedroom door, and Champ's light snoring on the floor beside me. I was contemplating how I would ever get off this shit. How would I ever find some normalcy in my life? When would I be able to face my parents with a clean bill of health? With no needle tracks down my arms and hands and without feeling that nagging gorilla on my back? Maybe things could get back to normal.

Finally I drifted off to sleep. But at 6:30 in the morning I woke up sweating profusely. My feet were cold, my head was burning up. I felt weak, and my heart was pounding. All I could do was faintly mumble that I needed help, but I couldn't get out more than a faint sigh. This was bad! I was one sick son of a bitch. I felt I was dying.

Champ was beside the couch. He had been nudging me, pushing his snout against my face and licking me. I heard him begin to growl. He seemed to be getting agitated, and he started to bark. He was jumping and scratching at the bedroom door. After what seemed like an hour I heard the bedroom door open, and Brian came out. He asked what was going on. I heard him say, "Tone? You OK?" I could only reach my hand out a bit. He leaned down to touch my head, and just said, "Holy shit, you're burning up, Dude." The next thing I remember was Brian carrying me to his car. He told me to hang in there.

Brian rushed me to the emergency room at the Milwaukee County Hospital. I woke up in a big room with about eight other beds. I knew this place, and I remembered the smell of it. I was in the same hospital I had been in back in 1961, when I had been hit by a car. There was an IV in my arm. I was feeling very weak, guilty, and despairing. As I lay there, I heard the sound of someone walking in the way I remembered my father's walk sounded. A man I had never seen before approached my bed. He was very tall with a serious look on his face and a cigarette hanging from his mouth.

He said, "Mr. Sicilia, how are you feeling?" I looked at him, wondering if he was a cop, because he didn't have a physician's coat. He told me his name was Dr. Rich and said, "You're a very sick man. But, you're also a very lucky man. You came close to making the grave." He explained that I had something called endocarditis. I gathered that was probably not good. He sat beside my bed and looked at me without any expression. He asked if I understood what that was. I just shook my head, no. He explained, "It's a bacterial infection around your heart, caused from bad heroin." I asked him why no one else got sick from it. He said, "You don't have a spleen. And maybe, just maybe, it's a sign for you to quit?"

I was appalled. He didn't know me. He went on to tell me he was giving me something called methadone, a drug used for heroin withdrawal. There was a clinic in the hospital for heroin addicts. He told me to come see him when I had completed the antibiotic regimen and had been discharged.

AMA

With the Fourth of July one day away, I was feeling a bit restless. Brian came to visit me in the hospital, and I told him the situation. I told him about my doctor and his offer of joining his clinic. He said that maybe it was a good option. Then again, we both knew the next day was the 200th anniversary of the Fourth of July. What the hell that had to do with anything, given my situation, is beyond me. I told Brian before he left that I had to have one last shot of heroin. He said he would see what he could do.

When he left, I remember lying in my bed looking around at the other people in the room. I noticed that the guy across from me was gone. I asked where he'd gone, and they said he had expired. WTF? Expired? That was the first time I had heard that term. I knew I didn't want to expire sitting in this place.

The room actually looked like a big hall. The windows swung open, as there was no air-conditioning. Out to the left was a big half-circle concrete patio which I knew would come in handy for the Fourth of July fireworks.

On the morning of the Fourth, I was getting sick from withdrawals, on top of the infection. My nerves were a mess. The methadone probably held it off somewhat, but I could still feel it coming on. Brian and another friend showed up around 1:00 pm. Brian motioned for me to go out on the patio and asked if I was I sure I wanted to do the heroin. "You were almost dead, buddy," he said. I said I wanted it now. I took the readymade syringe into the bathroom around the corner and did it. It didn't feel like I had hoped, but it did the job. I think the methadone had something to do with that.

Before Brian left, he told me my mother had found out I was there. I felt guilty and embarrassed by the thought of letting her down once again and the idea of her now knowing, if she hadn't already, that I was injecting heroin. I fought the hurt and guilt for hours. The next morning my mother called to say she was coming to see me. She sounded sad and said she was saying a rosary for me. Now I felt worse. I told her I was through with shooting up and that I just needed to get another job. She responded in a kind way, but not with what I wanted to hear. She told me that she and my father thought I needed to go into a treatment center for at least thirty days. To my mind I just needed to get a job and to curb my usage to weekends only.

When my mother showed up to visit the next day, she first spoke with my doctor down the hall and then came to see me. She was crying, which made me start to feel, and I did not want to feel. I fought so hard not to cry, but seeing her like this created a sadness in the pit of my stomach and my throat started to swell. I started to tear up for a moment and fought it back. After she left, I began to plan how to make a run for it. I felt that the infection was subsiding, and some oral antibiotics would finish it off.

I called Brian to tell him I was leaving, and asked when he could be outside to meet me. Hesitantly, he said he'd be out front in thirty minutes. Looking down the hall, I didn't see any staff around. I carefully pulled my IV out. I slipped out of my bed and started to grab my clothes from the cabinet. Just then, a nurse came in and asked, "What do you think you're doing?" I said that I had to leave, that I couldn't take it anymore. She said, "So, you're leaving? You can't do that! You need to wait for the doctor to discharge you." I told her that wasn't going to happen; my ride was outside. She replied, "You know this is going to be logged as AMA." I didn't know what 'AMA' was, and I didn't ask. I high-tailed it out of that hospital as fast as I could.

Brian's family had just returned from up north, so he told me I'd need to find my own place for a few days. I asked him to take me to my car, and I'd find a place. Brian then informed me that he had decided to sign himself into the Dewey Center, a drug and alcohol treatment center, for thirty days. I knew he was doing the right thing, but it gave me a bad feeling. The insane times we had shared were coming to an end. You'd think that I would feel relieved, but no. I didn't think for one minute that I could live without heroin. I really didn't think there was any way that I could function without it. This stuff owned me now. When I hung up the phone after Brian and I spoke, I decided to ride it out on my own, and try my best to drown out thoughts of attempting to quit myself. I just could not see any light at the end of this tunnel.

About six days later I received a message from the treatment center to call Brian. He said he was feeling great already, and that if he now did some heroin, he'd surely get off very well. With his system pretty clean, and his tolerance down, he said it wouldn't take much at all to get high. This was certainly not the point of his 'treatment.' He asked me to get a quarter-gram of heroin and bring it to the treatment center for him. He had called Stan the Man and arranged for me to run by and pick it up for him. The wonderful friend I was, I agreed. I was so f***ed up that the any idea of what a real friend would do escaped me.

When I arrived at the center, Brian was waiting out front with a big grin on his face. He looked pretty good for only having been clean for six days. He invited me in to his room. Sitting in a chair was his brother, Mark, whose street name was Marsha. He was as much a woman as any guy could want to be, as kind as kind could be, and funny as shit, with exaggerated feminine manners.

Immediately after we sat down, Brian was eager to get the heroin cooked up. He grabbed a spoon, poured in the dope, cooked it up, and drew it up into the syringe. Thirty seconds later he was on the floor. He had overdosed. Despite it being a rather small amount, the dose was too much for his decreased tolerance. Mark and I shook him and threw cold water in his face. We dragged him into the bathroom, rolled him into the bathtub, turned on the cold water, shook him, and slapped his face. He was getting as white as a ghost, and his lips were turning purple. His breathing had stopped, and I couldn't get a pulse.

I yelled to Mark, "Call an ambulance! He's not coming to! This f***er is going to die!" His brother darted out of the room saying, "I'm getting out of here!" He left! His freaking brother had just abandoned Brian! I ran down the hall to the nurse's station, shouting for them to call 911. The attendant at the desk called for help.

I ran back to Brian's room, pounded his chest, and slapped his face to see any sign of life. The nurse came running into the room and attempted CPR. I then began to scramble for any possible paraphernalia, as drug addicts do, trying to clear any evidence of drugs. Of course, in a treatment center, who would suspect a drug overdose? WTF? How stupid was I?

I gathered the syringe, the spoon, and the empty heroin wrap, and stuffed them in my pants. The ambulance was pulling in. I attempted to help the nurse perform CPR. The paramedics were in the room within minutes, though it felt like an hour. They asked what he may have taken, and one observant paramedic noticed the fresh needle marks on his arm. The nurse responded that his drug of choice was heroin, and the paramedic quickly grabbed a syringe and administered Narcan, an opiate antagonist. Seconds later Brian began to cough and gag. He had come to and looked horrible, but he was breathing. The paramedics asked him how much heroin he had taken. Brian just said that he didn't even remember what happened. He got belligerent and said that he was fine. He gave me a wink. He was a character.

As I left, all I could think of was how the thought of Brian's death wasn't the thing that affected me; it was just the idea that my using may have been threatened by this event. I loved Brian like a brother. In my heart, the most important thing was that Brian was OK. But in that sick corner of my mind, the thought of at least one more shot of heroin was foremost in my mind. How could any human being possibly even think that way? I was a prisoner to this stuff! I was its bitch!

Burnt Bridges

I had burned a lot of bridges, and I knew my days were probably numbered. I went to visit a few old friends near Jackie's old neighborhood. I met a guy named Bob whom I hadn't known before. He was a friend of a friend, and he had been in the Navy quite a while. We got to talking, and he said he had an old basement studio apartment that he was not using but was still under lease. For a mere $50 a month I could have it. I told him I could trade him some Percodan for a month's stay. He agreed, and we headed over. When we arrived at the apartment on

Twenty-Ninth and Atkinson, on Milwaukee's north side, I saw why it was only $50 a month. But who was I to argue?

He showed me the set up—an old box spring and mattress, some blankets, a small kitchen table, and an old gas stove. He even had some cooking utensils. Before he gave me the keys, he wanted to shoot some Percodan. He said he had done a lot of heroin and morphine, but never actually shot Percodan. I soaked some down, we did it, and he was amazed. Leaving, he gave me the keys, and showed me where he kept a loaded .38 snub nose revolver. It was for safety reasons, he said, and I was welcome to keep it close by in case of trouble. Nothing about the apartment or even the neighborhood struck me as a bad deal. What did strike me as bad was the gun. I'll repeat, I have never felt safe around guns, ever.

I did not leave the apartment for my first week there, with the exception of going to buy bacon and bread across the street. Out of Percodan, I was getting sick from withdrawals, the food, and the living conditions. I went to bed one night, and I kept thinking about the gun. I don't remember consciously contemplating suicide, but it may have been in that dark corner of my mind, along with all of the other shit. I grabbed the loaded gun, and as a lot of crazy shit was going through my head, I lay there with it in my hand and fell asleep. I woke up with the gun still in my hand. Things were bad and getting worse.

That morning Bob stopped by, and he asked if I had any Percs left. I told him that they were long gone, and he commented that I must be feeling sick. I hung my head and nodded. He said he had a good idea to get rid of the withdrawals. He showed me a blank prescription his girlfriend had taken from the doctor she worked for.

He filled out the prescription for thirty Dilaudid, asked for my driver's license, and added my name. I would have to show my license to the pharmacist. He drove me to a pharmacy in a decent neighborhood and parked his car around the corner. He said that if the pharmacist called the doctor, I should run out. As I went in the pharmacy, I was sick as a dog and scared as hell. Handing the pharmacist the prescription, I made small talk about the Milwaukee Brewers, and he went right about filling the prescription with no other questions. It worked!

Back home, Bob gave me five of the Dilaudid for following his instructions, and all I could think was, "WTF, five, really?" At least it was five more than I'd had lying in that basement sick from withdrawals. He also gave me $20. We did a couple of the Dilaudid, and then he left. Feeling a bit better, I went to a phone booth and called Jackie. She came over, and we spent time laughing a bit, something we hadn't done in months. Her father was out of town, so she decided to stay with me for a few days. During her stay I snuck into the bathroom each morning to shoot some Dilaudid, just enough to feel normal. We got along well.

But, eventually I couldn't even afford the $50 for the rent. Bob had mentioned that I needed to see what I could do about getting the money or some Percodan. Seeing that paying Bob would mean less heroin or Percodan for me, I found myself living in a vacant basement again. I would always pick a corner spot of the basement, and curl up in a blanket with a makeshift pillow made of bags, old clothes, or whatever was comfortable. I just wanted to lie down, and never wake up.

When things were so bleak, my thoughts seemed to drift back to my childhood experience when I was six years old and on my way out of this world, hovering over the people below. I was in a place where I could still be among the people I loved, but not have to feel, and not have to bring so much hurt to their lives with my destructive ways. But I believed that I deserved my punishment. I was no freaking good anyway.

I soon found myself in Jackie's basement. I began to go through withdrawals. It was cool and damp, as most old Midwest basements are. I was feeling physically sick, and the guilt and regret that was built up in that dark corner of my mind were immense. That room in my head had become a dark and gloomy place, bursting at the seams.

From upstairs in Jackie's house, I would hear the everyday hustle and bustle of routine activity—kids getting out of their beds, showering and brushing, the refrigerator door opening and closing. Then, complete silence with nothing but little settling sounds from the house. With Jackie at work, and the rest of the family gone to school or work, I would go upstairs to make a peanut butter sandwich and have some Kool-Aid. Jackie's mother was home most of the time. She was ill with some type of mental health issue. She was there for her kids' everyday needs, but there always seemed to be something else living in her head.

She was a very loving and kind woman, but another part of her was living in a different world. She would get up around nine o'clock in the morning and pace back and forth across the living room for hours and hours. Every once in a while she would take out a broom and sweep the carpeting. And then, pace again. For some reason I almost found this soothing as I would doze off listening to the repetitious sounds. When the kids returned home, I would wait for Jackie to bring me some food. She'd have a worried look on her face. I could tell she didn't know what to do with me.

Take It to the Bridge

I eventually wore out my welcome at Jackie's house and left. I knew my days with Jackie were short. I just didn't see it in myself to change anytime soon, or at all. I wanted to be normal—that's all I had ever wanted. But that dark corner of my mind, as always, reminded me of who and what I was. No good.

In thinking where I could at least lay my head for a night, I looked at the train bridge by the park near Jackie's home. This was a secluded area, at least three city blocks from any homes or other buildings. After surveying the area under the bridge, I decided it didn't look too bad. It was cover from the rain and pretty isolated. There was a little corner that wasn't visible to anyone walking by. It was early September, still warm so it would be OK to camp out for a while. And, it was only a three block walk to a little corner store, where I could get a loaf of bread, butter, and some cheap canned goods.

I set up camp, and made it home. It wasn't all that bad. I had my little nest, my makeshift pillow, my area to cook, and peace. I fell asleep to the sound of crickets and woke up to birds chirping. I sat with nature, away from judgment of any kind. Unfortunately, I knew what I had become. Maybe this was just self-pity, but I wasn't looking for that. I think I just wanted to lie in peace and go to the place I experienced after my accident when I was a kid. What seemed to always jump to the front of my mind was my family. I contemplated the effect of my actions on my parents. I didn't want to hurt or embarrass anyone.

For the first couple of weeks the withdrawals were mild, though they seemed to last forever! But, like my father always said, in ninety-nine years, you'll never know the difference. Still, it felt like it would be ninety-nine years before the aches, pains, and sleeplessness went away.

As time went by, and the little bit of money I had was nearly gone, I knew I would have to get back into society. It began to get very cold at night. One night, my hands and feet got numb and then began to hurt. I walked to a twenty-four-hour Laundromat, cutting through yards and parking lots. I had no clue whether I had outstanding warrants, but I couldn't be too careful. The laundromat was empty. I put a dime in one of the dryers, and turned it on. After it heated up, I shut it down and climbed in. For ten or twenty minutes it felt good.

That feeling, too, would pass. Just like everything else! If I enjoyed something, someone, or someplace, then I hated the thought of it ending. I think the problem was, and is, that when I experience pleasure my mind tells me it's not going to last. Instead of enjoying it for the time being, that dark corner of my mind always told me I was unworthy of it.

CHAPTER SIX

Time for Change

Shortly after the Christmas holidays that year, I walked over to my parents' home for a visit. They were sitting at the kitchen table having coffee, as was their custom. I could see by the looks on their faces they were shocked at how bad I looked. Yet they welcomed me. My father made me a sandwich, and he began to talk about the program he was working. He said that there were a lot of young people in some programs, similar to the one that helped him and many other people who felt hopeless. He said these programs were successful. Their slogan was, "Rarely have we seen a person fail, who thoroughly followed our path."

At this point I felt whipped. I knew that my father was right, and this program he spoke of was probably very helpful to some people, but I believed that I was different. I knew I needed someplace to go where I could dry out. So, my father then took me to a local treatment center located in a suburb of Milwaukee. Dad told me how proud he was of me for giving it a try, and he encouraged me to work the program. To be honest, I was only concerned about what they were going to give me for the withdrawals. The facility was comprised of beautiful old buildings, surrounded by a wooded area. It looked like a resort. I was hoping they would treat me well, leaving me to dry out in peace and quiet. After he checked me into the facility, my father gave me a hug and a kiss—the old Dago he was. He wished me luck and said that if I needed anything, I should call home.

I asked to speak with the doctor right away, and I badgered the staff until he came around. Once I had given him my conditions, the doctor half smiled, and said, "OK, let's start from the beginning." He looked at the paperwork I had filled out. I had minimized the information a bit, in case they were going to give it to the police. I didn't know how to justify the money I was spending on drugs.

My conditions were that I receive morphine, Dilaudid, or Percodan for withdrawals, rather than methadone. The doctor and I discussed it a bit, and my argument was that I had seen people have trouble getting off of methadone. The others were faster acting and shorter lived. He bought into it, and prescribed Percodan, at an initial dose he would then lower. This was the beginning of a new year. The doc had given me something that I actually wanted—not as many as I had wanted, but it was acceptable.

I went to my room, a very nice private room with a comfortable bed. Shit, I hadn't slept in a real bed in almost a year. It was a nice setup—until the next morning. They woke me up at 7:00 am. Did they know how sick I was? When I told the guy who came to get me, he just laughed and said, "Get washed up and ready, I will be back in fifteen minutes to show you the breakfast building." I thought WTF? No bedside service in this joint? He returned and I was feeling like shit, but ready to go. Along with about ten other people, I headed over to the dining area to eat a pretty good breakfast. I couldn't wait to get back and lay in that bed.

Back at the residential facility, I headed right for my room. There, I saw a calendar. My whole day was scheduled with group meetings and appointments. WTF? These people have got to be kidding! How is a guy supposed to get well going to meetings all day?

I attended the first item on the agenda just to see what these meetings were about. There were about fifteen people in the group. I noticed a couple of people I could identify with. I knew Bob from the streets, not well, but I knew he had some connections to pain pills. There was a physician and two young women I knew vaguely.

As the days went by, the meetings became bearable, even interesting. I got to talking with Bob because we knew a lot of the same people, and he introduced me to Ginger and Maria, the two young women in our group. Bob had a crush on Ginger. Maria and I laughed watching them. It was like high school all over again. I don't remember much about these meetings, except for one open meeting where we had a speaker who told the story of his battle with alcohol. There were about seventy people in the room. He sounded so calm and eloquent that I was convinced he took Valium or some other sedative. Nobody goes through withdrawal and is as happy as he sounded. It just didn't add up.

Finally, I hit day twenty-nine, and I was going home. But I wasn't leaving against medical advice. Is there a celebration in store for this? I wanted nothing more than to get a job and start fresh!

Making Amends

With my newfound freedom from the monkey, I headed to my parents' place. As I settled into my old room, I thought of my dog Peppy and days of normalcy. Brian stopped to see my sister, and he visited with me for the first time in over a month. He looked good. He always looked good, sick or well. It was in his genes.

On my second day home, my father took me to a club he frequented. This club didn't serve alcohol; they talked about the 'twelve steps' which my father said were a recipe for life. I sat in a meeting and listened. These guys were a lot older, and I wasn't too sure I could relate to them. But I listened, and I didn't drink or drug that day! It was a record twenty-four hours on the street without drinking or drugs.

The next day my friend Todd stopped by to see me and invited me to go to the old bar we used to haunt. I told him I'd quit drinking, but he said that was OK. We laughed about the days of going to see Dr. G., the

"You gonna pay me?" guy. We both agreed that Dr. G. was half the reason everyone in the neighborhood was strung out. We talked about all the crazy days behind us.

But things were different now. I was gleaming by this time, bound and determined to follow through on something I had learned in treatment. After all, I was an old timer at this stuff, with twenty days clean! One of the twelve steps they talked about involved making amends to the people you had wronged. I had a few.

My first visit was to Jackie. I owed her a big apology for all the years of grief and worry I had given her and her family. It had been months since I'd seen her. I succeeded in getting her to walk to the park with me, when she lowered the boom. She was engaged. I had a mixture of emotions. Regret, knowing I had blown it with her by my own insanity. But then, I was almost relieved. This was one less person in my life that I could hurt.

The guy she was going to marry was a small time drug dealer who lived right across the street from my good friend Mike. He had always rubbed me the wrong way. I asked her when and where the wedding would be held. I thought that my attendance would be taking the high road, and might be a way of making amends. When the wedding day came, I sat in the back. I discerned some hostile looks from people who may have expected me to disrupt the proceedings. But I needed to make amends, to show I still cared and that I had changed. I even went to communion, walking up in front of her and her new husband and her family. Nervous and embarrassed, I had to do it. I left crying, thinking of the wreckage of my past.

Copper Mine

The aftermath and the wreckage of ruining my relationship with Jackie haunted me. But there were new days ahead. I applied for a few jobs I found in the newspaper. In the meantime I took some part time work with temporary services. My friend Todd and I got jobs cleaning factory offices. We went through some basic training to learn the skills needed. After a couple of months, we began to celebrate our off days and weekends by visiting the local bars. The VFW Posts always had dime tap beers. And since alcohol wasn't my problem, I was able to manage getting up for work without a hangover. We worked nearly forty hours a week cleaning some big factories in the Milwaukee area. I felt that I could manage doing some Percodan, along with the dime tap beers, perhaps on weekends. Taking the pills orally, I really didn't see a problem with the usage.

We worked hard and enjoyed our weekends off. One Saturday sitting out by Glendale Park I noticed some teenage kids riding their bikes in and out of the wooded area by the train tracks. I asked one of them what was going on. He said they had broken open a train car, and it was full of beer. I walked back by the tracks, and there sat Mike with a bottle of Miller High Life.

I sat on a tree stump to have a beer and noticed a pile of what looked like big bars of iron., I began to scratch at one of them, and it started to shine. Mike and I rubbed off the dirt, and we could see the bars looked like copper. I picked one up and it was heavy as shit, possibly seventy-five to a hundred pounds. Mike said that they had to be worth money. They were pure copper ingots. We asked one of the older kids who had delivered them. He did not know but said the car they were in had moved. Then he said there were a bunch of them in a creek about fifty yards away. Mike and I went to investigate, and there they were—about thirty of them—submerged in three feet of water.

We called a salvage yard to find out the current price for copper and were told that pure copper went for seventy-five cents a pound. We jumped into his van, drove onto the landing by the creek, and backed to the edge. We had a few of the kids make an assembly line, handing us the ingots. With about thirty of them in the van, we headed for the salvage yard. The man there looked at one of them and said, "Holy shit! Where did you get these things?" He inquired whether we could bring more, and we told him we would see. He gave us a hefty check, which we cashed within thirty minutes.

We discussed going back for more ingots, but those things were heavy. We could always go back the next day. What we needed now was a celebration. We called Paddlehead—for old time's sake, you know. We bought a gram of heroin, and split the rest of the money. There I was again with the Hank! This time I vowed it would be different. I wasn't going to be doing this daily. That I knew for sure!

As the next day dawned, I found a wad of cash—burning a hole in my pocket. I called Mike, and before long, we were back to the old routine. See, I knew that treatment thing was just a bunch of shit! We went through that money so fast!

About two weeks later, Mike's brother contacted me and told me investigator from the Criminal Investigation Unit of the Milwaukee Police Department wanted to talk to me about the copper ingots. He gave me the phone number and said I needed to call them, or else they would come to see me. After much hesitation, I called the number and took a bus downtown for an interview with the investigator. He said that I was not yet under arrest; however, the FBI had directed him to investigate a case concerning train cars that had recently been burglarized and some related felonious thefts. The FBI had identified a salvage yard selling copper ingots to undercover officers. He asked me to tell him exactly what had happened. I just told him the truth—that some teenager I didn't know had shown me the area in the creek where the ingots were located. And that was that.

The Northwoods

It was close to the middle of June, and a bunch of guys were going up to a cottage in Marinette, Wisconsin. I was asked to ride along. I knew I needed to attempt to tame that gorilla, so where better to do it than hundreds of miles away from Milwaukee? We jumped in a couple of cars, equipped with a case of beer and a couple ounces of pot, and headed north. I rode with my friends Todd, Dave, Terry, and Jeff, better known as 'Woody.' He had a wooden leg, due to a lawn mower accident when he was a kid. As a result, he had a steady supply of Percodan. He kept them to himself, and was shooting them too. He was a very smooth operator, and I was told he was never to be trusted.

On the drive north, we stopped at a couple of rest areas to smoke some pot and drink beer. Finally, we arrived at a cottage home on a sixty acre lot along the Menomonee River. It was actually owned by the family of our friend Mark's wife. We had planned to do a lot of fishing, as well as hitting the small taverns in the area. I still had some Percodan which I planned to use for weaning down and getting off the Hank, once and for all. We did do some fishing, and I caught some frogs, just as I did as a kid when our family vacationed up north. At night we frequented the local bar, making our presence known as a pretty wild bunch.

After about a week I was already out of Percodan. I asked Dave to take me into town to find a doctor so I could try to get some more. All of us were doing Percodan, having all been patients of Dr. G. back in Milwaukee, so Dave wanted some, too, if I did score. We drove into a small town, where I found a doctor's office. I told the doctor I was visiting the area, working and fishing. At first she was very pleasant, but when I told her I had been prescribed Percodan, she seemed to get very short with me. She said she would give me something to help with the pain, but she didn't have Percodan. She told me to wait while she went to see another patient. When she left, I wandered out of the room to look around. There was an open door that sparked my curiosity. I glanced in and saw shelves with just about every drug you could imagine. Apparently she had her own pharmacy, which made sense, since there were no drug stores for miles.

I used the bathroom across the hall and then went back to the patient room. The doctor returned with a bottle of muscle relaxers. She repeated that she didn't dispense narcotics at her office, but these pills should help me get by with no problem. Apparently she didn't understand. I asked her to write a prescription that I could take to a pharmacy in town. She declined to do so, and Dave and I left.

The rest of the day, while fishing, I reflected on this. My psychological withdrawals were aggravating my physical ailments. This made me obsess. Now I really needed some. I asked Dave if he would take me to the doctor's office that night. I told him I would climb in the open window I saw at her office, and at least get some Valium or codeine to ease the pain. He agreed, and we headed out later.

There was a small, dim light on in the office. Sure enough, the window was still cracked open. Dave was nervous and said he couldn't do it. But I asked him to give me a boost up to the window, and I was in. When I went to let Dave in through the door, he was gone. Quickly, I went to the drug room and flipped on the light, keeping my ears honed for anything that sounded like visitors. I could feel my heart pounding in my head, like it was going to come out of my chest. But . . . I needed that stuff!

The shelves held barbiturates, codeine, and Valium, along with tons of other drugs, from A to Z. Grabbing a bottle of barbiturates, I saw a bottle of 1000 mg Percodan. I decided to leave the barbiturates, and grabbed the Percodan, a bottle of Tylenol with codeine, and some Valium. I was out of there in minutes.

When I ran back to the car, it was empty! I whispered loudly, "Dave!" Here he comes, out of a nearby bush. He had been so scared that he needed to take a shit. We laughed our asses off as we jumped in the car and headed back to the cottage. I knew I had put Dave in a position he didn't want to be in. And I violated the honor of Mark's in-laws by burglarizing a place near their home.

But I had what I wanted and needed. We all reaped the benefits of my score, as everyone had their hands out for the drugs. The people for whom alcohol was the drug of choice gravitated to the Valium, and the rest went for Percodan and codeine. Predicting that there may be police around soon, we headed back to Milwaukee.

A Leg Up

We drove about two hours out of Marinette before everyone wanted to stop and get off on some Percodan. Woody always had syringes with him, which made things convenient. We settled on an old hotel in Waupaca. This place was like something from the 1800's, with a saloon downstairs and the rooms at the top of a long, steep set of stairs. The six of us checked into a room with one double bed. We would make do, since it was just a place to flop for the night. When we parked the cars, we left our ounce or so of pot under the back seat of the old Chevy. We all did some Percs, then headed down to the bar for a while. After last call we each found a spot to crash for the night.

When we woke up, we did some more Percs before we headed out. Woody had already left. It seemed strange, but we figured he either went to another doctor's office, or had headed back to Milwaukee. Dave suggested we light up some pot on the drive back. When we looked, it was gone! We tore out the back seat and dug in every crack and corner of the car. And then Dave said, "Woody! That mother f***er!" He believed that Woody had taken it.

We drove for about five minutes, and then we saw Woody at a gas station, filling up his car. Dave pulled over and jumped out of the car. Todd also jumped out of Daves's car and grabbed Woody's wooden leg from the front seat of Woody's car. Woody had left his leg in the car and was using his crutches instead.

I almost wet my pants watching this. Woody came out of the gas station arguing with Dave, swearing up and down that he hadn't taken the weed. Dave was telling him he wouldn't get his leg back until he coughed it up. We drove off, Woody right behind us waving for us to stop. Dave kept driving until he saw a rest stop. We pulled in with Woody right behind us, yelling that he wanted his leg.

Finally, Todd reached out the window and threw Woody's leg into the other car. Dave and I approached Woody's car. The vehicle smelled like freshly smoked pot. Sure enough, there was a bag stuffed between the front seats. He did have the shit! I had given him the benefit of the doubt. By now we all felt like beating him with that leg. But, it was Woody. He was a pretty good guy, who'd had a bad break in life. We drove back to Milwaukee. Woody had his leg back and we had our pot.

Scriptomania

On my return to Milwaukee, I was haunted by the feeling of being sought by the law. I felt like my drug habit was King freaking Kong! Totally out of control. I needed to find a way to escape this creature. But how the hell was I going to do that, without this damn beast kicking my ass, and exposing my completely screwed up emotional state? I had been running from myself for so many long years, I feared that exposure.

I had a persistent urge to seek heroin, but the pursuit always got so messy. I always seemed to find myself at the mercy of the heroin dealers. There always seemed to be someone I had to work with to get money to buy it. I was just so tired of all the insanity of hunting it down.

So, I decided to go see Dr. G and get by with just the Percodan. Every time I got into heroin, I seemed to get this knot in the pit of my stomach. It always had me flirting with danger, including illegal activity. Often this involved the possibility of weapons, which I always feared. My fear was that someone else, most likely an innocent party, could get hurt. God knows I probably deserved the consequences, but not them.

Dr. G said he would give me sixty Percodan instead of 120. He said he would see me twice a month to monitor my back pain. It seemed the old prick was getting smart! Why not get the same money for half the amount of pills? Well, I needed more than that. I had the prescription he'd given me, and I had an idea—I would photocopy it.

I stopped over by my parents' house for a change of clothes, borrowed a car from my old neighbor Dennis, and drove over to a new copy store on Capital Drive. This had formerly been the restaurant where I had begun buying drugs at my lunch hour during my high school years. Strange how things turn around.

Going in I was very nervous. It was self-service, and they gave me a tutorial on how the copy machine worked. I made a copy, but it was obvious that the hand-written area was not original. I used some White Out to carefully obscure certain areas. As for signatures, I was a professional at that after years of practicing my mother's signature for tardy slips. I finished the White Out process and made new copies. They turned out great. Then I carefully cut them to size and made about five copies. All the while, I kept an eye out for any nosy people in the store, but it seemed pretty safe. I cleaned up evidence of my work, paid, and went to the library down the road to practice the handwriting.

I then wrote three duplicates and took them, along with the original, to a drugstore where there was a familiar face. I filled the original prescription and, since they didn't call Dr. G to verify, I figured I was good to try another drugstore. If a pharmacist chanced to call for verification, so be it.

That worked pretty well. But by this time I was shooting about sixty Percodan a day. I had gone beyond feeding the monkey—I was dealing with a gorilla. If that treatment center taught me anything, it was the truth of the saying that one was too many, and a thousand was never enough. I began to run the entire city to find a doctor to give me any amount of Percodan or Dilaudid. I would then go to the copy store to duplicate as many prescriptions as I could. I would fill them until a drugstore called for verification. Then I would find other doctors.

About a month later, my luck ran out. After I left one drugstore where the pharmacist hadn't made a call, I went to another. Apparently, that first pharmacist had waited until I left to make the call. I figured it was OK, so I proceeded to a Walgreens, and the pharmacist there said it would be one minute. And it was, almost to the second, until I heard heavy, fast footsteps, and keys jingling. The next thing I knew, there were two Milwaukee police officers grabbing me from behind and cuffing me.

I sure didn't see that one coming. But, then again, I wasn't the slickest guy out there. It was a hot July day in 1978. Here I was sitting in the Milwaukee County Jail, knowing that I was only beginning to get sick.

I ended up sitting in jail for seventeen days, until my court date. I wouldn't call my parents, and no one else I knew at that time could afford $50,000 to bail me out. I pleaded 'guilty' right away, in exchange for a four year stayed sentence in the Wisconsin State Correctional System. I was assigned a probation officer and released. I would have to report to him weekly, until further notice, and also comply with weekly drug screening.

Change of Direction

My friend Mark, whose place we had visited in Marinette, helped me get a job at the Capital Court Shopping Center. This was the same place my family and I visited when I was a kid to window shop with my mother. I was with a crew that did maintenance work—asphalt, grass, streets. The money was OK, and I actually liked the outdoor work. On Fridays, we had a card party with a lot of beer. I felt I could go this route, as opposed to the drug thing. I had been through enough.

I did want to comply with my probation, because in reality, I was so sick of my old shit! My life had been constant turmoil, and I was sick and tired of being sick and tired. I was back living at my parents' house, seeing my probation officer, and going to an occasional AA meeting at a place called the 'Twelve Step Club,' my father's hang out at the time.

I honestly had no interest in the meetings. I was twenty years younger than most the guys, and I believed that alcohol was not my problem. In reality, when I drank, I did it until I blacked out, so I couldn't really remember doing anything very bad. In those days, this thought process seemed to make sense to me. As for those Narcotics Anonymous meetings my father spoke of? I wasn't doing that anymore. But I had made some lifestyle changes, such as going to work, eating normal meals, showering daily, and going to bed at a reasonable hour. I was back on track with life.

Then one day at work, while I was cutting grass, I saw a number of police cars parked in the shopping center parking lot. Out of the corner of my eye, I saw an unmarked detective car pull up close by. Then about six police cars pulled up to my left and behind me. Two plain-clothed detectives approached me from the front. When I reached to shut off the lawn mower, I was grabbed and put to the ground, my arms pulled behind me and cuffs put on in seconds.

They lifted me to my feet, said my name, and read me my rights. I was being arrested for burglary. On the way to the police administration building, I asked a detective what it was about. He simply said that I would meet my new friend downtown. He was here from up north. I knew immediately that this was 'a friend' from Marinette.

When I arrived downtown, I was taken out of the detective's car, and put in another unmarked car. The driver of this car was an older man in his sixties. He asked me if I knew where we were going. I answered in the negative, and added that I didn't know why I was being taken either. He was quiet for about fifteen minutes of driving, and then said, "We're going back up to Marinette. You remember being there, don't you?" I just responded that I did not.

After another hour of driving, he said, "Dr. Lee remembers you." It was the doctor from up north, from whom I'd gotten Percodan. He went on to ask if I wanted to talk about it and he said, "We know it was you, I'll show you our evidence when we get to Marinette."

It was a long drive. He stopped at a restaurant on the way, and brought me in with cuffs on. I think it made him feel cool. He ate, drank coffee, and asked me some questions about my life. We left. It was a weird trip.

We arrived at the Marinette County Jail, where I was stripped, given my jumpsuit, and put in the cell block. There were about eight to ten inmates in the block, ranging in ages of eighteen to about fifty years old. The other inmates were apparently aware that I was coming. The eldest guy said laughing, "So, we got a Sicilian here. We heard you're a connected guy, Mafia! But we won't discuss that." He advised me not to tell anyone anything, saying there was a snitch in the block. So, I tried to make my time go as fast as I could by staying in my cell and sleeping. When dinner time came, I have to admit, I was amazed. They had some local cooks come in and make homemade meals three times a day. Many times they asked what we liked and offered more if we wanted it.

After a few days, I was brought down to a holding cell, where a public defender came to see me. He said that I was facing ten years in prison, that they had strong evidence on me, but that he could make a deal for five years, possibly. According to him, the judge was pretty tough on outsiders. The initial court date would be in about ten days.

By this time, I had called my father. I asked him to bail me out, and he just said he would see what it was all about. He told me to cooperate, behave, and keep my chin up. I think he wouldn't even have talked to me except that he knew I had been giving the sober life a shot. I asked him to call my attorney, and I gave him the attorney's name and number.

At my preliminary hearing, I pleaded 'not guilty.' The prosecutor showed the evidence. My fingerprints were on the on the bottle of barbiturates, which they had in a clear plastic bag. It was the bottle of pills I moved before seeing the Percodan. Well, they had the evidence, and the attorney told me it didn't look good. They set bail at $60,000. In those days, that was considerable.

The attorney told me he had spoken with my father. He said my father was a good friend of his cousin, who was a big name Irish attorney in Milwaukee. He seemed to be a bit more engaged in helping me because of it. My next court date was thirty-seven days away. Just the thought of sitting another month in jail was tiring. I called and asked my father if he could help, and he just said, "Stick it out, I'm doing what I can."

On day thirty-seven, my trial day arrived. I went into the court-room, and my mother and father were both there. I denied and denied, despite the evidence—my prints on the pill bottle and a statement from Dr. Lee identifying me as the person who visited her the day before the incident. In the end, the judge found me guilty. He ordered a pre-sentence investigation and withheld sentence for sixty days. The bail was kept as it was. However, my father signed a signature bond for my release. So, I was on my way home.

CHAPTER SEVEN

Clean It Up

Upon returning home to stay with my parents, and with thirty-seven days of being clean from chemicals in my system, I was finally ready for a change. I would need to clean up my act. I had a new girlfriend named Julie. She was a pretty little Sicilian woman who had a lot of devotion to helping me straighten out.

We spent time together visiting her friends and her family. I was again beginning to see the normal lifestyle of a family unit. I was intrigued by the whole idea of it and welcomed the change. However, when I was around her family or friends, I always wondered what they would do if they really knew who I was. Would they accept this drug addict and criminal? This young man who had so many dark secrets? There's a saying that goes 'You're only as sick as your secrets.' I was one sick SOB.

I even began to go to Narcotics Anonymous meetings with my old sponsor. I had originally met him while I was in the treatment center in Wauwatosa in early 1977. He was an 'Impaired Professional' as they were known, the physicians with either alcoholism or drug addiction. He was a pediatrician who had a long history of narcotic addiction.

When I went to these meetings, I just felt like a fraud. There was a part of their principles that read: Rarely have we seen a person fail who has thoroughly followed our path. Those who do not recover are people who cannot or will not completely give themselves to this simple program, usually men and women who are constitutionally incapable of being honest with themselves. There are such unfortunates. They are not at fault; they seem to have been born that way. They are naturally incapable of grasping and developing a manner of living which demands rigorous honesty. Their chances are less than average. There are those, too, who suffer from grave emotional and mental disorders, but many of them do recover if they have the capacity to be honest."

Well, that summed it up; I knew I was one of the unfortunates. I just felt that I was totally incapable of being honest. Because if I were to be honest, I would certainly be shunned from any person whom I were to divulge these deep dark secrets to, the secrets that I kept in that dark corner of my mind.

I had broken every commandment that God put forth as the recipe for life. I still wanted to be left alone to get some good heroin and just drift off into that place I had been, the place where I deserved to be. The place where I was that little boy observing myself being given his last blessings. And then sent off to whatever world it was to be, whether it was purgatory or hell.

When I left those meetings I always felt worse. I knew I was destined to complete my mission which was to destroy this sick and demented beast on my back. But I just couldn't see how sitting in church basements talking with alcoholics and drug addicts was going to help me.

I still tried to retreat back to my own little world, spending time alone with Julie where she could just take care of me. I felt safe with her. How was she in all of this? I now realize just how selfish I was then. It was all about me. I think I just felt sorry for myself.

In my quest to get myself ready for my sentencing up in Marinette, I contemplated that I was probably going to be going away to prison. With the burglary charge, I was facing ten years in prison. I saw a jail term as the inevitable outcome, since it was northern Wisconsin. The word was that they didn't go easy on people coming from a big city committing crime in their area. So I felt sure that this was going to be my time to pay for my insane fascination with narcotics. Of course I wouldn't play by the rules. I figured that if I received a ten-year sentence, I would find someone to smuggle me a lethal dose of heroin. If that didn't work, I would simply hang myself.

I began to scour the streets for some dope, as a going away present for myself. I found my old friend Terry had been getting Percodan from an old acquaintance of ours, Alice. She'd contracted polio and was in quite bad physical shape. She always had a source for Percodan, along with a monthly prescription from our old friend Dr. G.

When we bought the Percodan from Alice, we would head right for the bathroom, our shooting gallery. Alice had this mad crush on Terry, so he would try to console her and get her to relax about our shooting up in her house. Then, Alice would begin to nod off. She was herself on all types of meds. As soon as she began to nod off, Terry would dig in her pockets for the bottle she had. While he was checking her person, I would go through her cupboards, cabinets, and drawers. Terry told me this was a frequent occurrence with visits to Alice, and he said it worked every time. He said she would always take him back. He said she could always get more pills with her condition. What doctor would deny this poor woman pain pills? Just looking at her, you could tell she suffered a lot of pain. This was a pitiful display of humanity, but we felt that we needed the Percodan just as bad as she did.

My Day in Court

With my court date in Marinette coming up soon, I knew it was going to get tricky. I had to wean off this shit once again. I found five Percodan here and there, so as to wean off slowly. Even though it wasn't as hard to come off of this stuff as heroin, I still had raw nerve endings. Along with sleeplessness and legs flopping around like a fish out of water, I had a feeling of low-grade depression.

When my court date arrived, my parents and Julie accompanied me. My father mentioned that he had been in contact with my attorney's cousin, whom he knew well. The attorney was a longtime criminal defense lawyer in Milwaukee. I met with him, and he informed me that the pre-sentence investigation information the court gathered was favorable. He said that he had high hopes that if I pleaded guilty and asked for leniency in return for my plea, avoiding a trial would lead to a good outcome. He told me there were no guarantees that I wouldn't do jail time. Knowing that I was guilty as sin, I did as he suggested.

Having heard both sides of the case, the judge started with saying that he was not bound to make his decision on either the plea of the defense attorney, nor the prosecutor. He then asked if I had anything I'd like to add before he made his decision. I made a statement, telling him and the prosecutor that I was sincerely apologetic for my actions, and it was the most stupid thing I'd ever done. The judge said that what I had done was very offensive to the entire community of Marinette. He said that I was very fortunate to have him to dispose of the case. He was going to pass a stayed sentence of four years in prison and transfer the case to Milwaukee, which meant that if I was to be sentenced for any other crimes over the next four years, the four-year sentence would be enforced.

My probation officer in Milwaukee had left me to face my sentencing up north in Marinette. He took into consideration the fact that the crime up north came before the offense in Milwaukee. So, I was instructed to continue my supervision in Milwaukee as before. I did my weekly visits to the probation officer and my drug screens. I believe in those days, and from what I was told by a street savvy guy I met, that Percodan was not a substance that was caught in drug screens. This most definitely had to be the case, since I never heard anything from the probation officer stating that my urine samples were dirty.

Now, one would think that a person facing at least four years in prison might think twice before making the same mistake. But I was on a mission. At that time in my life, deep down I just felt there was absolutely no hope for any type of normal life for someone like me. Here I was, a young man who had probably broken all Ten Commandments by the age of twenty-five. A man whose physical health was declining fast, whose mental health was in a shambles, and who bordered on criminal insanity. A soul riddled with sin and disdain. I knew I was shunned by society, and I felt that I needed to complete my mission. I should just commit a quick suicide and be a self-centered coward.

My Maria

While I continued on the same hopeless and destructive path, I lived for one thing. That thing seemed to be a daily mission to have one last hurrah. I still had that monkey to deal with. My withdrawals were back and taking a toll on my health again. I did just enough heroin that I got from Stan to make it through work. But, I needed to find a way to wean off again. I found some Percodan to help me come off it, but it wasn't enough.

One weekend I needed to get a few more Percodan. The guy I usually got the Percodan from was out of product so I called my guy from treatment, Bob. He told me he would be getting some and asked that I stop by his house. When I arrived, he was there with his girlfriend, and they had been hitting doctors all over the area for Dilaudid and Percodan. He would send her into the office to get the prescription. He said it worked every time. She was a very attractive girl, and I guess that made it easier. He pulled out a bottle of Dilaudid and sold me two. He said it was a waste to drop them orally and that he had some new syringes.

I did the Dilaudid, and it was such a rush. It produced a crushing feeling on my shoulders, then an immediate feeling of euphoria and relaxation. It felt like a thousand-pound weight was released from my body. I absolutely loved it. If I couldn't get heroin, this was a good substitute.

I asked Bob about the girls we had been in the treatment center with. He said he had Maria's phone number and that I should call her. I called her that night. She said that she had relapsed and would like to see me. We planned a time to meet at her house the next morning.

Bob and I came up with an idea of going up to northern Wisconsin to hit some doctors' offices for Percodan and Dilaudid. The next morning, I got a ride down to Maria's neighborhood in the Hispanic area of Milwaukee. Maria happened to be Puerto Rican. I stopped at a phone booth to call her. She gave me the address, only a block away.

When I arrived at her house, she came to the door and invited me in. There were probably five other people in the house. She introduced me in Spanish and then brought me back to her bedroom. We spent time laughing and hanging out for a few hours in her room.

She told me about her family, some of whom were in Puerto Rico, others in America. She then brought up that she was going to get some heroin in about an hour. She also told me that her father had just been arrested on cocaine charges and that she was waiting for his call before we left. He called minutes after that, and they spoke for a bit. The conversation was in Spanish so I had no clue what was said.

We left for a house nearby where I gave her some money and waited out back. She came out minutes later, and we went back to her house to do the heroin. It was some strong stuff! She called it Mexican Brown heroin. She said that her friends had family members who would go to Mexico, ingest heroin-filled balloons, and then dig the balloons out of their shit once home. "So, I guess we're doing some shitty heroin, in the literal sense," I told her. She liked that one. I ended up staying at her house a few days, and we went at it until the money was gone. Then Maria said she was going to be busy with her uncles, trying to help her father get out on bail.

I went back to crashing at various old friends houses for a couple days, but I was already looking forward to returning to Maria's on

Friday. I kind of liked her, though there was somewhat of a language barrier and the fact that she was five years younger than me. On Friday, I called her house and a woman answered, identifying herself as Maria's cousin. She informed me that Maria had died of a heroin overdose. When I hung up, I felt sick. I didn't know what was what. That was a dark day that stuck with me for a while.

Doctor, Please

When I told Bob about Maria he seemed shocked. He told me to stop by later in the day. He and his girlfriend, Sandy, were going to hit a few doctors and asked that I come along with them. When I arrived at his house, they were all ready to go. Sandy was all dressed up like she was going to church. We visited some doctor's office on the south side of Milwaukee. We dropped her off and waited almost an hour and a half for her to come out. She had a prescription for ninety Dilaudid. That was pretty good, seeing that they were going for $25 apiece. But that was minus what we ended up shooting, which was usually most of them.

When we returned to his house, we did some of the D's (Dilaudid) and nodded out. I ended up staying there for the night. Bob told me that Sandy had been having sex with this doctor we had just visited. That's how she got so many of them. No wonder it had taken so long! She had been visiting him a couple times a month. He said sometimes she would be in there for two hours but always came out happy.

Over the next month or so, I made his house my new home. Bob and I began to take Sandy to quite a few doctors. We also began to see some ourselves. He and Sandy taught me well! They told me to ask for an antibiotic or a muscle relaxer to divert the doctor's attention from drug seeking. We scoured the entire three-county area around Milwaukee. I visited as many doctors as I could get to see me as a pain-riddled patient and begged for Dilaudid and Percodan.

When that became too much work, we just simply stole the doctor's prescription pads. It was cutting out the middle man. We would go to the nearest copy machine store, white out the phone number of the doctor's office, and insert a phone booth number. We had a girl waiting at the phone booth to answer with the doctor's office greeting and verify the validity of the prescription. I wrote the prescription with the needed pain pills at whatever amounts I was legally allowed. That seemed to hold me for a day or two. I was doing a hundred or more Percodan within a matter of twelve hours. I was now looking over my shoulder for police everywhere I went.

Careless Penmanship

I decided to call my ex girlfriend Julie for some possible refuge. Julie had been staying with a friend in West Allis, a suburb of Milwaukee. Julie and her friend invited me over to their new apartment. I got a ride over to their place. It was a spacious apartment with a nice layout and was decorated very well. As we sat and talked, they wanted to know if I could get a few Percodan for them. They liked to do a few here and there. They weren't junkies like me. They held jobs and lived normal lifestyles.

I told them I might be able to locate some. What I didn't tell them is that I had done over 800 Percodan myself in the prior week. I didn't even want to think about that. I consumed Percodan as fast as I could get it. I was embarrassed to say that I didn't have brains enough to save some or sell some for a meal. It all went into feeding my habit.

Knowing I still had some blank prescriptions, I told Julie that I would go check to see if I could get some Percodan. I left their apartment, stopped at a gas station, and wrote a prescription for ninety Percodan. It was about seven on a cold and very snowy evening. I left the gas station with my prescription in hand and $20 in my pocket.

Walking down Greenfield Avenue, near Julie's new apartment, I located a pharmacy. I knew where almost every pharmacy was in Milwaukee County. The pharmacist greeted me right away and was very pleasant. I handed him the prescription, and he said, "I will get it ready for you now, if you don't mind waiting." I kept an eye out to see if he would call the doctor. This was usually a sign to get out as fast as you could.

He never picked up the phone. He was going through the motions of filling the bottle with my Percodan when I heard footsteps from behind me. As I turned to look, someone grabbed me from behind by my right arm and then another by my left arm. Sure enough, two West Allis police officers had me dead to rights.

I was taken down to the police station, finger printed, and photographed for a mug shot. Then I was driven down to the Milwaukee County jail, finger printed, and photographed again. I was put in a cell block. I was feeling beat, imagining what my probation officer was going to say. This was my third offense in less than nine months.

The Judge

At my arraignment I met with my attorney, Russell S. He was young black attorney, thorough and aggressive. It seemed he had to be, given that he was somewhat new to the criminal defense arena. From my observation, Atty. Russell S. worked very hard on defense for drug offenders and sought a case for drug treatment as opposed to jail.

While awaiting my trial, I was taken to the House of Correction, a facility used as a work farm release, for midterm sentences of a year or less, and as a go-between for being sent to a state prison facility. I had been put on probation hold by my new probation officer, whom I will call Joe. Joe had come to visit me shortly before going into court for my preliminary hearing. He informed me that the judge I was going before was not one known to be lenient. He told me that he would be there for me, but only to represent his probation and parole department, with no recommendation either way.

When I was called in front of the judge, he asked a point blank question of both attorneys: "Why isn't this man in prison already?" My attorney replied that I was a perpetrator they were attempting to get straightened out. He added that the crimes I had been involved in were nonviolent and that he felt I needed to be in some type of treatment center. Mr. S. went on to say that he firmly believed that if the addiction was addressed, he felt absolutely sure that the criminal pattern would be eliminated from my lifestyle.

Given that I was already on probation for two other violations, the judge said that he would leave my fate in the hands of the probation and parole department. The judge sentenced me to four years in the Wisconsin State prison with a stayed sentence. The stayed sentence meant there would be an additional four years on top of whatever I was sentenced to serve by probation and parole. I was now once again sent to the House of Correction for a hold on my probation violation. There, my probation officer informed me that I would need to make this my dwelling for the next month, at the least, until his department decided what to do with me.

The House

My stay at the Milwaukee County House of Correction this time was pretty depressing. I was feeling lost in spirit, and I was emotionally and physically exhausted. I could not see any light at the end of the tunnel. I saw no hope for a way out of the way of life I had been living, even if I were to be released clean. I just felt that there were no avenues for me to live drug free.

So, while I sat awaiting my fate, I went about my way as best as I could. I stayed to myself, and I volunteered to work in the bakery. This was a way to make the time go faster and get away from sitting on my bed. My bed was one of sixty spaced out about three feet apart from each other. Sitting and sleeping in the same area with fifty-nine other guys like this, day in and day out, was absolutely miserable. I had a hard time sleeping in a room where almost half of the guys were snoring and smelled with body odor.

When it came time to work in the bakery at 4:00 am, I was more than ready to go. I was an assistant to the Master Baker. When asked if I had any experience in kitchen or bakery work, I answered yes to both. While I did have some experience in the restaurants where I'd worked, the only actual baking experience I had was baking bagels and donuts with my mother years ago. But, how were they to know?

I'm quite sure that the Master Baker soon caught on that I had little clue as to what I was doing. Still, I did catch on quickly, and he liked that. He didn't trust most of the other people sent to work for him. I always seemed to have a way about me that people trusted. I was comfortable in the role.

One trick I learned early on in the bakery was that there was an easy way to make friends and gain some leverage around the place. I met an older gentleman who had been there for about six months. He told me that he had limited duties due to some issues within the House of Correction. I didn't ask about that and didn't much care. He told me some old stories about the place and familiarized me with some of the ropes. He also gave me a recipe for something that could make things interesting and possibly bring fun to the place; it was called 'Apple Jack.' He had made this at another lockup he'd been in. He seemed to know quite a bit about correctional institutions. That was not really something I had hoped to learn firsthand, but I did find the stories interesting.

Apple Jack, he explained, was like a beer or wine. The main ingredient was baker's yeast. The yeast was very hard to come by and was watched very closely by the Master Baker. The yeast was locked away, and every bar of yeast had to be accounted for. He gave me the lowdown on how it was made. Since I was in a trusted position with the Master Baker, it would be up to me to acquire the yeast. When the yeast was in hand, he explained, he would have some large containers filled with apple slices, sugar, and water. He would then add the yeast and hide the containers on top of the large bread ovens, way in the back and out of sight. The heat from the ovens would speed up the process of fermentation. The end product would be a very nice alcoholic beverage.

The only problem was absconding with the yeast. It came in large bars about ten inches long, five inches wide, and three inches thick. Since bread was on the food line for breakfast, lunch, and supper, we made a lot of bread daily. The dough mixer was a huge bowl with large paddles. My duty was to combine large bags of flour, sugar, eggs, and water. After completing this process and starting the mixer, I would notify the Master Baker that we were ready for the yeast to be added.

The Master Baker would go to the locked area of the kitchen, grab the yeast bars, and bring them to me to complete the dough. When he brought it, he would watch me open it, and continue to watch me until it was in the mixer. I realized that this baker had probably had quite a bit of experience with missing yeast.

As the days went by, I was able to get some very small chunks of yeast off the top of the bread dough as the mixer was running. But the chunks I was able to get were only about the circumference of a quarter. I handed them off to my guy, and he would just give me a smile and whisper, "We need more, my man. We need a lot more."

About three weeks into this process, the guy said to me, "I'm going to double dare you to get a half-bar of yeast." He told me that would be enough for a nice batch of Apple Jack. Even enough to sell to other residents of this fine place.

Well, that morning as the Master Baker gave me the bar of yeast for the morning's first batch of bread dough, I unwrapped it as always. As I put the bar of yeast into the mixer, I turned away to tend to the cake batter I was also mixing. The baker, seeing me away from the mixer, turned towards his little office area. I quickly reached my hand into the big bread mixer in an attempt to get the bar of yeast before it crumbled. I managed to get half of the bar out of the mixer. As always, for a guy like me, half was never enough. So I reached in attempting to get the other half, and I felt a tremendous pressure on my hand. There was a crunching sound. The mixing paddle had cracked my right hand below the wrist. It hurt like hell! But, I did manage to get another quarter of the bar of yeast.

At the end of the day, I had the yeast needed to make a very large batch of Apple Jack. And I met the dare made to me. In some strange way, I felt like I was helping someone. I think that I wanted to feel needed, and maybe I wanted to be important. About a week later three large batches of Apple Jack were ready for consumption. It wasn't too bad. Even though I never really did like the taste of alcohol, it did appeal to me a bit. It gave me a buzz after having been clean for some time.

Now, the master brewer was elated on the score we'd made. He was very proud of this batch. He filled a bunch of little milk cartons like the ones we drank in grade school. He said that he was going to put a dollar price tag on each carton, which was a substantial price at that time, in this place.

To be honest, the money making part of this had no appeal to me. As with heroin, pot, or other narcotics I obtained on the street, selling it did nothing to make me feel fulfilled. It was never about making money for me; I just wanted to escape from reality and numb myself to the boredom and pains of life.

The Big Escape

As my days passed and I awaited my fate, contemplating what my punishment would be from the probation and parole department, I continued to make bread and cakes in the bakery. I continued snitching a bit of yeast, here and there. Still feeling the pain in my hand from the mixer, I was more cautious. I worked as many hours working as I was allowed. As I got to know the ropes better, I saw more of what was going on.

One week I caught wind of a couple of guys who were plotting to escape. This was amusing seeing that this place was pretty well locked down. If you got outside of the building, there was a twelve-foot-high fence with an additional three feet of razor sharp barbed wire on top. I didn't think much of their plot. There are always people in jail plotting an escape.

One morning in the bakery I saw the two guys who were plotting. They asked me to distract the Master Baker. They wanted me to try to keep him busy by the bread ovens for five full minutes. One of the guys mentioned was originally from Mexico and was facing a twelve-year term in Wisconsin state prison. The other guy was facing a six-year prison sentence.

When 6:00 am came, I was working with the Master Baker, and I didn't have to distract him because he was already distracted. He was showing me some of his tricks for making cakes and bagels. I think he had become comfortable with me, because I worked hard. Anyway, he was distracted, as the two would-be escapees hoped for.

It was about 6:15 am when we heard the garbage truck pull into the back of the bakery area as they did twice a week. As the Master Baker went back to unlock the two gates, I looked around and noticed the two guys were nowhere to be seen. The baker opened the gates, supervised the garbage trucks, the dumpster was loaded, and another one replaced it. Once this was done, the truck began its way out.

The two guys had managed to hide under all of the garbage. When the truck pulled out, they leapt out of the dumpster and made their way to the fence. Up the fence they went, with multiple aprons from the kitchen to pad them from the barbed wire. This was the funniest thing I had seen in quite some time. I was told the guy from Mexico actually made it out and had a car waiting. Word was that he got back to Mexico. I never heard anything about the other guy.

These stories have stuck with me over the years. Why are they important? They're just crazy memories. And I would most definitely not want to relive them. Still, they are memories that built the character I am today.

CHAPTER EIGHT

Alternatives

It was a spring day in 1979, and I had just finished a day's work in the bakery at the House of Correction when I received word that I was to report to the office of the Wisconsin Correctional Service. This was a department within the facility that handled recommendations for inmates. It housed a group of social workers who dealt with various types of issues relating to most every criminal problem, including sexual abuse, violent behavior, mental health issues, drug and alcohol abuse, and many other behaviors within the criminal justice system.

I was escorted to the office to meet with a young lady named Nancy. She explained that her role was to evaluate people based on their crime and their potential for rehabilitation. Nancy had me complete a questionnaire on my family history, health history, and lifestyle since the age of twelve.

After my evaluation, Nancy told me about a facility that might offer me the possibility of changing my lifestyle and becoming free of substance abuse. It was called the Wisconsin Family. She explained that this facility was not just a place to sit in a cell. She said it was a grueling, boot camp style therapeutic program. There was no promise that I would be accepted, but if I was, there would be no turning back. If I aborted my stay there, I would have to complete my sentence in the Wisconsin State Prison. She finished by saying that she would work with my probation officer to see if there would be a possibility of recommending this to the court.

About three days later my probation officer, Joe, came to visit me and informed me of his conversation with Nancy, the social worker. He told me that I would need to spend thirty days in a detox facility before admittance to the Wisconsin Family treatment center. When Joe left, I had a lot of thinking to do. I knew that this was not going to be just a slap on the wrist. I was going to be going away somewhere.

The next morning, Joe visited again and told me I was scheduled for evaluation at the Wisconsin Family—unless, of course, I wanted to stay in jail. Sitting another day in that hell hole was not my first choice. So off we went to visit what was to be my new home for the next eighteen months.

Emotional Boot Camp

The facility was an old eight-unit apartment building on the east side of Milwaukee, only blocks from downtown. At the locked front door, we were greeted by the director of the facility, Chris. He gave us a short tour of the building and then introduced me to one of the residents who was considered one of the trustees. The trustees, I learned, were residents who had some tenure and had earned privileges by having good standing in the program.

I was escorted to my room and introduced to my four future roommates. The trustee then showed me to the communications room, where he took my basic information and explained the rules of the program—which were many and very strict. The daily schedule was regimented. There was a 6:00 am wake up and a 9:00 pm lights out. There was to be no deviation from this schedule.

The day began with a morning reading of sorts, very similar to prayer. All the residents made a circle and did a recitation together. I cannot recall, or find, the entire prayer. But it went something like this: "We are here because we have no refuge finally from ourselves. Until we confront ourselves in the eyes and hearts of others, we are running.

We are neither the giant of our dreams, nor the dwarf of our fears. We are human beings, a part of a whole, with our share in its purpose." I recited this every morning, but for the life of me, I just couldn't decipher or process its meaning. Not until years later did the words make sense to me.

After our morning prayer, the kitchen crew (selected by the senior residents) and staff would go to the kitchen to prepare breakfast for the twenty-five or so residents. While the breakfast was being prepared, the rest of us would go to clean our rooms and make our beds, military style. That is putting it mildly. Everything was inspected, and it needed to be perfect. Even if your own work was perfect, you were not exempt from further work, because if any resident was the slightest bit faulty in their housekeeping, we all paid. When we were finished with our work, we were called down to breakfast. I must admit, it was always very good. It sure beat the hell out of jail food.

We always began our breakfast with a prayer of thanks. I felt a person could disbelieve in prayer and just go with the ritual, which is what I did. No one was ever forced to kneel, bow, or chant. With that out of the way, breakfast commenced.

A group of four or five residents were assigned to 'tighten up' following breakfast. The cleanup had to be absolutely impeccable; there could not be one granule of sugar or salt on the floors or counters. It was inspected by the senior residents and usually one staff member. If they found the slightest imperfection, or they were just not in good mood that day, they would tear up the kitchen. I mean they would empty the cupboards; dump molasses on the floors, counters, and shelves; and throw flour on top of that. The kitchen crew had to go back to scrub and clean on hands and knees. This was their attempt to break us down, to become a 'shell of a human being.' They called it emotional boot camp.

As the 'tighten up' crew cleaned on hands and knees, we had to yell at the top of our lungs things like, "I'm just a crawl-from-under-a-rock dope fiend" and "I'm sick of my life being a no good drug addict." If we were not loud enough or we were not cleaning fast enough, they would proceed to douse more flour over the floors, counters, and shelves. We would have to do everything over, yelling at the top of our lungs. We always had the option of leaving to complete our prison term. There were a few who chose that route rather than be demeaned, humiliated, and belittled.

The entire program was based on breaking a person down and then helping them build a whole new self-image with a new way of thinking their way through problems. There was a classroom style course held weekly called 'Rational Behavior Therapy.' It was aimed at helping a person learn to work through situational issues. It actually did make a lot of sense, though at the time, it seemed to me like brainwashing.

During my time at this place, I saw quite a few people break down emotionally, some to the point of no return. A few were transferred to other places such as mental health facilities. Conforming to this program, for some people, was just plain impossible. If a resident displayed any sort of negative behavior, there were consequences. People were made to scrub toilets with a toothbrush for hours while reciting statements about what they did wrong and what they were going to do reform.

Each and every day was highly structured with a full schedule for the residents. The people who ran the program seemed downright cruel. Still, I found some aspects of the program to be helpful—maybe not at the time, but years later.

One warm summer day, after about three months of this place, I felt I could not take it anymore. I went into a counselor's office to inform him that I wanted out, that I had learned what I could from the place. He reminded me of my court order and said he would need to call my probation officer. He opened the front door—which was always locked—and let me go outside to think about my decision. I sat on the lawn looking around at the trees swaying in the wind, with the sun shining down through a beautiful blue sky, and I felt so damned depressed. I wanted to leave in the worst way. I felt that after being clean for all these months, I was ready to live a normal life. I was absolutely certain that drugs were a thing of the past. But, I had the dark cloud of prison hanging over my head.

While I sat on the grass thinking, two of the counselors, as well as two residents that I had become close with, came out to talk with me. One counselor told me to take some time and think about where I had been six months ago. "Think about how long you were living the life of insanity that got you where you are today," he said. He went on to say that he felt that I had been making very good progress and that I was probably halfway through the first phase of the program. At the pace that he saw me moving, he said that he could see me doing very good things in life, if I gave it a shot. At the time, all I could think of was to get out of the hell hole I was in. I'd been clean for almost six months, I was feeling physically fit, and I longed to be with a woman. I just wanted the hell out.

But, after about an hour of listening to the counselors and my peers, I decided to go back inside and give it a go. With jail as my only alternative, I could stay where I was. The only positive thing I had ever seen jail do for a person like me was to lengthen their time away from drugs. So, I was back in, and I didn't have to serve any consequences for my near desertion.

After this incident I felt like I had experienced some growth in my spiritual and psychological outlook from many of the valid things pointed out from the staff during our conversation. I became more involved in the program, and about a month later I was given additional privileges. I was promoted to a trustee, of sorts. This meant that I, along with two other residents, became senior residents with positions similar to staff members. We pretty much ran the facility after the staff went home for the evenings at 10:00 pm. There was just a night watch person, usually a student, whose only duty was to be at the facility in case of break-ins or a resident attempting to leave. They usually just studied for an hour or two and then fell asleep until 7:00 am.

After a month or so of being one of the senior residents and having input on making decisions as part of staff, I became close with the other two trusted residents with whom I shared responsibilities. We spent time coming up with schedule changes, consequences for negative actions by residents, and an occasional outdoor activity. There was a small park with a picnic area and a baseball field about a block away. We planned picnics for days like Memorial Day and the Fourth of July.

I, along with two other residents, made a grill out of a fifty-gallon barrel. We had one resident who was a self-proclaimed grill master and loved to cook soul food, especially barbecued ribs. We set our dinner menus to include Edward's soul food. Occasionally, I made some Italian style dinners. We would compete about whose dinners were better. I insisted that black people didn't really learn to cook until the Italians came to America. Edward claimed that we Italians had stolen their recipes.

All in all, it became a bearable place, and we even had some fun. It was still very strict, and I still had a problem with their 'consequences.' If we got too lax, the entire facility went back to a 'tight house' condition, enforced by the staff. We all had to clean from morning to lights out, using four-by-six-inch rags to scrub every part of the facility: the walls, the fixtures, the floors. When the tight house was deemed to be over by the staff, it came as a big relief. It seemed the tough times made the more lax times that much better. Perhaps this was part of their strategy. It was almost exhilarating—as crazy as that sounds.

There came a day that I got to talking with the other two resident trustees. We felt we had worked very hard and that we had earned a night out on the town. Could we pull off a way to sneak out some night? After dinner and clean up were completed, the two other trustees and I met to discuss some house business. And, we made our plan for getting out for a while. We would wait for the night watch person to doze off, and then we could climb down from the back second floor balcony.

Here I should explain that there was a process in place for any resident who might be having thoughts of leaving the treatment program or had some pressing issues that needed to be addressed promptly. They would ring 'the bell.' The bell was an actual bell with a handle that was always on an end table in the main living room area. Every resident was well aware of the bell, and we all knew that it was there for anyone in case of an emergency. If the bell was rung, it signaled that every single resident was to report to the main meeting room within five minutes. No matter if it was two in the afternoon or two in the morning, you needed to be there quick.

On the night of our escapade, everyone was in bed by 9:00 pm as usual. At about 11:00 pm the two other trustees and I met in the back stairwell. We went downstairs to check the night watch person, and sure enough he was snoozing with his head on his book. We went to the storage closet to get some of our money. With that in hand, we proceeded to the second floor balcony and climbed down. Off we went, laughing like some teenage kids escaping a grounding.

Our first stop was a corner bar about three blocks away. John was dead set on getting drunk. He went in to buy a six-pack of Pabst Blue Ribbon beer. He had spoken about his relationship with Pabst quite a bit over his months in the program. I was just happy to feel free. I declined on the beer and told the other two guys to enjoy it. We then took a walk down Brady Street which is a busy area of Milwaukee that had a bar on most every corner. We people watched, smoked cigarettes, and laughed. We discussed the possibility of bringing some women back to the facility, but we knew that would be a sure way of getting caught. As the hours went by, John bought yet another six-pack of Pabst. We enjoyed our short-lived freedom, but inevitably we needed to return to our quarters.

Once back in the facility, a big problem presented itself. John was pretty toasted from his Pabst. He went into the living area, grabbed the bell, and began to ring it. I was shocked. I was sitting on a chair in the main room as all the residents came hustling in. Here it was about three o'clock in the morning, and he smelled like a brewery. As everyone gathered in the room, including the night watch person, to find out what the emergency was, I was cringing. I had no idea what John was about to do.

When everyone's attention was directed toward John, he just stared. One of the residents asked what the emergency was, and John simply said, "I want you all to know that you're a bunch of low-down, drug addict assholes." One resident shouted out, "You a drunk mother f***er!" And some others jumped in and began to yell about being woken up for this kind of shit. The night watch person had to jump in front of a potential fist fight. And John began to bark out consequences that he was going to hand down to people.

Well, I quickly saw why John was in this program in the first place. Though I found what I was observing absolutely hilarious, I knew we were in for trouble. The night watch person instructed everyone to go to their rooms, and he began to write up a report for the staff director. I knew we were f***ed. John stumbled up to his bed, all the while calling out who was facing consequences. Well, all I could think was, yes—the consequence was going to be ours.

When all the staff arrived the next morning, the two other trustees and I were called into a meeting. The director, Chris, asked all three of us to write a paragraph of the prior night's incident—and he separated us while we wrote. I had no clue what the others were going to say, so I just said the bell rang, and I came down. I also said that when I came to the room, there were some words exchanged, and I just saw John as being depressed. Apparently John wrote that he drank some vanilla extract and got light-headed. And that he may have said some things to one of the residents who he had resentments about. The other guy, Freddie, also wrote that he just heard the bell and reported to the meeting area.

Needless to say, John was stripped of his privileges and received some toilet duty as punishment. But, he never did say anything about leaving.

Longing for Home

As time passed in the program, I began to feel stronger emotionally and physically, and I began to experience some moments of clarity and serenity. The moments of clarity were times that I felt like I was really getting life. I hadn't felt that in myself for many years, and never to this extent.

While in the first phase of the program, which was six months, residents were not allowed visitors. But, one late afternoon, my father stopped by to see if he could get an exception to the rule. Of course my father would attempt it. And he no doubt used his salesmanship on one of our staff members, because he made his way in the front door in no time. My father was still wearing his sharp suits and always could be mistaken for a mobster. It was a Robert De Niro type look. The counselor came and told me he needed me to come to the front door. And as we entered the front vestibule, he said that he would let me spend five minutes with my father.

When my father and I met, he gave me a kiss as always. He told me how proud he was to see me stick out the program, and he made mention of how healthy I looked. We chatted a few minutes about my mother and the rest of the family. And soon enough he had to leave. It was a very nice surprise, and as he always was, my father was very upbeat and complimentary.

Another month went by, and I was nearing the six-month mark, coming to an end of the first phase—that is, if I was compliant in all aspects of the program. If I were fortunate enough to move to Phase Two of the program, I would be transferred to another facility. At that facility, the residents were allowed to obtain a job and begin to live a life like that of a more normal individual.

I began to feel like I was very capable of moving forward with life. I was getting praise from the director of the program as well as from the other counselors. It was around this time that I learned from some other residents that a few former residents had left the program against the advice of the director, and the probation and parole department. Further, I was told that these individuals had not been sent back to jail. They had been given a chance to make it on the street with strict supervision of probation and parole. This really got me thinking. Why would they send me to jail? I never committed a violent crime. I never hurt anyone physically. And, I had been clean for almost eight months, counting the time served in the House of Correction.

The day came when I got up the nerve to try to make it on my own. I waited for the right moment when there was no staff in house, and I made my way out. I called my former girlfriend, Julie, to pick me up. I felt very nervous about my decision, but I did feel I was done with the old lifestyle. I knew that I had to call my probation officer the very next day to inform him I had left the program and that I felt very confident that I was going to make it this time.

When I did call him early the next day, he voiced his concerns, but said that he would go along with my decision. He told me that I would be expected to visit him twice a week and comply with weekly drug screens, and I agreed. When I hung up the phone I was feeling so free and so relieved. I was finally done with all the shit in my life. My girlfriend agreed to allow me to stay at her apartment for a couple of weeks until I found a place of my own.

For Old Time's Sake

The first couple of weeks with my girlfriend were great—especially the feeling of a woman next to me in bed. But, it quickly became something I took for granted. For me, I would routinely crave something I knew was out of reach. And when I felt I had it in hand, the obsession would fade.

Becoming comfortable with the thought that I could have a woman when I chose, I ventured off to see some old friends I hadn't seen in a while. Some of these people were ones I felt I needed to make some amends to, and some others, I just wanted to say 'hi' to.

I stopped by Mike's house. It was always good to see him, and his family was always very inviting. Both his mother and father were very nonjudgmental, even knowing about my insane habits of getting into trouble.

Mike and I laughed about our old drug dealer, Paddlehead, and our escapades to Florida, as well as the other people who had crossed our path. We reminisced about our heroin days, and I told Mike that was the one thing I really missed. And, of course, in just talking about it, I got the itch. The next thing I knew, we were out driving around looking for a heroin dealer. Mike admitted he had been chipping occasionally over the time I was gone. Somehow he juggled work and using once in a while. It seemed his willpower was much better than mine. For me, willpower was nonexistent. It was always that old theme—one was too much and a thousand never enough.

So, we found a phone booth, called his guy Barry, and the games had once more begun! We were at his place in a matter of fifteen minutes, buying a half-gram of heroin. I knew this was not what I needed to be doing, but that dark corner of my mind, that seemed to have sat dormant, had awakened. It said, why the hell you wouldn't want to feel ultimate euphoria, if only for a matter of hours? It told me that I had earned it for all the time I had spent clean. And it would definitely drown out that old thought of being a useless son of a bitch. It made sense to me, even though it wasn't rational, especially since I had been given a second chance on life, and I had a hell of a lot to lose.

But nothing was going to stop this obsession I carried with me. I wanted what I wanted, and I wanted "IT" now. And, "IT" was my fix to escape from the world I knew I didn't deserve to be in. The things I had done in life dictated that I needed to pay for my sins. I thought if people only knew who I really was, they too would understand my need for self-destruction.

When Mike and I finally got the dope, we did it up as fast as we could. And I must say that it felt so freaking good. I was puking my guts out, itching, and nodding off all the way into the world of the ultimate dream-state.

The consequence was waking up the next morning, knowing exactly what I had done. I had ruined over eight months of clean time. The problem was that I was clean but not sober in my thinking. What I had learned in the Rational Behavior Therapy class had taken a vacation. It was drowned out by the thoughts from that dark corner in my head. What a freaking shame! The only remedy I knew was to get more, in the hope of erasing my guilt. I found myself calling Mike the next day and saying it was time to do it all over. There we were, driving to Barry's place for more Hank.

These trips to Barry's became a daily thing and even twice a day sometimes. It was very unlikely that I would stop unless of course I got into legal trouble. My money situation had become an issue. When Barry would no longer front us some heroin on an 'I Owe You,' there was only one alternative—to substitute with Percodan or Dilaudid.

I began to visit doctors again, asking for pills for my fictitious migraines or backaches. I was back to Dr. G in no time, begging for prescriptions. And when I ran out of the ninety Percodan he gave me, which took only one day, I was on to other doctors.

When I visited doctors, I made sure I was very presentable, well-dressed and well-groomed. I couldn't go in looking like a drug seeker. On one visit I told the doctor that I was a minor league baseball player for the Cleveland Indians. Why I did this and why the Cleveland Indians, I have no freaking clue. But whether this doctor believed me or not, he wrote me a prescription for sixty Percodan. I continued this on a daily basis, until one day I was striking out at every doctor I visited and began to go through withdrawal.

At this point I figured the doctor and the pharmacist were just middlemen in the mix that needed to be eliminated. Just simply visiting as many local pharmacies I could locate in the yellow pages would be easier. Now we're talking burglary. I would enter the store and when the coast was clear, I would jump the counter, grab as many bottles of morphine type drugs as I could locate, and then run out. I didn't hurt anyone and never used a weapon, so what was the harm? Then off I went to the nearest friend's house or safest cheap motel to melt down and inject my gorilla's feast.

This way of doing business had its downside. People could identify me. The local detectives had my description come into their stations almost daily. It got to the point I couldn't even walk into many pharmacies without the clerks and pharmacists identifying me.

By this time word on the street was that I had a plethora of Percodan. The problem was that I didn't want to sell any. I didn't give a shit about money, but I did need to pay for the motel stays. Mike usually came by to buy small amounts for himself and some for other people. Other than Mike and a couple of other friends, I really didn't even want to see anyone. We had some laughs while doing the Percodan. But by this time, I was way out of hand. I was probably doing over 100 Percodan daily.

I went from motel to motel, fearful that I was being sought by the police. My veins were being destroyed from shooting them so much. In my stay at one motel, I had left for about two hours to hit another pharmacy. When I returned, the manager of the motel asked me what the hell was going on in that room. The maid had showed him my bloody bed sheets. It had become so hard to find a good vein to use that I began to use the smaller capillary veins, which were hard to hit and bled more. I told the motel manager that I had my girlfriend over, and she'd had a bad period. He just said, "Holy shit, I thought someone had been cut up in the room."

It was probably time to hit another motel. I gathered my plastic garbage bag I used to carry the little bit of clothing I had, my syringes, and a couple bottles of Percodan. I walked about two miles down the road to another cheap motel that was a bit tucked away. I always preferred that kind, as I felt more secluded and out of sight.

As I went about my daily business of scoping out pharmacies, my life was getting crazy. This habit of mine was way out of control. It was like I resumed right where I left off when I was locked up a year ago. I stopped going to see my probation officer, although I would call him to check in. When I did call, I was always hoping to get his voicemail. If he answered, I just told him all was well. I didn't have the balls to say there were issues. He would say, "No craziness going on?" and of course I would say no. His lack of concern told me was that he hadn't been contacted by the police.

I was carrying the section of the yellow pages with pharmacy locations around with me and driving by each one to survey the area. I wanted to get a feel for the traffic, the neighborhood, and the people working behind the counter. I would walk into the pharmacy to check out the pills, vitamins, or whatever was near the counter. Pharmacies kept the pill bottles in alphabetical order, so there were two designations I would home in on: 'D' or 'P' for Dilaudid or Percodan. Over my years of frequenting drugstores, I could pick out those bottles from 200 feet away.

I had been hitting pharmacies all over Wisconsin by now. That itself became an obsession. I was way out of control. On the street, junkies were talking about me. People I barely knew were running around town searching motels to find me. Everyone wanted Percodan, and Percodan prescriptions were pretty hard to come by, as doctors were tightening their pens and had become very reluctant to write them. I had quite a few people who sought me out to ask if they could be the getaway driver for me if they found a drugstore that they thought was easy prey.

But it was getting old, and I was getting very tired. I knew my life was out of control, and my gut made me think back on my time at the Wisconsin Family. I had some fond memories. I felt like I had finally learned how to live right, at least while I was there. And I remembered how good I had felt without drugs in my system. But with this gorilla on my back once again, I was not able to regain that feeling. And there was no way I wanted to go through the wicked withdrawals. I had never once gone through complete withdrawal without being locked in a cell, or in a hospital.

So with my habit once again dictating my life, I was pretty much stuck in this world of addiction. All my best intentions and dreams of being clean had been futile. That dark corner of my mind made sure that I couldn't do it.

I continued stealing from every drugstore I came across. These thefts carried a maximum nine-month sentence. I never used a gun or any other weapon. At the time, however, I hadn't researched the penalties; I just saw it to be an easy way to get more drugs. After each theft I committed I honestly felt bad for the employees. Most of the time they didn't realize what had happened until I was out the door. I never really planned these events, so it was amazing that I was never caught.

At one drugstore, I went through the swinging door to the pharmacy area while the pharmacist was filling a prescription. As I walked back and took three 1,000-count bottles of Percodan, the pharmacist asked if I had a delivery. Without thinking, I responded, "No, a pick up." The guy's expression said that hadn't registered. I'm not sure any of it registered with me either, other than the fact I had the Percs in my hands. I was that insane. By now I knew that this was insanity. I knew that someone would eventually be able to identify me, and this would all come to an end. But every time I went to do it I believed it was the last time.

As this continued day after day, I could think of only one plan that might work. I promised God that this would be the last time, and if He would let this go through smoothly, I would honor Him, go as far north as I could get in Wisconsin, and clean up. What a deal for Him, I thought! I always had some conditional offers that I put forth to my God with the hope that He would fall for it. Back then I was sure that was the way it worked. God would allow me to rob drugstores, and I could just annihilate my health.

Knowing this, I felt I had to eventually give in and do my part of the deal. I packed up some clothes, Percodan, syringes, and some money, and headed north. The plan was to go to Upper Michigan where an old friend of mine, Al, had an older brother living in a trailer home. My friend Al knew what I was going through. He too had been struggling with heroin, cocaine, and other narcotics. Also Al and I had previously visited his brother at his mobile home up north, and all the way up we hit doctors, pharmacies, and clinics attempting to extract some narcotics.

One of my most memorable times with Al, unfortunately, had been when Al had a good buddy over at an apartment on the north side of Milwaukee. While there, Al invited me up to do some cocaine and asked that I bring some Percodan. Well, as the night progressed with a group of people shooting cocaine for hours, I got to the point of paranoia and began to feel sick. I pulled out a big bottle of Percodan and quickly swallowed down thirty of them just to mellow out from the excessive cocaine binge. It was about ten minutes later that I walked out on the second floor balcony and heaved my guts out. The sickest part of the incident was that the Percodan were almost still intact, and as I was leaning over puking, I could see the Percodan in the snow bank below. Al and I looked down and together decided to see if we could salvage them. The pills were a bit swollen but we could still read the label imprint "ENDO 122." Now if that isn't sick. . . .

CHAPTER NINE

Northwoods Hideout

So I headed north. I made some quick stops in small northern Wisconsin towns to see the pharmacy setups. In one town I visited, I stopped to see an old doctor I had convinced a year or so earlier to give me Percodan for my supposed bad back. He had written a prescription for ninety Percodan which I considered a good score in those days. I was informed it was his day off. That just didn't sit right with me since I needed the stuff now! I left his office and thought the guy had to live close by since it was not a big town. I laughed to myself thinking how crazy an idea it was as I stopped at a phone booth to look him up in the White Pages.

With the address in hand I headed over to visit the good doctor at his house. It was a nice little Cape Cod-style home with a white picket fence and a big screen porch. I jumped out of the car, and up to the door I went.

The old doctor opened the door, stepped out, and with a bewildered look asked, "How can I help you?" I smiled and said "Hi Dr. C, it's good to see you again. I'm very sorry to bother you at your home. But, I was just at your office, and I drove a long way to see you. My back is killing me, and the last time I saw you, you gave me the little yellow pills called Perco something, but whatever they were, those were the only pills that worked for me."

There was a pause between us, and he gave me a look as if I were freaking crazy. He said, "For this you come to my house? You can't come to my home! Come to my office tomorrow." I sighed and asked if he could please just help me out this one time. I told him I would never have come to his home if I wasn't hurting so bad. Well, he finally caved in and wrote me a script for sixty Percodan. Junkies aren't real keen on backing off and accepting no for an answer. It's just the way it is.

On my way up to Michigan, I had 500 or so Percodan sitting in my bag. If I were really to quit while I was up there, these Percodan needed to go. I sure the hell wasn't going to toss them. So I made a stop, soaked down about twenty-five of them, and shot them up.

One stop that I made always stuck in my mind. It was near a little brook along a desolate area of northern Wisconsin that looked like an old commercial I remember seeing as a kid, 'The land of sky blue waters.' I hadn't any water to soak down the Percodan so I just used the water from the brook. After all, some of the water we used to soak them down or shoot heroin back in Milwaukee probably wasn't any cleaner than the water from this stream, so why not? Every hundred miles I did it again and again until I arrived to a very small town in Upper Michigan.

I found a small resort type area with about four small cabins. I stopped in to pay for a week and settled into a cabin. It was a studio-style, one-room cabin with an old bed, a wood burning stove, and small kitchen area, as well as an indoor bathroom. Musty and damp, but nevertheless a place to stay.

Within forty-eight hours all 500 Percodan were gone. I was messed up, nodding out, and scratching my face until it was completely raw. My reflection in the mirror looked like I had a very bad case of wind burn. I knew that I was in for one hell of a case of withdrawals.

The next day, after finally going into a good deep sleep the night before, I got up and took a walk down by the lake behind the cabin. It was called Mirror Lake. I saw why they named it that. Looking out at the lake, I saw the reflection of a deer, and it was truly like seeing the deer in a mirror. As I sat down to think about what my next step was going to be, I became more and more depressed. I knew that I would eventually going to have to face the music back in Wisconsin.

I wasn't feeling any withdrawal yet, but I knew it was inevitable. I probably had so much in my system that I was running on the fumes from the amounts I had used in the past two days. In addition to the physical withdrawal symptoms from oxycodone (the narcotic in Percodan) there were also psychological withdrawals. Depression set in. It was like losing a loved one. The drugs had become my best friend, my lover, and my lifeline.

Eventually I ended up at a place called Bears Lounge to eat and drink beer. For me, one of the worst things in the world was to drink alcohol while hoping to make it through withdrawal. Not only did it push the opiates out of my system faster, it made me feel sick. It seemed to exasperate the ill feeling of the withdrawal. Some people I knew liked to drink away the withdrawal, but I did not—maybe because of the quantity of the stuff I took.

Nevertheless, when I got back to the cabin, I drank a six-pack, hoping to fall asleep. I did end up falling asleep, only to wake up about an hour and a half later. The withdrawal was really beginning to take its toll. All I could do was lie in the bed flopping around. My bones were aching, my nose was running, I had stomach cramps that wouldn't stop, and I felt feverish. Looking outside, I could see the rain coming down, and it was very chilly.

The rain continued nonstop for almost four days straight, and I was getting really sick. I felt that maybe I should had saved some of the Percodan to wean myself off more slowly. But for me, that was never an option. I never did save opiates. If I had them, I did them. I was now paying seriously for my abuse of opiates. I felt absolutely horrible. I was deeply depressed, had suicidal thoughts, a slight fever, and every bone in my body ached. Though I wasn't feeling hungry, I knew I needed some nutrition. But without enough energy to find food, my thoughts instead began to center on getting to a phone booth to search for doctors and pharmacies.

Somehow, I got up and dragged my ass through the nasty, cold rain to my car. I was shivering and my teeth were chattering, but I made it to a phone booth. I tore out the phone book pages of doctors and pharmacies. I knew the odds of getting away with a theft, in my condition and not knowing the area well, were not good. Better to seek out a doctor. At this time, I really did want to quit. Having another thousand Percodan in my possession would be a big mistake.

I grabbed my map and headed to the nearest hospital emergency room as it was getting late to find a doctor's office open. When I met with the ER doctor I told him my lower back was hurting badly. I told him that I had been up north fishing for a couple of weeks and forgot to bring my Percodan. He said that he would give me a prescription for something similar, which turned out to be Darvocet, a milder narcotic. I had the script filled for sixty and went back to the cabin.

I started out taking four of the Darvocet, along with a couple cans of beer. I didn't feel much of anything, although my bones didn't seem to ache as much. And I got a couple hours of sleep, always crucial when going through withdrawal.

During the next few days, the weather remained rainy and cold. I sat alone in the cabin and began to experience what I believed to be 'cabin fever.' I was going absolutely nutty! I felt depressed enough from the withdrawal, but with the seclusion, the lack of nutrition, and no one to talk to, I had gotten really sick. I was stir crazy. Three weeks of torture was enough. I packed up my stuff and headed back to Milwaukee. There had to be a better way.

Hotel California

When I got back to Milwaukee, I stopped at a drugstore on the east side. I had thought about this one a few times, but being in an area close to the inner city, I figured the security to be a bit much. But, I was still feeling quite a bit of withdrawal, and running around town looking for heroin was not feeling like the way to go, plus I was quite low on cash.

As I drove by the drugstore, it looked pretty empty. I parked about a half-block away and walked into the store. There was one customer speaking with the pharmacist in an aisle about 100 feet from the pharmacy. There was no one else around, and I thought, "How lucky can I be?" I looked back toward the drug shelves and saw that bottle that stuck out like a full moon in my eyes. I crouched down and crawled behind the pharmacy counter. As I reached up for the bottle of Percodan and slid it off the shelf, I noticed not one, but two more bottles. By the time I crawled back out from behind the counter, I had all 3,000 Percodan under my shirt.

I was about to run out when the pharmacist looked my way, smiled, and said, "I'll be right with you, OK" I just said, "That's OK, I left my wallet in the car; I'll be back in a couple minutes." He smiled and said, "OK," as I walked out of the store with three sealed thousand-count bottles of Percodan. I thought, "Why they all can't be like this one?"

With the bottles in hand, my withdrawal seemed to lighten up, even before I did any Percodan. That is why I say that the psychological part of withdrawal plays such a big part that can't be dismissed.

As soon as I left the drugstore, I stopped and called my friend Mike. We sat down, talked awhile, did some Percs, and laughed a bit. We then drove around the old neighborhood where my ex-girlfriend Jackie lived. I stopped in by another guy I use to run with, Terry S., and we, too, did some Percs. Terry and Mike didn't always hit it off too well, though they could be civil.

The three of us sat and talked about what had been going on around the neighborhood. They told me that another old acquaintance of ours who lived about a block away had been selling heroin. Both Terry and Mike said he might be interested in trading some Percs for heroin. We stopped by to check to see if he'd do it. When we arrived, he told the three of us not to stop over again without calling first. He was paranoid that having too much traffic at his house would arouse suspicion.

We sat at his house shooting heroin, and Mike and Terry began their feuding. Mike was teasing the guy's cat, and Terry began to yell at him, "Mike! Leave that cat alone! Or I'm going to gas you!" Sure enough, these two were up in each other's face ready to go to blows but fortunately it didn't come to that.

When we left, Terry offered to let me stay at his house where he lived with his parents. However, I would need to stay in the garage. It was summer, so I didn't see a problem with a cot in his garage. As the days went by, I was getting low on Percs already. So, I went to scope out a few more drugstores. I took a ride out to a northern suburb of Milwaukee and came back with another 1,500 Percodan. That wasn't too bad, so I felt at ease with my habit for at least a couple days. But this, too, was going to be the last pharmacy I robbed. I can't believe God fell for "the last store" bit again!

When I was back at my new home in Terry's garage, he told me some guy we knew from way back was interested in getting some heroin. And he asked if I wanted to take him to get some from the guy who lived nearby. Terry couldn't leave the house because he needed to take care of some things. So, I agreed to take the guy to get some heroin for him, as the dealer didn't want anyone he didn't know coming by.

Well, this old acquaintance of ours came to pick me up. When he arrived, he was with another person I didn't know. I got in the car with the two of them, and he introduced me to the guy driving. There was something about this guy that struck me the wrong way. I felt it in my gut. This guy had an aura about him that I just didn't like at all. And, sure enough, as he was talking small talk shit to me, he pulled out a bottle of a drug called Talwin. He took two of them and began to go on about how he really needed to get some heroin or cocaine.

Now, I knew all about Talwin. It was a narcotic; however, it was an opiate antagonist. So, if a person was addicted to heroin, Percodan, or any other opiate, they would go into withdrawal from taking Talwin. It has the same effect as Narcan, a drug used by emergency rooms to administer in the case of an opiate overdose. And, not to mention, anyone telling you that they needed heroin or cocaine is probably full of shit. Heroin and cocaine are in classes of their own. They're very different drugs.

Well, I now had a very strong gut feeling that this guy was a cop. I told him to park on a side street which was two blocks away from the dealer's house. I wasn't bringing this guy anywhere near that dealer. The guy handed me a hundred dollar bill and said, "Now make sure you come back with the stuff, OK?" To play along, I said, "I'll do what I can."

When I got out of the car, I walked the opposite way of where the dealer lived, cut through some yards, and I sat in someone's backyard for a few minutes, thinking it through. I didn't want to abscond with a cop's money, but I sure wasn't going to get dope for him. And, I didn't know why I was doing it in the first place. I wasn't getting any free dope or making money off the deal. My honest intention was just to do what I saw as a favor. Yes, I was that stupid!

After about ten minutes, I headed back to the car. As I got in the front seat, the guy reached under his seat while he asked to see what I got. I told him the guy was out of heroin. After telling him that, he pulled his hand back out from under the seat. He didn't have anything in his hand, though I felt sure if I had dope for him, it would have been a badge or a gun that he was reaching for. He was very disgusted, and said, "Who else can we get some from tonight?" He said he wanted to party, and he would share it with me. Well, I knew the only thing this prick was planning to share with me were handcuffs. I just told him I was quitting, and I hadn't seen too many people selling as of late. He sighed and said he would drop me off. The whole time I was with these guys, the one guy I knew, who sat in the back, had been quiet as a mouse. Or, what I should say: quiet as a rat!

When he dropped me off at a corner near Terry's house, I stopped at a phone booth and called Mike to tell him what had just happened. When I told him who I was going to help get some heroin for, he said, "Holy shit, Tony!" That guy had been arrested for selling eight ounces of cocaine to an undercover a few weeks back. It was a setup for sure. This guy we knew was trying to get out of his drug sale charge by turning on one of us. I don't think the cop cared who he got; he just wanted a bust. Years later I read in the newspaper that that same undercover had been stealing drugs from the seized drug storeroom at the Milwaukee police administration building. What an idiot.

Well, after that, I wasn't feeling too good about my situation. I had no clue what direction I was going to take in my life. The only thing I knew for sure was that it couldn't possibly have a good ending. I had tried everything I knew to stop. That dark corner of mind had become a large room full of guilt, regret, sorrow, and pain. It had succeeded in all but completely destroying me.

One morning I was sitting with Terry in the basement of his house shooting up some Percodan while his father was at work and his mother was upstairs. The phone rang and shortly after, Terry's mother called downstairs for him, and she was crying. It was a call from the hospital where his father worked as a security person. His dad had just died of a massive heart attack. Needless to say this was a tough day for Terry and his mother. So I knew I needed to find a new place to hang my habit for a while.

As I looked around for a place, I knew it needed to be inexpensive and somewhere I could hide out from the world when I needed. I came across a rickety, old rooming house with very small, nasty rooms. The bed had a mattress with springs sticking out of the top padding, and there was a rotted, drafty window right by the bed. And the community bathroom was pretty gross. But, I had before settled for a spot under a bridge, so what the hell?

As I sat in this crazy room, I almost became a part of the surroundings. I lay in that bed day in and day out, only leaving to find another score of Percodan or a loaf of bread, peanut butter, and some juice. That was it. There was nothing more to my life at this time. And as this room seemed to become my entire life, it became known as the 'Hotel California' to me and the people that knew me.

When my intuition told me things were getting too risky in some areas of Milwaukee, I began to venture out to the suburbs. I felt that these areas were less inclined to have a lot of traffic in their drugstores, and I would then have an accomplice who would lure the pharmacist out from behind the counter by asking questions about an item away from the pharmacy area. I would then crouch down and hurry back to grab the Percodan.

I was becoming bolder, and my habit was spinning more out of control than ever before. I completely cut off contact with my probation officer. I knew the day I would have to face him, and my sins, was right around some unknown corner. To be honest, I knew I had to be locked up if there were any hope of staying alive. But, I sure wasn't going to just walk into some center and ask for help of my own accord. And the fear of facing my PO wasn't related to the threat of being incarcerated; it was a sense of shame. He had given me so many chances, and he seemed to believe in the fact I was a decent human being who just couldn't grasp the concept of a normal life.

I heard through friends that there were detectives visiting my parents' house and asking them where I may be living. I was jumping around from motel to motel, to abandoned houses, to basements of apartment buildings that had unlocked doors. I remember waking up some days in basements of buildings when a washer or dryer would go on, and I knew it was time to head out.

I began to make visits to an old friend's pharmacy. By a fluke I found out he was in town and had opened a pharmacy. I knew this guy prior to all of my narcotic insanity, and he felt indebted to me for some past favors. I told him what I had been doing with the drugstore thefts, and asked for help to wean off the Percodan. He began to give me bags of Percodan, sometimes as many as 500. And he'd also throw in $500 in cash and tell me to get out of town.

The trips to his pharmacy became more frequent. I would ask him to give me another chance to wean off. It was always the last time I would ask this of him. Of course I would do it again, and I would need cash to get out of town. It was getting more and more insane with me visiting the pharmacy two or three times a week. He had a hard time turning his back on me, and I could sense it. I'd do whatever it took to get what I wanted, and I would stop at nothing to satisfy my never ending thirst.

Eventually, he told me that I was crossing the line. Hearing that from him, I knew that I was walking a very thin line and could very well find myself on the bottom of a river with cement shoes. I never doubted the extent of what he could do. I just felt I would know where the edge of the cliff was and would be able to back off if necessary.

Knowing I needed to step back from him for a while, I went back to the hunt. I was lured back to drugstore thefts. I scoured the Wisconsin area looking for any drugstore I thought was vulnerable enough to get in and out safely with their Percodan.

On one such occasion, I picked out a large Walgreen's pharmacy. I parked my car a block away in a residential neighborhood and walked around the fenced in area to the store. As I walked in, I saw that it was extremely busy. It was about six or seven in the evening, the time of the day that normal people were traditionally off work and out shopping.

I shopped around for a while. The store had a closing time of eight or nine. It was probably about a quarter to eight that I went into the bathroom. There were too many employees in all of the back rooms, and there was no way I could access to the storage area or basement without being noticed. So, the bathroom it was. I went in one of the stalls and tried to decide my next move.

I had no intention of leaving the store at that time, because I was beginning to feel withdrawal coming on, and I was desperate as hell. I closed and locked the stall door, climbed up on the tank, and put my feet on the toilet bowl. What an amazing evening! OK, it was some sick shit. What human being with any common sense whatsoever and with an ounce of decency (as my mother would say) would spend an evening crouched up on a public toilet?

After being crouched over and kind of dozing off, the lights went out in the bathroom, and it was very quiet. All I could hear was the very faint hum of the fluorescent lighting. I had no clue what time it was. I carefully and quietly stepped down off the toilet, unlocked the stall, and made my way to the door.

I looked up and down the aisles of the store and listened for any signs of life as I made my way to the pharmacy. I crawled under the swinging door of the pharmacy so as to not trigger any alarms. I took out my garbage bag and began to shovel in bottles of Percodan, Valium, and any opiates of significance to me. I crawled back out under the swinging door with my bag in hand and made my way to the main public door.

When I turned the deadbolt and opened the door, a loud alarm bell went off and scared the shit out of me. I had so much adrenaline, however, that I felt light as a feather and flew out of there. I ran to a wooden privacy fence that was about six feet high, separating me from another fifty yards to my car. I was over the fence in a matter of a few seconds, hopped into my car, and took off.

Just as I was turning the corner to the main street toward the freeway, I heard police sirens, as well as the alarm blasting. I was just then realizing what I had actually done. Yes, I had it planned out for the most part, but it was like a half-ounce or so of common sense came into me. It was like I had been under a trance. But, whatever it was, I did it, and I sure wouldn't be able to explain any of my trance bullshit to a cop, if I were caught.

I made my way to the Parklawn Housing Project near where I grew up. I tucked my car in a secluded parking spot and figured it would be safer there than anywhere else. Not only was I avoiding police, I also didn't want some of the people I knew to find me and my large haul of drugs. I made my way to an old friend's girlfriend's place to lay low.

The next day I was afraid to even walk down the street. I felt sure the police were keeping an eye out for me. It probably was not as dramatic in reality as it was in my mind. But just the same, I was very fearful of being caught this time as I had a very strong habit going, and I knew going through withdrawal in jail would be hell. I was one very sick man.

As I waited a few days in the house I was staying in, I just bided my time shooting dope. I then called Mike and told him what I did. He just laughed and said, "You crazy f***er" and then asked if we could meet up. We came up with a plan to trade some of the stuff I had in exchange for heroin. Mike had a lot of heroin connections so he made a few calls, and within a couple hours we had a gram of good heroin. We ended up doing the gram that night, and nodded off into heroin land, the place of no worry and no hurry.

For the next few weeks, Mike and I were off and running with our heroin escapades nightly. But, the money goes quick, and our requests to have the heroin dealer front us dope got old. He expected us to pay him before he would give us more heroin. We were just not able to come up with the cash to pay him for the stuff from yesterday, much less what we wanted the next day. So, it was back to the drawing board.

Boxed In

As I continued my downward trend in life, things took a turn for the worse. I got hooked up with a guy we knew as Jimmy F. This guy was living in the upper of an old house in the inner city of Milwaukee. There were also three other women living there too. All of them were doing Percodan or heroin. One was a lesbian, one bisexual, and one just curious.

Well, the house was quite an interesting place with all the crazy activities happening there. And, this guy Jimmy F. was quite a character. Story I heard was, an old girlfriend of his overdosed on heroin. And he wrapped her up in an area rug and put her in a dumpster. And then, from what I heard, he just went about his way as if it were just another day.

As the insanity went on in this house, the lesbian and another girl held up a drugstore with a pistol. That was a bit much for me. I never liked weapons of any kind and certainly didn't want to be involved in that shit. In all honesty that stuff scared me. I ended up leaving; the others were being evicted anyway.

I wound up going out and hitting a few drugstores. It got to the point where small pharmacies I hadn't been to were getting hard to find. I was so desperate one day that I walked into a Walgreen's pharmacy in a high traffic area. I scoped out the counters for what was what on the drug shelves and where it was.

I knew I'd be hard pressed to do this one. I would probably have better odds of robbing a bank than to get out of this place without being nabbed. I began to walk out of the store, thinking I might need to go to find a smaller drugstore, but then I had a better idea. I saw a double swinging door to a back room. I looked around to see if anyone was within view, and when it was clear, I slipped into the back room. I saw a stairway to a basement area, and I headed down there. As I was going down the steps, I said aloud, "Hello?" I was thinking that if anyone was down there, they'd answer, and I could ask where the bathroom was. There was no response, and I felt this was where I needed to be. I said another prayer, asking God to help me out one more time, just one more time. This would be it, I promised.

As I walked through the basement, I saw it was a storage area with boxes stacked in aisles. I came across a big empty box, and I climbed in. I tried to settle into it and not make any noise. I lay in this box for hours, and I dozed off. Finally, a clicking noise awoke me. Someone had turned off the lights. I sat there for at least another hour, all the while thinking how the hell I was going to find my way out of this dark basement without knocking something over and possibly setting off an alarm.

When I finally climbed out of the box, I could see very faintly the outlines of the aisles of other boxes. My eyes seemed to have adjusted enough to make my way out. I found my way to the stairs and quietly walked up. I literally came close to shitting myself, I must admit.

As I got to the swinging doors, I peeked outside into the store. It was dim, but I could see enough to make my way to the pharmacy area. I crawled to the back of the pharmacy and began to scoop up all the Percodan and Percocet, as well as some Dilaudid, as fast as I could. I stuffed them in my shirt and made my way to the door.

Pulling the door open, I looked to my right, and there was a police car parked on the street about fifty yards away from the door. I saw a small flashing light at the bottom of the door, but luckily there was no audible alarm going off. I walked out the door and turned to my left, keeping an eye on the police car out front. I began to run across the parking lot and behind the store. The police car didn't budge. Maybe the alarm hadn't triggered. The police car just sat there, and no one ever got out. I ran down the block to my car, jumped in, and headed to a motel that I had just checked into.

When I got inside my motel room, I quickly soaked down twenty-five Percs and began my little ritual. I injected myself over and over, and it became harder and harder to find a clear vein. I had been shooting in my hands, my wrists, my forearms, my upper arms, and then I started to go into my legs and feet. I was a freaking mess.

I knew I would be caught eventually. And I knew that I would be embarrassed to face my probation officer, Joe. I felt he had gone out on a limb for me. I am sure that it's not common to hear a parolee speak affectionately about their PO, but I felt gratitude for this man. My actions didn't reflect this, and I'm sure it didn't appear this way, but there was a lot of guilt in that corner of my mind surrounding this relationship.

So, as I sat in this motel room injecting nonstop until I nodded off, I knew it was insanity. I think I was trying to drown out part of my brain by doing more and more Dilaudid and Percodan. But it just didn't seem to ever go away completely. There were blood soaked towels lying by my side as I kept trying to get one last good hit. I thought that if I were to find one good vein where I could get a good big dose, I'd be satisfied. But, it just didn't happen.

And again, that old saying of one is too many, and a thousand never enough, rings so true to this period of my life. Not to mention that it seemed to happen with every facet of my life. From the beginning with the quest to get Hank Aaron and to anything else I had a fondness for (whether it was relationships, sex, a special food, sports, or even just working), I just never stopped. There was seemingly a black hole in my pleasure node. And through this addictive personality trait I had, I became more and more selfish and self-centered.

That night I remember very well. I would nod off and when I came back down to earth, I continued to do more and more. I finally dozed off into a sleep mode while watching Monday Night Football. The next thing I remember is waking up to *Green Acres*. Why I remember that so well, I have no clue. It was just that Mr. Ziffel and Arnold were pretty amusing. It may have been that the humor of the moment took me away from reality which was getting gloomier by the day. I just could see no end to this insanity.

As the sun came up, I felt the need to do more dope to escape the chaos of a new day. My thoughts raced to the fact that I should have some type of responsibility in my life. I sure hadn't been working like the normal people. And that feeling just added to my guilt.

So, what did I do? Of course, I did more dope in an attempt to drown out the guilt.

When noon came around, for some reason, I walked to a nearby park. I used back alleys to avoid seeing police on my way to the park. When I got there, I went to the little par three golf course which was empty. It was a little course where I remember carrying my brother's golf clubs as a kid.

With a bottle of 500 Percodan stuffed in my sock, I played golf. And every step I took, every swing I made, I heard the rattle of the pills in the bottle. There was some guy playing who came up from behind me and asked to join along. I was sure he was a cop, or what I should say is my mind told me he was a cop. Now, why in the hell would a cop walk alongside me golfing and not arrest me? WTF was I thinking?

As we walked along the course, I felt so self-conscious and embarrassed. I had a large blood-spotted Ace bandage wrapped around my left hand. I had on old dirty jeans which also had blood stains and the pill bottle rattling in my sock. I have no clue what possessed me to golf, and I'm sure the guy who joined me was just bewildered as hell. I probably looked like the walking dead. However, this guy never said anything other than small talk about his shots.

When I completed my nine holes of golf, I walked through the alleys back to my motel room. I made a call to Mike to tell him about my adventure the night before. He stopped by my motel room, gave me a few bucks, and we rattled off some Percodan (like I needed more). Mike told me I should probably have someone look at my hands as they were terribly swollen. My only response that I remember was, "OK, sure." When Mike finally left, I began to think about where I could go to live my next few days or so. I knew I couldn't stay here long, as it was only a couple blocks from the pharmacy I just burglarized.

CHAPTER TEN

Hospital Visit

When I checked out of the motel, I went to another small motel about a half-mile down the road. It was set back from the road and pretty dilapidated. As I sat in the small room, I began to shoot more Percodan. My veins were all collapsed and had begun to look purple. I had very little feeling in either hand; because I am right-handed, the left was battered pretty badly.

I knew I needed to do something about my health, and fast. As I pondered what my move needed to be, thoughts of my mother kept popping into my mind. Since she was a nurse, I thought I might want to call her. But, what the hell was I going to say, and how would she take seeing me like this? I thought that was not a good option, so I decided to make a trip to the emergency room at the Milwaukee County Hospital.

When I arrived, the doctor examined my hand and said that he wanted to get the advice of another physician. After this doctor examined my hand, he told me that he thought the only option may be amputation. As strange as it may sound, that didn't seem to faze me. I told the doctor that I wanted to make a call, then reluctantly called my mother. When she heard my voice, she immediately said "Tony? Are you OK? We have been worried sick." I explained the situation to my mother the easiest way I knew how, trying not to give her a stroke. I said that I had been back into the Percodan, and my hands had been losing feeling. And I also told her that I was at County Hospital and that the doctors were contemplating a possible amputation of my left hand. Hearing this, my mother told me not to let them do anything until she got to the hospital.

Very shortly, she arrived at the emergency department. She told the doctors that she would like to see me admitted to a detox rehabilitation hospital. My mother told me that my older sister knew a doctor who was connected to a twelve-step program and a rehab hospital. After a few calls, it turned out that I was going to be transferred that night. Well, I was in a lot of pain, and I knew that I would be getting weaned off the opiates once I got to the rehab hospital. So I took a bottle of Percocet that I had left over from a drugstore theft that I had stuffed in my sock, of course.

Percocet is basically the same drug as Percodan, except for the fact that Percocet is bound with Tylenol, whereas Percodan has aspirin. Percocet pills were not preferred by my circle of acquaintances because they were much more difficult to soak down for injection. We just took Percocet in the case of withdrawal, and we took it orally. Well, this was one of those times for me. I took the entire bottle which had about forty left.

After I was transferred to the rehab hospital, I was greeted by the doctor friend. He examined my hand, and said that it didn't look good. He gave me a piece of crumpled up newspaper, and instructed me to slowly try to squeeze it until my hand was tired. After only about five times of doing it, my hand seemed to tire and swell more. The doctor told me to work up very slowly to doing it for one hour. He said that he wouldn't like to see it get too swollen, as that would my cut off the circulation. And he said that the whole idea of the exercise was to attempt to bring the circulation back into my hand.

I did as the doctor told me through the night until I dozed off. About seven the next morning I woke up to a nurse taking my vitals. She gave me some kind of a vitamin B shot and told me that the attending physician would be in to see me at about eight. When the doctor came in, he told me he would like me to stay in bed for a few days, and to continue the hand exercises with a sponge ball he brought in. He also told me that I tested negative for infection, which he thought to be a positive sign.

After a few days of lying bedridden, I was given a schedule of appointments and group therapy sessions he had set up for me. The appointments I understood. However, the group therapy stuff I wasn't too thrilled about. The way I figured, all I needed to do was rest and exercise. After all, I knew what was best for me. I felt that sitting with a bunch of alcoholics and drug addicts would just be a waste of time. What were they going to tell me that I didn't already know?

My first appointment was with a doctor who was going to be meeting with me a couple times a week. I will call him 'Dr. Dolphin.' He was a fairly young guy and seemed to be pretty sharp. In our first meeting, he went over my health and drug history. When I told him about my Percodan habit, and my intertwining heroin escapades, he shared with me his history. He said he was a former gynecologist. He also told me he had been doing about 300 Percodan a day, by way of heating the pills in a kettle on the stove so that the active ingredient in Percodan, would come to the top. And he would inject it. I felt like I finally met someone in the medical field who understood my fascination with opiates. He went on to ask where I came across the quantities that I had been doing. When I told him, he just snickered and said I was crazy, but emphasized that he didn't mean really sick crazy. Just wild crazy.

As the days went on in the hospital, I began to attend the group sessions. I could relate somewhat to some of the other people who were patients—and others not so much. I thought I was different because of the quantities I was doing, and the way that I went about getting my drugs. But, I was beginning to see that it wasn't the drug habit that made me crazy. Maybe I had been crazy before I even began to use opiates. Maybe it was because of my crazy mind. Maybe that dark corner of my mind could be the culprit in this whole drug addiction thing?

In my last session with Dr. Dolphin before I was going to be discharged, he gave me his direct phone number, and said I could call him if I were to relapse again, or better yet, he said, before I relapsed.

On that last day, I was also instructed to go to a twelve-step meeting of some kind. When I left my room to attend an AA meeting, I was met at the elevator by a guy who introduced himself as Jeff. He said he would be my temporary sponsor. He explained that a sponsor is a person with a similar problem as I had, but with some experience in staying clean and sober by going to these twelve-step meetings. On the elevator heading down to the meeting room, he said, "You'll find that a sponsor can be a very good support person as you begin your journey of sobriety." He then said, "One thing I have to tell you—a sponsor is not, and won't be, your mother or your babysitter, and they won't be your bank. A sponsor is to help you get the most out of this program, and I will be here for you if you need to talk." My initial thought was, "Hey, sponsor, go f*** yourself."

Well, I attended the meeting that night and listened to all the program stuff, and all the other people telling their stories, how they made it work. I still wasn't convinced that this shit was for me, because after all, I was different.

When I was discharged from the hospital, I immediately called my probation officer. I told him what had happened, and all he asked was where I was planning to live and if I committed any crimes in between the time he saw me last and the time I was admitted. My immediate response was, of course, "no" to the crime thing. I then informed him that I was going to live with my girlfriend. He asked me to come to his office the next morning, to do a drug screen, and to give him a phone number and address of where I would be. After hanging up with my PO, I called my then ex-girlfriend and asked if I could stay at her house for a short while and use her phone number to give to my PO. She agreed to let me stay at her apartment for a couple days.

Pissed

So, I didn't lie to my probation officer about where I was staying; however, what I didn't tell him was that it was only a few days and, I never told him just how messed up I really had been, or what insane things I was doing. This type of stretching the truth was just like all the other times I swore that things were going to be different. It was more deceit to add to that dark corner of my mind. It was so much the dominant part of mind by this time that I had trouble deciphering the truth from the lies I told. Even though I had been clean for about thirty days, my mind was one terrible mess.

While I was staying at my ex-girlfriend's apartment, I discovered she had been doing Percodan quite regularly. I had also heard through the grapevine that she had been seeing quite a few different men while I was gone. I was told that some of the men she had been seeing were guys that were supposedly friends of mine. It seemed that with or without drugs and alcohol in the mix of failed relationships, when you split with a woman, there was always some guy that you thought you knew who would jump in. And it usually happened pretty quickly. Maybe it's just part of the human condition? I'm not sure, but this practice seemed pretty tacky to me.

I packed what little belongings I had, and we said our good-bye. But before I left my girlfriend's apartment for good, I felt a need to leave behind my reaction to learning of her activities while I was away. It was a reaction of vindictiveness, typical of how I always treated what I perceived as betrayal. When I left her apartment, I went right to her unlocked car, opened the driver's side door, and pissed on her car seat. What a guy! I'm quite sure that my actions just exemplified what a nice guy I was. Leaving my mark, like a dog. I guess I sure took the high road!

The Sisters

About a week later I found myself staying with Shelly and Lori, two sisters I had known from my crazy past. They were both pretty good looking women, and both were into Percodan. They told me that they heard I was back on the street, and they figured I may have access to some Percs. They offered to let me stay at their parents' house where they lived with both parents and their younger brother. The girls had an attic room in the house.

The girls took me to their home, and as we walked into the kitchen, we were greeted by their parents. Their father was a firefighter in Milwaukee. He was a big and very tough looking man with a stern voice. He took one look at me and said, "You better behave in my house, son." I guess I was in pretty rough shape—very thin, shabby clothes, a bandaged hand.

Well, I knew I was walking into a situation that could turn out to be risky—in that if I didn't keep my nose clean around this house, I'd soon be answering to this big firefighter. As we went up to the room I was to stay in, the one sister, Shelly, told me she was going to stay up there with me. Right away I thought, "Shit, all I need is their father walking upstairs and finding me and his youngest daughter under the blanket." But, I felt lucky to have roof over my head.

The first morning in this house, as soon as I woke up, the girls started asking me where we could get some Percs. And, they said they had an idea. The sisters had some friends who wanted to meet me, two of whom were with a motorcycle group that had a bad reputation.

So, one of the guys from that motorcycle group did stop by the sisters' house to meet me. After we were introduced, he named some people that he and I shared as acquaintances. He also mentioned that he heard about my 'luck' with hitting pharmacies. He said he thought that together we could do some drug hunting, so to speak. He went on to say he knew of a pharmacy where we could snatch some Percodan. But, of course he would only drive me there and play getaway driver for half of the haul. I thought, "What the hell, if it turns out to be an easy hit, why not?"

He drove me down to an area that was new to me, and the pharmacy was one I wasn't familiar with. The area looked really busy, and there was a lot of traffic. But, it was getting to the point that I didn't care what happened. If I got caught, so be it. I was so tired of running. If we got the Percodan, it was something to get me by till I quit. That is what I said, and I swore to God, that I would quit if He would allow me to get away with it one more time. And that's how it was every time— just like the last twenty or so drugstores I hit. It was always the last one I was going to do.

This guy dropped me off at the pharmacy. He told me he would be right there and he wouldn't leave me, no matter what. Well, I went into the drugstore and saw a female pharmacist behind the counter. When I approached the counter, she asked if she could help me. I just said, "Yes, I need these," as I was already behind the counter with two 1,000 -count bottles of Percodan. She said loudly, "The police are on their way." I just remember saying, "OK, say 'hi' for me," and I ran out. I really didn't say what I said to be funny; it just came out of my mouth.

I ran to the car, and the guy was right where he said he would be.. Almost as soon as we drove away, he wanted to pull over to split up the pills. I thought to myself, "Are you freaking crazy?" All I said was that we needed to get farther away from here before we do the split.

Willy

Doing this store with this guy led me to another guy I had known previously in this biker group. Now this guy was crazy as they get. His nickname was 'Dirty' but his real name was Willy. He was into everything—heroin, morphine, cocaine—everything. He was definitely the tough type. He had a look on his face that seemed to say, "F*** with me, I'll kill you!" He had piercing blue eyes and an aura that you could almost feel when you were around him.

He asked that I sit down with him to do some dope. What was I supposed to say? "You will say yes," is what I picked up from him. So, we commenced to shoot some heroin. As we got to talking, it came to light that he had heard that I might be a guy he could trust to be there for him, for a number of things. And now, he told me that he, in fact, he did trust me. It was probably not a compliment. But, I did feel honored and a bit relieved that this guy did not have ill feelings toward me.

A couple weeks later Willy's girlfriend called me to let me know my presence had been requested by the one and only 'Dirty.' Willy's girlfriend was a registered nurse, and she seemed to be an extremely gentle, kind, and caring woman. Also she was very attractive.

When I arrived at their apartment, she greeted me at the door. She was getting ready to go to work at the hospital for a twelve-hour shift, and she explained that Willy had asked for me to be there with him to help him maintain. She said he had specifically asked her to get ahold of Tony which was a compliment to me in a strange kind of way since she said he trusted very few people.

I knew I was walking into a strange predicament. Willy had locked himself in a spare bedroom. His girlfriend showed me to the room while thanking me for coming over. When she knocked on the door, Willy asked if she had Tony. She assured him that I was with her and that he could open the door. She told him that everything was OK and that she would be back right after work. I then heard the deadbolt lock turn and some furniture moving, and a few minutes later, the door opened. Here was Willy looking paranoid, agitated, and ready to do battle with anyone. The look reminded me of a caged tiger! His girlfriend gave him a kiss and told him again, "Tony is here, and everything will be OK." She thanked me again, and left.

Once I was in that room with Willy, I knew this would be a long night. And it wasn't going to be a party. This had the feeling of the twilight zone. I sat in the big chair that was wedged against the dead bolted door, and Willy paced back and forth. He would stop every couple of minutes and peek out the corner of the closed window blinds, and say to me, "I dare those mother f***ers to come in here!" He told me that he was being watched by the police. When I saw a .45 caliber pistol on an end table, I just thought to myself, "Why the f*** am I here?" I just wanted out.

Willy was on a cocaine binge. He had a good sized bag of rock cocaine, a syringe, and a spoon, sitting next the gun. Willy thanked me for coming by. He told me he needed to come down off the cocaine. I told him I had some Percodan with me, and it may help him relax a bit. I really wanted this thing to tone down as I, too, was beginning to believe we were being watched. I was worried that at any moment the place was going to be raided.

Willy took me up on my offer of the Percs, so I pulled out fifteen to soak down for him. He asked if I could get him some Valium to ease the crash of coming down. At that point I thought this might be a way to get the hell out of there. But looking him straight in the eyes, I knew I better not lie. So I told him I didn't have any but could call. He told me the phone was tapped and said, "Forget it; we'll stick with the Percs." Well, so much for me getting out of there anytime soon. Willy finally began to settle down as he did more Percodan. He told me that he knew the cocaine was killing him and said he should have just stayed with heroin as his drug of choice. Good choice, I thought. Then maybe I wouldn't be there babysitting a grown man.

As the night turned to morning, I kept throwing out the Percodan to keep Willy settled down. I remember hearing the birds chirping just before daylight, and soon both of us began to nod out. Finally, I heard the jingle of keys and Willy's girlfriend call out that she was home.

What a relief! Even though I was pretty buzzed up, I was just the same very anxious to get the hell out of there. It was nice that I was chosen for this task because he trusted me, but WTF—I wanted out! I said my good-byes and headed back to the sisters' house.

Murder on Sixty-Ninth Street

When I returned to Shelly and Lori's house, the neighborhood was swarming with police. They appeared to be at the girls' house, so I knew that I needed to move on to find a new home.

At this time, I was so physically sick that I just wanted to get somewhere to lie down, go to sleep, and hopefully never wake up. So, here I was walking the streets with a bottle of Percodan and a couple old syringes strapped in my sock. My clothes were stained with blood from all of my shooting gallery binges. Ace bandages were wrapped around my right hand and left arm to cover the swelling and needle marks, and a deep infection caused by injecting in my forearm. And I had two broken 27 1/2 gauge needles embedded in my arms, one in my upper left arm and the other in my right forearm. The needles were so deep that I couldn't see where to begin to dig them out.

Since I couldn't go back to Shelly and Lori's house, I jumped on a county bus but with no idea where I was going. I rode the bus to an area of the inner city of Milwaukee where I got off to look for anyplace warm to lie down. I saw an old apartment building and discovered the entrance door was unlocked. I slipped down to the basement near the locker area, found an empty storage locker, and made a little nest in the dark corner, out of plain view in case someone came down. There I was like a little rat, huddled up in the corner of a dark cool basement. I know that it sounds so gloomy, but at that moment I felt so safe and peaceful. I could be alone in this dreary basement corner with just my thoughts of fear and gloom.

I reflected on all the wreckage of my past and the people I hurt, especially my family and myself. I thought of what I learned growing up, that our body is the temple of the Holy Spirit. Well, if there was ever a Holy Spirit in this temple, he surely was holy no more. I had desecrated any likeness of anything holy in this temple, and I doubted that there were any cracks in the door for any Holy Spirit to find his way back in. It was just me and my demons in this dark corner of my mind and soul.

I had finally had a couple hours of sleep, I knew I needed to go back and face this ugly world once again. I only knew of one place close by where I could go—it was a heroin dealer. I walked down alleys making my way to this guy's house with the fear of being seen by police. When I arrived at this dealer's apartment, he reluctantly let me in and immediately asked what the f*** I was doing, coming unannounced. I told him my situation. He looked me up and down, and he just said, "You are a freaking mess!" I asked him to front me some heroin until I could pay him in a day or two. He was again very reluctant but gave in to my pleas. When addicts are hurting bad, as I was then, they can be very persistent, pulling stories out of their asses to get what they want. I walked out with a half-gram of good heroin.

As soon as I got the dope, I headed back to the apartment building that I had slept in, went directly to the utility sink in the basement, and cooked up about half of the bag. I searched for a vein in my leg and injected it. It was an instantaneous rush that was so powerful, it literally brought me to my knees. All I remember is that I vomited and gagged until my stomach was completely empty. When you shoot good heroin you tend to puke your guts out. And the sick thing about it is that it feels great.

After I cleaned the utility sink of the vomit, I climbed back into the empty locker room, made my nest, and nodded off into the world of no worries. It temporarily cleared my mind of the emotional pain and all the fear that awaited me back out in the real world. The reality of the broken off needles, my infected forearm, my swollen hands and feet, and my frail body, were all eliminated from my mind.

The sad thing was that a few hours later I was awakened by a light and the sound of footsteps. My first thought was that it was the police, but it was just another woman coming to do her laundry, humming as she worked. And here I was back to reality.

As soon as she left the basement, I headed back out into the real world. I was a complete mess—completely bankrupt physically, mentally, emotionally, and spiritually.

I headed to the nearest phone booth to call Mike. When Mike answered, he said, "Oh, f*** Tony, did you hear about Shelly's dad? He was murdered yesterday!" I told Mike I had been on my way to her house when I saw the neighborhood swarming with police. Mike told me that they found her father with a slit throat and beaten over the head with a baseball bat.

Shelly's father had been a fireman for years in Milwaukee, and he seemed to be a wonderful husband and a good family man. He seemed to be a guy who wouldn't have had an enemy in world. We he met me for the first time he looked me up and down and said, "Holy shit, what the hell happened to you?" He warned me that if I were to bring drugs into his house, we would have a problem. He was a very big man, built like a bull! He sure wasn't a guy I wanted to piss off.

About a week later, after much speculation that the murder was a break in and attempted robbery, Shelly's younger brother and a friend were arrested for their father's murder. What a shock! Apparently the two young guys, who were about seventeen years old, were in the house smoking pot when the father came home unexpectedly. The story is that the boys were surprised and scared when he came in, so they panicked and hit him over the head with a baseball bat. Then they apparently decided to make it look like a suicide and slit his throat, and he bled out. What a way to go. And now, here was a father in his fifties, dead, and two teenage boys with their lives changed forever, not to mention the man's widow, as well as Shelly and her sister without their father. All of this over smoking pot. This was a huge story at the time, and I remember feeling so sad for Shelly and her sister. All I could think of was how f***ed up the drug life was.

CHAPTER ELEVEN

The Good Doctor

Shelly's older sister Lori, had just moved into a house on the north side of Milwaukee, which was where I made my way to after the devastating news of their father's passing. Shelly told me that she was going to stay there for a while also.

We had been hitting doctor's offices for prescriptions of Percodan. It seemed easier for the girls to get the doctors to write for Percodan. I had been struggling to get a doctor to write scrips for me, as I was in pretty bad shape, with tracks up and down my arms. I pretty much had to depend on the girls for a few Percodan here and there. While they were in the offices, they always made a habit of trying to get their hands on blank prescription forms. When they got the blank prescriptions, I would write for some Percodan or Dilaudid.

When going into pharmacies to get one filled, I didn't stick around too long if the pharmacist would stall. It was too risky. I usually engaged the pharmacist in a conversation while waiting for my script to be filled. In my conversations, I let on to the fact that I had cancer, in hopes they would feel bad for me and fill the prescription quickly. If the prescription thing wasn't working, there was always my counter leaping thing. That was where I would hop over the counter, grab a couple thousand Percodan, and run out.

One day I stopped by my friend Bob's house to say 'hi' to his mother and see what he had been up to. While I was at his house, Willy (Dirty) stopped by. He told me he wanted to do a drugstore with me. He told me that I could have 75% of all the narcotics, specifically the opiates. And he said he mainly wanted the cocaine. He suggested a doctor's office in a small town about fifty miles north of Milwaukee, which he thought had its own pharmacy. His plan was that I could go into see the doctor, while he waited in the lobby to scope out what it looked like and maybe slide in.

We drove out to the office late that afternoon, and I walked in to see the doctor for back pain while Willy looked around. The doctor wrote me a script for twelve Percodan, which was pretty much a doctor's way of telling you good-bye and please don't come again. I asked if he could fill it for me so I wouldn't have to go to a pharmacy, but he told me that he didn't carry narcotics in his store. When I told Willy what the doctor said, he told me that the guy was lying. He said he saw a bottle of Percodan on the shelf. We left but we returned about ten that night. I wasn't real keen on the idea of doing this place, as I figured it was no doubt alarmed (even though Willy said he saw no sign of an alarm system). We went up to the back door, and Willy immediately kicked it in with his boot, right near the deadbolt lock. The door opened right up, and we entered. We found a very large storage area filled with pharmaceuticals. This guy probably supplied other offices or nursing homes with his drugs. There were way too many for his small office. There was cocaine, which was Willy's, as we agreed. And there were bottles and bottles of Valium, Percodan, Seconal, and morphine, liquid and dissolvable.

By the time we headed back to Bob's house, I was sick to my stomach. The insanity of my actions—ridiculously wrong and even dangerous. From what I could tell, Willy couldn't have cared less if there had been someone in the place when we were there. I felt quite sure he would have had no problem snuffing them out. I never wanted anyone to get hurt or go to jail. My habit, however, was so out of control that I was associating with people who, in my sober days, I would not. (And most likely, I would not have been anyone else's choice, either.)

When we returned to Bob's house, we went in the back bedroom, out of sight from his mother, to split up the stash. We sorted everything in its proper category—opiates in one pile, sedatives like Valium in another, and Willy's cocaine. There was one large bottle of liquid morphine, which I dug into right away. I had a syringe full of this stuff in my arm so fast, even Willy said, "Slow the f*** down, you're going to end up dead by tonight!" And, he was probably right. But, at that time, I think that was possibly my mission. Though I loved the physical feeling and the temporary black out of my guilt, I wanted out. I floated off into my dream world from the morphine injections and dozed off into the night.

When I woke up in Bob's back bedroom, I began to reflect on the prior day, as well as the past couple months. I remembered some of the things I learned in my last stay in the treatment program, as well as the Wisconsin Family program. Though I hadn't put into practice what I learned in those places, it was still in my mind. It seemed to be telling me there was a chance I could clean up, though the chances may be very slim. I knew that if I were to choose that path, it would not be easy. I would no doubt have to face my demons. This path almost looked impossible, given the fact that I would likely have to spend quite a bit of time in prison, first and foremost.

I thought about all my options and tried my best not to weigh any of the options based on my fears. Fear, as I was once told by an old man I met, was basically just "False Evidence Appearing Real." That struck a chord with me, and I never forgot it. With these thoughts at that moment, I decided to take the offer of help from Dr. Dolphin, the doctor I met at the thirty-day hospital treatment program I was in just months before.

I took a chance and called the doctor, and though it was a Saturday morning, he did answer. He asked me where I was staying. I explained my situation, that I was way out of control and that I had been robbing drugstores, and he told me to stay put, he'd be right over.

About forty-five minutes later, Dr. Dolphin arrived at the house. He was dressed in a suit and tie, and carried a big physician's bag. It all looked very official to Bob's mother, who knew I had been struggling with a drug problem for years.

He asked me what kind of drugs I had been doing through this binge and if I was still carrying anything. I reached under the bed I was sitting on and pulled out the very large duffle bag full of pharmaceuticals. When I poured the bottles out on the bed, his eyes opened wide and his jaw dropped. He then told me I needed to go into the hospital right away. He said that he could not in his right mind wait until Monday or I'd probably end up dead. He also told me that I needed to pack some clothes, and he would take me right to the hospital and admit me himself.

I looked at all these bottles of opiates, and thought to myself, "Maybe Monday would be better." But, I could see in his eyes, he wasn't going to leave without me in his car. He took another look at the drugs and told me that he had a friend who was in the DEA (Drug Enforcement Administration) who would dispose of them without asking questions. I very reluctantly said OK.

So, off we went, with the doc carrying the bag of treasures—there was no turning back now. We arrived at the hospital on Milwaukee's south side, and Dr. Dolphin took me through the entire admission process. He was most helpful with everything. He prescribed methadone for me to withdraw. I thought that was the right way to do it. What junkie wouldn't? And the dose was high enough for me to ease off the shit very slowly. And, before he left, he said he would see me as his patient, later the next week.

Well, Monday came along, and I received a sheet that had a schedule made up for me. But, before I was to attend my first group, I was called to the physicians' offices. When I arrived at the lobby area, I was greeted by a doctor I was not familiar with. He asked me to sit down and began to ask questions about my admission. He asked what my relationship to Dr. Dolphin was and went on to ask why I was on methadone.

Not having a clue where he was going with this questioning, I just told him that I was fortunate enough to have been admitted on a Saturday, because I was a physical wreck. As far as the methadone choice, I told him the status of my habit and the enormous amounts I had been doing. I didn't mention the drugs I gave to Dr. Dolphin, as I didn't feel it was necessary. When our visit concluded he just thanked me and told me I was free to go to my next group. I had a strange feeling that something wasn't right. But I attended my groups for the next few days, and all seemed OK.

That Thursday came around when I had an appointment with Dr. Dolphin on my schedule. When I went to his office, Dr. Dolphin told me he had just come back from a skiing trip in Colorado. He asked me what happened at the hospital while he was gone. He looked at me somewhat bewildered, and said "Did you talk to anyone about our meeting at your buddy's house?" I told him that I said exactly what he requested I divulge, which was basically that I had called him and begged him to get me admitted, and nothing more. And I also told him I was asked about the reasoning for the methadone for withdrawal.

As we were talking, I noticed he was clearing out his desk, and he had boxes filled with books and pictures. He looked at me and said, "I just got shit canned!" I responded, "What the f*** for?" He told me that he had just come back from four days off, and they asked him to do a drug screen. And he went on to say, "Yeah, they made me drop urine. And then they shit canned me." He then asked me if I mentioned the stuff I gave him for his DEA buddy, and I told him absolutely not!

Well, stupid me, this guy was a dope fiend just like me. There was no DEA buddy, and I doubted that there was a ski trip. He probably did all the dope I gave him. It was then I realized that no matter what a

---

person's professional status is—doctor, lawyer, banker, or janitor—those who share the disease are all the same. We will lie, cheat, and steal if it is necessary to get our habit fulfilled.

Well, with my buddy Dr. Dolphin gone, I was set up with a new doctor named Dr. Z. He reviewed my health and drug history, and he then asked about my relationship with Dr. Dolphin, just as the first doctor did when I first arrived. I told him very little about it, just basically the same story I gave the first time. As we talked, he began to share some of his past history. He told me not to be embarrassed about some of the crazy things I did out on the street while I was using. He told me about the parties he used to have. He said that he would walk around the party with an IV in his arm, dragging around the IV pole, with a bag full of pharmaceutical cocaine solution. After telling me how crazy he had been through the years, he then began to ask me how I got my drugs. He mentioned that for the amounts I was doing, I must have some extraordinary access to the drugs.

After this type of questioning, I believed that he may be trying to get information for the police. I began to shut down when he again asked me about Dr. Dolphin and the relationship he and I had. He knew about the stories that Dr. Dolphin had shared with me about his times doing about 300 Percodan a day, by soaking them down in a pot on the stove at low heat. As he went on about his knowledge of Dr. Dolphin's drug history, I figured he may know him better than I originally thought. He said that Dr. Dolphin had come up dirty on the drug screen when he came back from his four days off. And that was the reason he was canned. I just responded that it was too bad. But, in the back of my mind I thought to myself, "That prick took off for four days doing my dope."

When I sat and reflected back on what transpired over the prior couple of months, I could see pretty clearly how messed up I really was. I realized just how powerful this stuff was. I had become a prisoner of this shit. And apparently the good doctor couldn't shake it, either. I thought, if this guy who worked so hard, for so many years, to become a board certified obstetrician / gynecologist, had still risked it all for this stuff, it is not only me it takes prisoner.

So, as I was coming up on twenty-eight days in the hospital, I was going to be released. I knew I would have to go see my PO. I had called him to check in. I didn't say where I was, though I would have told him if he asked. I was honestly too afraid to tell him and just too embarrassed.

This time when I was released from the hospital, I knew I had to do something different, as the 'same old, same old' hadn't been working. It seemed that every time I went back out and relapsed, I started off right where I left off. It was just like I heard in some of the meetings I went to. But, I felt that I was different; I was just an unfortunate soul with some deep-seated problems.

When I was released from the hospital, I found a place to stay at an old friend's house—Terry, the guy I had been staying with before until his dad passed away. Now, Terry was helping his mother more around the house, but he was still chipping drugs. He kept his habit somewhat under control—about five to ten Percs most every day.

Terry and I talked about going on the methadone program. But, I just wasn't sure if it would suffice for me. I tended to need a quick boost, whereas methadone was a one-dose-a-day drink that did the trick for withdrawal, but just didn't feel like what I needed. Plus, it was too much of a commitment. I'd have to get up and go in every morning, and then give a urine sample when asked. It seemed that I wasn't only addicted to the opiates, but also to the lifestyle—the hunt, the capture, and then finally, the well-deserved feast at the end of it. I was still attempting to run from that bulging room in the corner of my mind, which was storing all the doom and gloom from my guilt, and feelings of uselessness. But when I used, I would seemingly go from 100 miles an hour to an abrupt halt in my feelings of despair. It made the process feel so rewarding and so euphoric.

I ended up going along with Terry to the methadone program the next day. I hadn't used drugs for almost thirty days, so there was no need for me to do the methadone thing. I was just there to support Terry. I watched Terry go to work and do his methadone daily while he did a little chipping here and there. He smoked pot, took an occasional sedative, and was satisfied. I myself didn't get the moderation thing.

Break Time

At that time I started hanging out with my friend Mike again. This guy seemed to have very good willpower and kept a job. For him, heroin seemed to be a hobby. He'd go to work every day, he'd go home to his family, and go on an occasional heroin binge. How the hell he did that, I didn't know; it was just foreign to me.

It was right around that same time that Mike and I somehow came in contact with a guy named Larry. He was a pretty good guy from what we could tell. Larry carried himself pretty well, like a professional of sorts. He had been working as a salesman. He was intelligent, handsome, and well-dressed. He was also a very assertive guy, bordering on aggressive, when he felt the need. Especially if heroin was the need!

For several months, Mike, Larry, and I were out running the streets hunting down heroin. We had limited amounts of Percodan that was quickly diminishing when our runs with Larry began to escalate. We would scrape up cash for heroin any way we could. It soon became an everyday thing, and many of the days, there were two or three runs to the heroin dealer. Our habits were once again becoming that daunting gorilla tugging on our backs. More and more, every day, we were devising ways of coming up with a couple hundred dollars here and there whether it was from borrowing money, hitting a drugstore for Percodan, or Larry going off on his hold ups. Though Mike and I still didn't use weapons, our tactics were no less devious or crazy. At the end of the day, we ended up in the same place as Larry, giving our daily wages to the same master—whichever heroin dealer was available and had the best stuff.

By now, Larry's car had broken down, and he decided that stealing a car was the convenient way to go, plus, if he knocked off some place, what would be better than a car with plates that had no connections to him? We were all crazy, but Larry was like a character from an old movie about cops and robbers. He even looked the part in his business clothes and full length, black cashmere overcoat.

So, Larry continued with his daily scams, and Mike and I continued to work our magic. We all grew more desperate as the days zipped by, we knew we had to get something going to keep up with our habit. One day Larry stopped by to see Mike and me with a proposition. He told me that he would supply the getaway car and do the grunt work if I were to give him the ins and outs of robbing a drugstore. He asked that I let him know what to look for and where it would most likely be on the shelf. As I knew Larry was getting absolutely crazy and out of control, I told him that weapons could not be part of the scenario. He simply said no problem.

Later that afternoon, Larry was ready to roll. It all seemed to happen so fast, and I was feeling very unsettled. Every time I did one of these things, I felt nervous as shit, but this unsettled feeling was different from those other times. I felt unsure of Larry and his way of doing things. Any time I did one of these crazy ass deals, I had to do it 100% my way.

Regardless of my feelings, I knew he was going to do something with or without me. And, I knew we were all very desperate, and any ounce of logic was completely gone. So, I agreed, and we were soon on our way to the event that would change our lives forever.

The Big Event

Larry showed up in a later model Ford station wagon, which he picked up, or stole rather, from the car lot where he had been working as a salesman. I had been waiting along with my friend Jerry, who was a good friend I made from my thirteen months at the Wisconsin Family. So, the three of us took off onto our journey to test fate once again.

We headed to our spot which was a pharmacy on the northwest side of Milwaukee. It was quite a busy pharmacy, one that I had been in before. And the time I was there, I saw a bottle of a thousand Percodan sitting right on the ledge of the pharmacy divider, clearly visible, and within reach. The place had been so busy I just reached over, grabbed it, and slid it in my coat. Among all the busy chaos, no one even noticed. Now that was the kind of deal I liked doing. Not the strong armed or weapon kind of thing which just never appealed to me. But this time, with Larry at the helm, I had a feeling we were in for a wild ride.

When we arrived at our destination, Larry got really anxious. He just said, "Ok boys, this is it, I'll be right out. Don't leave." Jerry and I were both nervous as hell, and I could feel that something wasn't good. And I don't mean the anxiousness of the fact we were pulling off a robbery. I just knew there was something more to this whole day. My gut was turning a mile a minute!

About three minutes later, which felt like an hour, the front door of the pharmacy blew open. Out came Larry running like a rabbit, with some guy in pursuit. As Larry ran our way, he made a ninety degree turn away from us and toward a gangway between two houses. Right as Larry grabbed for a gate toward the alley behind the homes, he glanced back and saw this guy reaching out to grab him. Larry reached in his coat, and in a flash pulled a .38 snub nose pistol, put it directly in this guy's face, and pulled the trigger. Jerry and I were shocked at what we were seeing, especially not even knowing Larry was armed, and we both just cringed. All we heard was a click, and Larry yell out, "F***!" The gun had jammed.

Jerry took off in Larry's station wagon and quickly turned through the alley that Larry had been heading toward, but there was no sight of Larry. We weren't sure if he had been nabbed or if he was running just that fast and was already on his way to safety. Jerry and I drove to an area about halfway between the pharmacy and the neighborhood I grew up in. We gave the station wagon a quick wipe down for prints and then dumped it near a creek. Jerry ran in the direction of a bus stop, and I ran along the creek toward my parents' house. By the time I arrived at my parents' home, I was physically exhausted and sweating like a pig. And I probably smelled like one too!

My mother was at home, and when I walked in the door, she just said, "Well, look who's here." She asked what the grand entrance was about and commented about my appearance. She told me I looked like I just ran through a sprinkler. I just responded to her that I had been running and asked if I could take a shower. I was trying to act as calm as I could, and I just wanted to jump in that shower and think things through. Everything happened so fast that I wasn't sure what side was up. I needed to think hard on what I was going to do if I were picked up in connection with the crazy Larry ordeal. And I also needed to think of what the hell I was going to do with my life in general. When the panic of something like what just happened was so fresh, I always seemed to have an awakening and swear I would straighten out my life.

As I stood in the hot shower for what seemed like an hour, I contemplated my next move. I knew I needed to talk with my mother for a bit and assure her I was doing OK. And, after that I was going to need to talk with Mike. He always had an ear on the street and would generally know what kind of crazy shit was going on out there.

After I finished showering, I went into the kitchen with my mother. We talked for a bit, but I honestly couldn't tell you one word of what we discussed. My head was crowded with all the insanity that had taken place over the past couple hours. I then went downstairs to call Mike. He immediately said, "What the f*** happened?!" He told me that Larry had run to his house and asked to hide out. Larry had apparently filled Mike in on some of what had happened. Mike went on to tell me that Larry wanted to stay there, at Mike's parents' house. Mike told him that it wasn't an option, but he offered to let Larry stay in his van in the garage. Mike told me that he had made a steak dinner for Larry and brought it out to the van.

I told Mike that I was going to head over to the old basement apartment that I had been using occasionally, and where Larry had been staying on and off. When I arrived at the apartment, I went downstairs only to find that the entrance door had been kicked down. The door was completely torn off the hinges, and it was broken into pieces. That very minute, I knew the police were on to Larry. I headed out to the tavern across the street from the apartment building to use the pay phone to call Mike.

When he answered, I could tell by the tone of his voice that something was wrong. He said, "F*** Tony, the freaking cops were just here and swarmed my house!" He had been in the living room watching TV with his parents when there was a knock on the front door. It turned out to be a tactical squad of police with their shotguns drawn. They instructed everyone in the house to be still, and Mike heard the garage door being kicked down. He then heard a police officer shout that they had Larry trapped in the van. When the squad stormed the van, they found Larry lying face down with his clothes stained with blood. Mike explained, "That crazy f***er stabbed himself with the steak knife I gave him!" The police handcuffed Larry and shortly after, they loaded him into an ambulance.

Having heard this whole bizarre story about Larry, all I could do when I hung up the phone was to just sit down on a bar stool. I ordered a tap beer and sat with a feeling of doom and gloom. I pictured Larry bleeding to death. I pondered the thought of me being picked up at any moment and on my way to prison. I didn't know what to do. I was sick, withdrawn, cold, and just physically, mentally, and spiritually exhausted. It seemed that my whole world was caving in on me, and it was happening faster than I could even think. It was as if I was frozen in time. So what did I do? I ordered another beer. Something was needed to drown out life at this moment. I kept thinking, "Maybe it'll all go away. When I wake up, I will find it was just a miserable dream."

Well, when I did finally wake up after drowning myself with beer, along with the little bit of heroin I had, I found out that nothing had changed, except for me having a pounding headache, the chills, and more fear and anxiety that I'd experienced in a very long time. My life was at one of the lowest points it had ever been. I was physically, spiritually, and emotionally at a point of no return. I felt this may be the end of the road where I needed to end the insanity once and for all. I needed to get up the nerve to destroy this monster inside me. When I began this journey, heroin stole my heart, but I had also allowed it to steal my soul. I was hopeless and powerless over the insane life I made for myself.

While the cloud of darkness was hanging over me with fear of the unknown, I was obsessing over the possibility of Larry implicating me in our crazy caper. But regardless of what happened with Larry, there I was, as miserable as a human being could possibly be. I was of no use to anyone including myself. In fact, I was just a miserable waste of oxygen.

Desperate Times Equal Desperate Measures

With Larry sitting in police hands, I was very unsure what may lie ahead for me. I was already AWOL from seeing my parole officer, Joe, so I knew my status was not favorable.

What I was sure of was the fact I had no place to live and very few options readily available. I knew that going back to the old basement apartment was out of the question as the door was ripped off the hinges, and the police may very well be back to see what else they could gather about Larry. I walked along the old familiar path by the railroad track bridge that I had once called home and tried to think of where I could lay my head for a day or two. When I arrived at the bridge, I went to my old little nest. It brought back some old memories, some of which—those of my old love Jackie—brought tears to my eyes. But, for some reason I felt so safe and so grounded. Outside looking in, I am sure the thought of living under a bridge doesn't sound very inviting, but I felt so peaceful there. It was an escape from the outside world.

I made my way to a pay phone to call Mike again. He told me his brother had asked if I was interested in hitting a drugstore he knew of. Not having any money to speak of, and out of drugs, I said I was absolutely interested. I told him I would be sitting at the park near his house and that I'd be waiting for his brother to hear the proposition.

I sat beside an old willow tree smoking a cigarette, impatiently waiting for Paul, Mike's younger brother. I was as grubby as could be. My hands were swollen from the circulation being all but completely shut down. I had needle tracks up and down my arms and my hands. I had a needle lodged in my upper left arm that had broken off. I had been shooting Percodan over and over trying to find a clear vein. Well, I found one. And the one vein I did find was very deep into my upper left arm near the armpit. I heard the needle break off deep into my arm. At the time, all I thought was, "I hope I have another syringe." The needle was still lodged in my upper arm while I grabbed another syringe and began shooting more Percodan. It didn't seem to faze me.

After about thirty minutes Mike's brother Paul arrived. I got in his car, and as we drove off, Paul told me about the drugstore he had in mind. It was on the east side of Milwaukee, just a little drugstore off a busy corner with only one person working, the pharmacist. He was an older gentleman probably in his mid-sixties.

Paul and I drove around the block a few times to check out the area. We found a path between the side of the drugstore and the old brick building next door. It was a dark pathway that led behind the store into to an alley. Paul parked around the block so we had a straight shot through a yard, across the alley, and through the dark pathway to the store. We looked at each other and laughed nervously. I was anxious, but my gut told me it was going to be OK.

After sitting for a moment, I looked at Paul, paused, and said "OK, let's do it." As I was getting out of the car I said, "Do not move from this spot!" I took a deep breath and said a little prayer asking my God to help me through this thing. When I entered the drugstore, I noticed that the pharmacist was behind the counter, and he was working alone. It was just he and I.

Without any hesitation I walked through the swinging gate and behind the pharmacy area. When the pharmacist saw me coming back into his space, he had a look of shock on his face. I just walked right to the shelf where I saw the Percodan, and I grabbed the two bottles. The pharmacist stepped back and said, "What the hell are you doing?" I quickly blurted out, "Please don't try to stop me!" And I was out the front door in a matter of about forty-five seconds. The whole thing happened just that fast.

As I turned the corner I glanced back through the store window and noticed the pharmacist hunched over the counter with a look of death. My immediate thought was that I gave the guy a heart attack. Nevertheless I ran through the gangway, across the alley, and through the yard, and literally dove into Paul's back car window. As I ducked in the back seat Paul drove away laughing. "Did you get them?" he asked. I responded affirmatively. The only thing I could think of was the old pharmacist. I was sure I gave him a heart attack.

Paul and I quickly returned to our old neighborhood and headed over to a big house where our old friends, the sisters Lori and Shelly, were living. Since I now had a couple thousand Percodan, I knew I could probably buy myself a few days under the sisters' roof. It was still winter, and living under a bridge didn't feel like an option to me.

The girls opened up their home to me with open arms. With a laugh they said, "Now what did you do?" I had a feeling that whether I had drugs or not, these girls would have invited me in. They were sympathetic people with big hearts, much like their father. The first thing I did when I got into their house was grab the telephone. Lori asked what I was doing, and I responded, "I'm calling the drugstore I just robbed." She laughed, but I wasn't kidding. I called to see how the pharmacist was. When he answered the phone, I told him I was sorry and just wanted to be sure he was OK. The pharmacist told me there was a detective who wanted to talk to me and gave him the phone. The detective asked if I would give him my name. I told the guy that I just wanted to be sure the pharmacist was OK and that giving him my name wasn't happening, and I hung up. (In those days there wasn't anything like caller ID.) Lori looked at me and said with a smile, "You really didn't just do that?" I smiled back at her and said, "Yes I did." She told me that I didn't make a good crook.

And with that out of the way, we began shooting the Percodan. Everyone in the house had shot glasses full of soaking Percodan and syringes ready to go. I could finally relax knowing that I had my fix and a place to sleep.

After poking my arms and hands for hours with Percodan, Lori showed me to my room—a basement storage area filled with shelves of paint and tools. She gave me a blanket and a pillow and told me that it was the best she could do. Her new boyfriend wasn't real keen on my staying in the house. So, here I was with another cool and damp basement palace for a while. I remember cuddling up on the floor in a corner of the room like a rat—a rat with drug bottles tucked in my pants and syringes in my socks. It's all I needed at the time because I had something else that I always brought with me that no one could take away. It was the dark corner of my mind that was mine, and mine alone.

Drastic Measures

One evening during this time period, I met up with Mike to shoot some Percodan. Neither of us had any working syringes, and it was about one o'clock in the morning. With no twenty-four-hour hour pharmacies in those days, finding a place to buy syringes was not an option. The day before, however, I had thrown a couple old dull syringes into a nearby sewer. Mike and I looked at each other and had the same thought of trying to retrieve them.

We went out by the sewer with a cigarette lighter to check if we could see them. Sure enough, they were there. I reached down with a stretched out coat hanger and just barely got ahold of one. We took it in the motel room where I was then staying and attempted to revive it. The plunger was stuck from being worn out, and the tip of the needle was so dull that it would almost take a hammer to puncture a vein. We got the plunger out and tied the rubber plunger to the plastic top with dental floss and wiped it with Vaseline. We filed the needle tip on the flint of a match book, and we were ready to go. That is just one of the desperate measures we took to get high.

Desperation seemed to trigger an electrode in the brain opening a whole new path of thinking and creativity. Mike and I could get very creative in our quests to get things done back in those days.

Since there didn't seem to be many other options available, I figured that I would give my old pharmacy friend a call. Now this took balls of steel to even consider calling him, as I felt had certainly burned my bridge with him. The last time he and I spoke, he made it very clear I was to take the 500 Percodan, $1,500 in cash and leave town to clean up my life. I knew crossing this guy wasn't a wise thing to do. The thoughts that went through my head before picking up the phone to call him were definitely red flags.

One of the red flags was that it was only a couple months earlier that he had grazed my leg with his 45 caliber pistol that had allegedly, accidentally misfired while I was in his bathroom taking a leak. He was supposedly cleaning the gun or loading it when it misfired and the bullet went through the kitchen wall and into the bathroom next to where I was standing. I distinctly recall the sound of the bullet coming through the wall and the burning sensation I felt, as the porcelain wall tile shattered in front of me. It was probably very lucky I wasn't sitting on the toilet or it would no doubt have gone through my back.

Well, despite my fears I decided to call him, and as soon as he answered and before I let him talk, I told him that I just needed one more favor of him before I left town. He responded by telling me that he warned me to get out of town and clean up. I somehow convinced him to give me one more chance to explain my situation, which, in reality, is just an addict's attempt to say 'One last time, I swear!' I told him that I had run into a snag with a woman I was seeing, and it screwed me up. He allowed me another visit to his pharmacy where he gave me a paper lunch bag filled with Percodan and wads of cash. Even with the load of guilt I was feeling, taking advantage of his soft heart beneath that steel armored exterior, it didn't deter my pet gorilla from taking charge. Regardless of how dangerous this man appeared to the outside world, I knew that his heart was made of gold, and his intentions were genuinely good. It was just that he was so good to people that he became an easy target—because of his goodness. And I was one of the ruthless f***'s that exploited his vulnerability. If there were anyone I needed to make amends to before leaving this earth, it would be him.

CHAPTER TWELVE

Familia

It was September of 1980. I was twenty-five years old. I had been on another pharmacy run, jumping counters for a few months, which allowed me the luxury to graduate from sleeping in damp basement corners to local motels. Once again I was living life with the dark cloud of fear of the law hanging over my head. My physical health, which I had revived while locked up in jail, was right back to the critical stage. My arms were swollen with no sign of any visible veins. My hands were again scarred and swollen to the point of being "like two big balloons, comfortably numb" to quote Pink Floyd. I was a f***ing mess!

In an attempt to get ahead of the law and to rid myself of the continued self-destruction, I made a preemptive move. I took myself back to the therapeutic community, the Wisconsin Family, and begged for another chance to right the ship and change my life. I knew it would be just that much more difficult this time, mostly because I knew what I was walking into. It would be back to a strict regimen of rules and some very difficult soul searching. They knew junkies like the back of their hand at this place. As much as I wanted to think I was unique in my habits and manipulation, they had seen it all. This was going to be hard work, physically and mentally, and it would demand a deep down look into the core of my soul.

When I arrived at the facility, I met with the staff to plead my case for reinstatement into their program. When the staff further examined my physical condition, they told me that they did not have the resources to accommodate my health problems. I had a low-grade fever, swollen arms and hands, and my weight had dropped considerably since they last saw me. They pled with me to seek hospitalization, adding that they felt I was critically ill—and that if I did this, they would seriously consider having me back. Well, in my mind, the hospital thing wasn't going to happen that day.

I thanked the staff and headed back out to the cold, hard streets. I was so very physically tired and spiritually exhausted, once again. But, I knew I could remedy all the aches and pains, and drown my soul's hurt with one visit to a local pharmacy or heroin dealer. That always worked very well, at least temporarily. They say insanity is doing the same thing over and over, expecting different results? F*** them! I expected the same results every time, and my opiates never let me down. I got the same results that I expected. Tried and true.

Well, I was back to the drawing board to see what I could come up with to get myself out of the hole was in. Yes, I do have to admit that the true definition of insanity is exactly as the old saying goes. My problem was that I really thought I was taking a different approach each time. That's just how messed I was. I would try taking a few Percodan every couple hours. I would try shooting just a small amount of heroin. I did anything I could to just get by without the physical withdrawal, and I thought that maybe, just maybe, I could get off this stuff once and for all. The problem was that I didn't want to feel any discomfort at all. In addition to the withdrawal, I was pain due to my ill health. I just attributed any pain and agony to the withdrawal. I didn't know how physically sick I really was.

Even if I were able to get clean once and for all, I would then need to face the string of criminal offenses that resulted from my selfish behavior and left a trail of wreckage from my past. So here I was again, hopping pharmacy counters and hiding out at cheap motels.

That September night, Terry was with me in a motel room, curled up in the corner with a blanket and pillow, while I nodded off in the bed. At one point, Terry shook me awake. He said I was screaming in my sleep. Not giving it much thought, I just nodded back off into my dream world.

Then, at about five o'clock in the morning, Terry and I were awakened by someone pounding on the motel door. I saw a spotlight shining through the closed window drapes. And suddenly the door was rammed open by police with their shotguns drawn. And as a bright light was pointed directly at me, all I remember hearing after the door burst open was, "Freeze, you mother f***er! Don't freaking move!"

Well, I knew this was coming sooner or later, but it shook me just the same. One officer told me to stand on the bed with my hands on the ceiling. I was standing there in just my underwear and they still frisked me down, while two of them had the shotguns pointed directly at me. And Terry was put face down while they cranked his arms behind his back. This poor guy already had a couple broken ribs and was battered from head to toe from his prior beating.

The police quickly cuffed me and put me on the floor face down, while they ransacked the motel room. I heard one cop say, "My, what the f*** do we have here?" He was holding up a bottle of a thousand Percodan. I almost felt like asking if I could just have a few before they confiscated them. Man, I was hurting. I just wanted to drown this shit away. And I also remember thinking that I should have taken heed of my earlier nightmare when Terry woke me.

The police put us in the paddy wagon and we were on our way downtown to the police administration building. As I was being booked at the police station, a detective came walking by with a heavy set woman who was in handcuffs. It was the lesbian who had stayed in the same house with me in the inner city of Milwaukee. It all made sense now—she had been arrested for armed robbery of drugstores and gave me up as a plea for leniency. All I could do was shake my head in disgust. But in reality, this woman did me a favor. I needed to be locked up to be saved from myself. In all honesty, I didn't hold a grudge. I just felt a fleeting sense of betrayal.

After I went through the booking and mug shots, a homicide detective came to take me for questioning. He began to ask me what I had been up to for the past year, and then he asked a few questions about some Italian guy who had been whacked on the east side of Milwaukee. He stared right into my eyes, and he just said, "You know, if you were ever to come clean with all of your past crimes, you might just move beyond where you're at right now. You're very sick, my man."

It was then, while he moved on to some other cases, that I drifted and didn't listen to what he was saying. My mind was stuck on his first question, and something dawned on me for the first time in a couple of years. It was during a period of a time in 1978, when I was in very deep with heroin, morphine, and booze, and I was living for months in a near blackout state. During that time, some guy on the east side of Milwaukee gave me a gun to dispose of. I remembered it because the gun, a .22-caliber, long-barrel pistol, was equipped with what looked to be a homemade silencer. And, the guy was almost frantic. He offered me a few hundred dollar bills and told me to dispose of it good and far away. Even in my drugged condition, I sensed at the time that something bad had just happened, something more than a quick holdup. And for some reason, while this detective mentioned some dates, and my whereabouts, it was then that the incident popped into my mind.

But, apparently the questioning was just a procedure because he didn't keep me very long. I'm very glad he didn't go deeper. What he did say, as he took me back to the bullpen for holding, was that he thought I needed to be looked at by a doctor.

A short time later, a jailer came and pulled me out. He noticed how purple and swollen my hands were. He then put his wrist to my forehead and said I was burning up. They shackled me and loaded me into the back of an ambulance and headed for the hospital. During the ride, I just felt worn out and spacey. Everything seemed to be a blur. The detective asked me if I believed in God. I nodded my head 'yes.' And he told me that I needed to pray that I would make it to the next day. When we arrived at the hospital, the detective looked at me and said, "If you do anything today, you might want to make it that you read the Bible." That was the end of his conversation with me.

Doctors examined me in the emergency room and then I was escorted to a hospital room and shackled to the steel bed with another deputy who would be shadowing me during my stay. I was quickly hooked up with an IV inserted into my jugular vein, since they couldn't find a clear vein anywhere in my arms or hands. I was embarrassed and disgusted with myself. It was almost as if a moment of clarity hit me.

A couple doctors came in the room to inform me that I was going to be with them for at least a few days. They told me I had endocarditis, the infection of the sack around the heart. Here I was all over again, with the same infection I had in 1976 that nearly killed me. So, I thought, maybe this is it, maybe I'll die here. Oddly enough it didn't seem to faze me. I wanted out anyway. And my hospital room was warm and somewhat comfortable. I hadn't been use to that for a while. I just didn't feel like I gave an f*** about anything. I only felt guilt and embarrassment about what I had become, but maybe this too would go away once my heart stopped for good. Or, would it?

My thinking about death included a lot of 'what ifs.' What if you die in a stage of life where you are carrying guilt? I had been dragging around a heavy burden of guilt for the all the deceit, suicidal thoughts, and having hurt so many innocent people by my path of destruction. What if you leave this world in the state of complete agony? Does your soul agonize for eternity? These were some of the questions I wasn't really ready to get the answers to. The Bible says that if you think of a sinful act, you're as guilty as if you did it. Shit, if this is true, I'm f***ed.

Well, I did end up rebounding from the infection after six days in Froedtert Hospital in Milwaukee. When I was released from the hospital I was sent to the House of Correction once again. My probation officer, Joe, came to visit me, and after seeing the state I was in physically and mentally, he told me it was time to head back to the Wisconsin Family program. He told me that this time my stay there was going to be different. There was not going to be any of the old shenanigans, such as wanting out after six months or so. He told me there were no negotiations to be made.

I was to complete all three stages of the program, which was six to nine months of in-house treatment, then three to six months of the second phase, which was like a halfway house, where you needed to secure gainful employment. While in the second phase, you worked, went back to the living quarters, attended meetings and groups, did household chores nightly, and satisfied the staff that you were ready for phase three. Phase three was where you had the steady employment, found suitable living arrangements, and attended outpatient groups, until you were deemed cured.

Joe went on to inform me that along with this recommendation, which was actually a demand, that I would also need to face the music on the theft of drugs charges. Those charges carried a maximum of nine months in prison. That was always the point of jumping pharmacy counters instead of holding the pharmacy up with a gun. No weapon, no physical harm to anyone, and no forgery. Just grab and go.

So, there I was again joining up with the Familia—the Wisconsin Family or what had become known as Wisconsin Correctional Services. The first thirty days in this place were very difficult for me. I was still feeling the effects of mild withdrawal with aching bones and sleep deprivation. But, overall the thing that bothered me most was the idea of not having an option of getting out soon.

And it was especially difficult knowing that it wouldn't be all that hard to just walk out the front door. The main deterrent at this place was that if you did walk, you'd soon be on your way to prison. This time things were going to be different for me. This time I really was sick and tired of being sick and tired, period. And since I was going to be isolated from drugs and alcohol for an indefinite period of time, or face eight years in the prison system, I chose to give it my best.

I knew doing time here was not going to be easy. It actually wasn't doing time, either. In this place, time did you! It was back to a very strict regimen of constant activities which included household chores done the way the staff wanted them done. Sometimes the same chore had to be repeated as many as four or five times, just to build character. And the group sessions many times became very heated. They would never let you leave a meeting without having to share something about yourself that played a part in why you were there. And it wasn't something like what you stole, who you hurt, or any other war stories.

They insisted it be something that had to do with internal personality issues which led to your behavioral problems. If you were a guy who closed down to the point of being mute and not sharing, they'd dig until you opened up, broke down, or blew up. Becoming physically violent was considered a cardinal sin at this place and would result in an automatic ticket back to jail. It took a lot of restraint to hold back sometimes, but it was a necessity.

Some of the practices were a bit strange, to say the least. As residents of this facility we were required to button our shirts up to the first button. Another rule was that we had to make eye contact with any other resident who talked to us. If ever we saw another resident with the button thing off kilter, or if there was no eye contact when in a conversation, we were required to make the person aware of it immediately. It would go something like this: "Jerry, I'm making you aware of not giving me eye contact. Give me ten push-ups." And the person was required to say, "Thank you" and give you ten push-ups, no questions asked. There were consequences for every little bull shit thing that was out of place. And if there were any arguments about any of the 'Awareness System,' there would be further consequences such as having to clean a toilet with a tooth brush for thirty minutes straight while people were yelling at you. It was some messed up stuff. But, of course this was to teach humility and character!

After I made it through the first thirty days, I began to get to know some of the other people that were in the facility. There was one in particular that I wasn't very fond of. I thought of him as a real condescending asshole. His name was Jerry, my old friend from my previous street activities. He and I went against each other like polar opposites. I despised this guy and looked for any reason to get him consequences. But, as time went on, we actually became close, and we were able to laugh at each other and also at ourselves. We both began to change for the better. We were clean from drugs and alcohol, and we were now building structure in our lives both behaviorally and health wise.

In March of 1981, after being back in the Wisconsin Family for about six months, I had a sentencing court date for the theft of drugs charge that stemmed from the days I was counter hopping. My parole officer, Joe, told me I would have to do the time, and then return to the Wisconsin Family to complete the program. This was the day that I would see what the sentence would be.

I was shipped to the Ozaukee court house to appear before the judge. First I met with my court appointed attorney who, strangely enough, was a pharmacist as well as an attorney. He owned a pharmacy in the same community where I committed my crime. It's just the way the cards fell that he was appointed to my case, as far as I knew. He was pretty stern with me—I felt as though I was meeting with the prosecuting district attorney instead of my defense attorney. My attorney seemed to want to see me punished as much as the DA. He told me that the word on the street around Ozaukee County was that they wanted to send a message about committing drug crimes in their community. And he went on to say that he, too, didn't appreciate my actions around his neighborhood. Though I could understand his view, I just didn't see this as an appropriate gesture, given he was supposed to be defending me.

When my case was called, we entered the courtroom and sat front of the judge. This judge was known to the guys I met in the county jail, as the hanging judge—tough on sentencing. He was a big man with a stern voice. After the pre-sentence investigation was read, the district attorney gave his speech and opinion about me, and his plea to give me the maximum allowable time in jail, which was nine months.

I had already spent ninety days in their jail awaiting trial. My attorney said next to nothing about my rehabilitation efforts, so the judge began to give his view. He said that he found my behavior in Ozaukee County completely unacceptable. He handed down the maximum sentence of nine months in the Ozaukee County jail, with credit for time served, which was the three months, making the final outcome that I finish out the additional six months. The judge went on to say that he felt that this crime, in his view, should mean that I spend at least a few years in the state prison. He finished by saying that he did not want to see me in his court again. I thanked him and went with the deputies to my new home for the next six months.

While I was getting settled into my new abode, which was an eight-by-ten-foot jail cell, I noticed that I had begun to feel safe. It was a feeling I hadn't felt in years, if ever before at all, just knowing that I was away from that self-destructive part of myself. In this place there was no way of getting drugs. The jailers were these country type, straight laced guys who you knew were not about to buy in to any type of bribe or misconduct.

During my time in there, I learned an even stricter routine than what I previously experienced there. It was a regimen in which someone controlled what time you ate, slept, and showered, day in and day out. I found myself reading books, which I just never had time for while on the streets. I started writing letters to my mother. The letters were my way of apologizing to my mother and father for the sick lifestyle I had been leading for years. And I then began to get letters back from my mother and father, just simply telling me to keep my chin up. They also gave me forgiveness in each letter I received. I just remember thinking that if they knew the extent of the shit I had been doing, would they really forgive me? I believe the answer would be a definite 'yes.' They were so patient in their love and understanding of me. And God knows I had my issues!

One day I was visited by a local minister who frequented the jail to console inmates. At the time I just saw this as a way to break up the day and get out of the cell block. What I didn't know was that this gentle-man would play a big part in my life. His name was Pastor George. On my first visit with George, we sat and talked about why I was there. And his first order of business was to let me know that God forgives. I just remember thinking, "OK George, if you can convince me that I'm worthy of being forgiven for murder, robbery, theft, and the crimes of my ill passions, I'm all ears." But I did have my doubts.

George began to visit me on a weekly basis, even twice a week sometimes. I eventually began to welcome his visits, and our prayers at the end of each visit seemed to be calming. I wasn't completely sold on this type of help, but there was a glimpse of hope that seemed to come from the visits.

George and I agreed to keep in touch after my release, though I didn't see any real benefit to come from it. I didn't really see this guy getting any heroin or morphine for me on the streets, so what was the point? Still, truth be told, George did hit on something deep down, spiritually.

Upon my release I felt very healthy. I had a clear mind, with a new spiritual outlook from my visits with good old George, and physically, I felt better than I had in many years. I had been doing a thousand pushups and sit ups daily, along with reading books and writing to my mother. I felt like a new human being ready to face the world once again.

When I left the jail I remember thinking that taking the high road was what I needed to do. I actually thanked the jailers for being good people and wished them the best in wherever their lives may take them.

The Final Phase

I then returned to the Wisconsin Family to continue with my treatment program, so that I could once and for all tame that beast that I had invited into my life for so long. When I arrived back to the facility that had given me such a great start to a new life of sobriety, I felt exhilaration. As crazy as this may sound for someone who had been incarcerated in different capacities for over a year, it was my reality. I felt safe and very grateful that I had been waking up above dirt, not to mention that I remembered what I did the night before. Whether the night before was in a cell or a rehab facility, I knew I hadn't hurt myself or anyone else. That was called progress in my book.

During my first week back, I learned that I was moving on to the second phase of the program, and I would now move to a halfway house facility located on the south side of Milwaukee. I would now be able to pursue employment and make an attempt to live the life of a productive human being. It was kind of like what we learned in the Morning Prayer we recited daily: "Neither the giant of our dreams nor the dwarf of our fears, but a human being, part of a whole with our share in its purpose." Wow, what a change for me! My old motto seemed to be: "The dwarf of my fears I am, so f*** you all, and on my path of self-destruction, I'll show you MF's just how bad I can be!" I had been this insecure little boy wallowing in self-pity and not making any attempt to change because I believed in taking the softer, easier way of life. And I seemed to dismiss the fact that life wasn't easy, but it could be good if you just try to make the right decisions and not give up. But I had given up many years earlier.

In my first month at the halfway house, I noticed that most of the fifteen or so residents in the facility were living pretty productive lives. They got up every day for our early morning meeting and prayer. They ate breakfast, helped with cleanup, and left for work. At first I thought some of these guys had to be getting high, or at least chipping a little bit. I could not imagine that after being an inpatient for six to nine months, they wouldn't take advantage of the freedom. Well, I sure thought about it. I was a dope fiend.

As I completed my first month at the facility, which is a time of reflection on what you learned in the first phase of the program, I began my job search. During the first thirty days we had also been schooled on what to expect during our search and coached on how we might answer questions on the work applications about previous convictions and gaps in work history.

I found a temporary staffing agency that worked with a few factories and foundries in the local area to find workers for special projects or as fill-ins for vacations. For me, even temporary work would be great. Just getting up in the morning and having a job to go to was a wonderful thought. After what I had been doing for the years past, not even wanting to wake up, this was nice. I didn't have to worry about looking over my shoulder for police. I didn't have to cover my arms for fear of people noticing tracks up and down my arms. No more sleeping under bridges or waking up in strange basements, which was so foreign to me, though it was such a relief from years past.

My first gig was at a foundry on the near south side of Milwaukee, just doing menial jobs like sweeping and assisting the die cast guys. It was hot, it was filthy dirty, and it was tiring. But at the end of the day when I got paid, I felt great. It's amazing how I felt, having my own hard earned money. My father always told me free money was great, but if you worked hard for it, you cherished it that much more, and I did. And I won't lie—one of the first thoughts after cashing my check was how much heroin I could get with the money. What if I just did this gig daily and bought a half gram of heroin at the end of each day? No police asking where I got the money, no hopping pharmacy counters, or selling stolen goods. What a thought!

However, on second thought—how do I eat, buy essentials, and pay rent? What a messed up thought process I still had going on in that dark corner of my mind. But it was there, so I needed to deal with it daily or I would be overcome by the beast once again. It's just that easy to relapse. I knew if I let that stinking thinking get the best of me I'd be toast.

After a few months of working daily at the temp agency and actually having a bank account which was monitored by the staff, I saw progress that I hadn't seen in years, and it felt wonderful! By now I was being encouraged to find a steady job with some type of future. I finally received my G.E.D. after months of studying in my spare time, and things were looking up. But this was still foreign to me. I realized that after so many years of being miserable, that the very misery that caused me so much trouble became my comfort zone. I always seemed to expect the worst and then disappointment wouldn't be an issue. In my habitual thinking, in that dark corner of my mind, I knew that I was no f***ing good anyway. Why should I expect good to come anywhere near me? So, when the good did begin to happen, I felt out of my comfort zone. I think that is why I was always drawn back to the thoughts of self-destruction. After all the shit I had done, I felt like that's what I deserved.

Feeling the need to follow the staff's advice to seek permanent full time employment, I reached out to a few successful old friends from my younger days, and my old boss when I worked for the Milwaukee

School Board maintenance department. That was the best job I ever had, with full benefits, great pay, and an early retirement option and a pension. When I stopped in to see this guy, he was sitting at the same old desk, and he welcomed me in immediately. He was very open and kind—as he had always been—and he asked how I was doing.

I disclosed my whole story of drug abuse and the fact that I had made vast progress in my recovery. He was very sympathetic to my story, and he told me that he and some of the guys had thought about me over the years. He said that I had been one of his top workers and they all enjoyed working with me. However, as much as he would like to consider having me back, there were no openings at that time. He said he would let me know if one were to become available. We said our good-byes and off I went, back to the drawing board.

My next call was, reluctantly, to my old neighbor Johnny, the guy who initially introduced me to drugs. But I had heard he became very successful in the real estate business, and that he was looking for someone to help him rehab some buildings that he recently purchased. The buildings were close by the facility I was at, so I thought I would give it a shot. Since Johnny was never into heroin or morphine, and his drug days had been behind him for ten plus years, I didn't feel uncomfortable doing it.

When Johnny and I met, he explained that he was going to convert an old apartment building into sleeping rooms for single adults who were financially strapped. He showed me a layout of what he wanted it to look like and told me I could begin working for him on the conversion the next day.

I began working with Johnny, building new walls separating the apartments into a number of rooms. Days turned to weeks and weeks to months. We were making pretty good progress, but when it came time to get paid, Johnny had some excuse to hold back the pay until the job was completed. That was Johnny, and I should have known there'd be some underhanded stuff going on.

After a few rooms had been completed I was finally able to squeeze a partial payment out of Johnny. I needed to show a paycheck to the staff at the treatment facility. And, I wanted the money. Shame on me for not having the insight to realize what working for Johnny was going to entail. I knew what Johnny was like, but I opted to believe that after ten years and some success, he would be a different person. It was then I began to realize that dishonesty was not only in the world of alcoholics and drug addicts, it was everywhere. The thirst for money is like a drug that makes some people stop at almost nothing to get it. Well, that would include Johnny, as I found out.

At least I had work even though I had to lean on him to give me a paycheck. Having a steady job would soon become my catalyst to move on to the next phase of the treatment program. Phase three was where I would be out on my own with gainful employment and proof of a stable living environment. And while out on my own, I would be responsible for attending weekly groups at the treatment center.

Playing With Fire

While still at the facility I got to know another young guy who I will name as Geoffrey. This guy was somehow different from the other residents. I picked up a sense that he may have some mental health issues. At first, as Geoffrey and I began to spend time together going down to the Mitchell Street shopping area in Milwaukee's near south side, I saw another side of Geoff that differed from the demeanor he displayed at the facility, which was that of a tough and apathetic guy. He was actually a very kind man, even though he had the appearance of a very muscular, street gang type of guy. Geoffrey also seemed to be very intelligent. He was street smart but also seemed to have a pretty good education under his belt. What I began to notice about Geoff was that while we would be having a normal conversation he would seem to be a bit distracted, and out of nowhere he would laugh, then immediately return to a very serious expression.

I began to see quite a bit of Geoff's other side when we were sitting around people watching. There would be a strange smirk on his face that would turn to a stone cold serious look almost instantly. When I would ask Geoff what was so funny, he'd turn to me and say, "Nothing" as if it never happened. It was then that I realized there was more to this man than what I initially saw. There was definitely a mental health issue that was completely foreign to me. But, it seemed that it was this very flaw in Geoff's personality that drew me closer to understanding him, and I became protective of the Geoff I now knew. I felt horrible for this guy, and I seemed to want to help him during my every waking moment. I think my concern for him took me away from my own ills and flaws, which began to seem minimal in comparison.

One morning when I was getting ready to go to work with Johnny, I asked Geoff if he wanted to accompany me and possibly make a few bucks helping out. Geoff agreed to tag along. Once we arrived, I introduced Geoff and took Johnny aside to let him know a bit about Geoff. I asked if I could have him assist me in my work for the day, and Johnny agreed.

As we went on about our day of hanging drywall, Geoff told me that he would soon be moving on from the second phase of the program and asked if I thought Johnny would consider renting him a room at this building. My initial thought was that this type of arrangement could work out well for both Johnny and Geoff. But, then on second thought, I went a bit deeper in considering what that situation might look like.

I had to keep in mind the fact that Johnny was who he always was, an opportunist. And as I thought of the fact that Geoff was pretty vulnerable, it brought out the protective side of me. Johnny was like a shark, and if he smelled the blood of anything he could exploit from someone, he'd pick up on it quick. Needless to say, I was very apprehensive about letting Johnny exploit this guy, so later that night I spoke to Geoff. I told him of the possible pitfalls of dealing with Johnny and gave him fair warning to rethink his decision to rent from Johnny. But, I also knew Geoff wasn't dealing with a full deck, and in his view it was a done deal.

So, Johnny and Geoff worked out a deal in which Geoff would be doing odd jobs and daily caretaker type chores around the building, and in exchange, he would live in the building rent free. But, in dealing with Johnny, nothing was free. There was always a big price tag on what Johnny would offer as 'a favor.' I realized that after the many years of not seeing Johnny, there was only one change in his behavior patterns: He had become more opportunistic and more devious, drugs or no drugs.

About a month later, Geoff moved on from the treatment facility into Johnny's rooming house. I myself had secured a job with another one of the residents at the facility who had started a painting business. I was getting full time hours and began to receive a weekly paycheck consistently, as opposed to what I had become accustomed to with Johnny, where I had to beg like a dog.

Working the full time painting job with Mike, I began to make money, and I was actually able to see my bank account grow a bit. It felt good to be working like a normal and productive member of society. After work I would go back to the facility and shower, have dinner, relax, and then attend our evening group sessions. The routine seemed to work wonders for my soul. This change in my lifestyle felt so good in comparison to my days of being a slave to heroin, when my whole selfish world was centered on dope. I began to realize just how much my life had been just a big bowl of 'me.'

And now, after learning to interact with people and to live on life's terms, I saw a whole new world. I began to understand my life as "being that part of a whole, with my share in its purpose" just as we always recited in the Morning Prayer every day. When I first began reciting that prayer every morning, it was just that—reciting. But I had come to realize what it meant.

One night when I was done with the evening group, I took a walk over to Johnny's building where Geoff was staying. It was only about a half-mile away, and I had been thinking about how Geoff was doing. He had been popping up in my mind occasionally as I was out painting during the day. I had come to like this guy, and I felt that he wasn't going to be able to make it alone out there. I felt he needed some human contact other than Johnny.

When I arrived at the building, I found Geoff sweeping and mopping the halls of the rooming house. On the first level of the building there were two corner taverns, one on each end of the building. This in itself was a worry I had thought of in terms of Geoff being here alone with only his seemingly crazy thoughts. Being alone is OK, but there has to be some positive interaction occasionally for people with our history. I knew that from my own times of solitude. When a guy like me had too much alone time, it seemed that that old committee in my brain would convene for a session. And when that happened, it usually meant trouble. Those f***ers in that committee would always seem to rule on the side of self-destruction.

As I visited with Geoff, we laughed about some old times back at the residential facility and then gradually began to talk about the here and now. To me, it seemed that Geoff's here and now wasn't such a healthy place. I noticed that he was more distracted than he had been in previous weeks. While we talked, he became very distant, and his laughing spurts were shorter than in the past. I remember feeling so helpless in trying to think of a solution for him to get well in his mind.

It seemed that out of nowhere in our conversation, Geoff mentioned that Johnny had said something to him about torching the building. He said that the occupancy was down, and that Johnny felt that the rooms were not how he wanted them done. The bottom line is that we just did what he told us to, when constructing the place. It seemed that Johnny was again looking for someone to blame for any misfortune that came his way. That's just the guy he was.

Geoff suddenly changed the subject from Johnny to his father, whom he hadn't ever spoken much of. Geoff said his father wanted him to come to live back at his old house with him. After leaving Geoff back that night, I could feel his confusion and emotional pain. He seemed so lost. As I lay in bed that night, I couldn't help but obsess about how to help this guy.

About a week later, I stopped by my parents' house after a painting job in their neighborhood. My mother and father were both in the kitchen having breakfast before my father was to travel to Atlanta for work. They welcomed me in with open arms and told me that I looked great and that they were very happy for me.

As we were having breakfast, my father mentioned a story in the morning newspaper about a fire at an apartment building on Milwaukee's south side. He said that someone was killed in the fire. When I looked at the article, I saw that it was Johnny's building and immediately picked up the phone to call him. He said, "Hey Tony! Did you hear about my building? Someone torched it!" My immediate response was, "Please tell me Geoff wasn't in that building." He assured me that Geoff was not on the premises when the fire occurred. I was very relieved when I heard Geoff was probably OK. However, when I hung up the phone, all I could do was sit at my parents' kitchen table and stare out the picture window with a thousand different thoughts going through my head.

I regretted getting involved with Johnny again. And I thought about how ironic it was that the news of this incident unfolded while I sat in the kitchen of my parents' house. This was the very room of the house where I had spent so much of my younger years listening to my mother and father warn me about my decision making when it came to the company I chose to keep. And one of the most frequent warnings from my parents was about my association with Johnny.

That one hour of sitting in my parent's kitchen on that day was a very sobering hour. I knew I needed to take a good hard look at my decision making skills. At the end of that work day I walked by Johnny's burned building. With that distinct smell like none other enveloping me, I thought about the horror it must have been for the guy who died there. What a f***ed up mess. As I walked back to the facility I knew I needed to get ahold of Geoff somehow to see if he was OK.

After our group meeting that night, I looked up Geoff's father in the phone book, and I left message asking him to call me. It was about three days later when I returned from work that there was a written message for me to call Geoff's dad. I immediately returned his call, and when he answered, he asked how I knew Geoff. I told him that Geoff and I had recently got to know each other pretty well at the facility we were in. And Geoff's father just responded in a very soft voice saying, "I'm very sorry to tell you that Geoff shot himself last night, and he's gone." As I could hear the grief in his voice, I could only say how sorry I was to hear the news. I told him that if there was anything at all I could do for him during his time of sorrow, not to hesitate to ask.

When I hung up the phone, my emotions were very intense but so mixed. I was torn between deep sadness and great anger. I felt horrible when I thought of how much emotional pain Geoff had to be in that he would take his own life. I could not even imagine the depth of his pain that led him to do what he did.

The anger came from the fact that I suspected that somehow Johnny was partially responsible for this. My feeling of anger centered on thoughts of the possibility that Geoff may have torched the building himself and then felt devastated that someone died in the fire. There were only two people that knew the answer to the real truth of this tragedy. And one of the two people was lying dead in the morgue, and the other person would never talk.

The next day I called Johnny and asked him to meet me at the building to look at the damage. Truth be told, I wanted to look Johnny in the eyes when I asked him about Geoff's possible involvement with the fire. I felt very sure that I would be able to get the truth from Johnny by the look in his eyes, even though I knew that he would never tell me the truth in words.

As I walked over to the building to meet Johnny, my thoughts were on Geoff and the pain he must have endured just prior to pulling the trigger. I thought of my state of mind when things in my life were difficult, and my way of dealing with suicidal thoughts. I knew that when I was in that frame of mind, I would just think, "F*** it" and put my proverbial blinders on, with no worry of death, and jump to my imminent death by way of 'don't-stop-till-you-drop' type of thinking.

That type of thinking was more careless and cowardly. But for Geoff, it seemed that he just said, "F*** it" and pulled the trigger. Though I knew Geoff had been suffering quite a long time in his battle with the demons that resided in his head, it was a tragedy just the same. And I couldn't help thinking that Johnny prompted Geoff's demise. The questions in my head were: Did Johnny actually pull the trigger and make it look like suicide by guilt? Did he terrorize that poor guy with guilt after the fire, not expecting that someone would actually be in the building? Did he tell Geoff it was his only option, knowing that Geoff was mentally unstable? These were questions I'd probably never get the absolute truth to, but I needed to ask Johnny.

When I arrived at the building, I saw Johnny's car parked outside, and I entered the side door of the building which had a stairway to the rooms upstairs. Johnny was on his way down the steps, and he waved me to come upstairs. As we walked through the hall along the doors of the rooms that housed the residents, he pointed to the charred remains of the room where the guy had burned to his death. It was a very eerie feeling thinking that it was just seventy-two hours earlier some poor guy was probably sleeping in his dream world, and moments later fighting for his life, only to lose his fight.

As we moved on to the room Geoff had occupied a week earlier, I asked Johnny point blank if he killed Geoff. Johnny turned and looked at me and said, "No," with a sheepish look on his face. Then he just looked away from me, and seemed to retreat inward, just looking at the floor. Johnny said, "Geoff was a troubled guy, that's all." It was at that very moment my gut told me he may be guilty. I felt he surely had some guilt surrounding Geoff's death, not to mention the poor f***er that burned alive.

After that short conversation we had about Geoff, Johnny seemed to dismiss my presence as he guided me back downstairs and out the door. He became very quiet. I had expected something more in the way of sadness or guilt, but this felt more like anger toward me. And maybe he felt some betrayal by me. Maybe he expected me to condone his actions, regardless of what he may have done. When I left our meeting, I felt a bit guilty for asking him the question about Geoff so bluntly, but I also had a feeling of vindication about my suspicions.

I still could not possibly know precisely what happened on that tragic day. And I may never know what the final straw was that pushed Geoff over the cliff of life. But what I was very sure of was that my decision making process, in terms of what company I would choose to keep in my life ahead, would need some thorough revamping.

CHAPTER THIRTEEN

Stepping Out

In my treatment program, I felt I was making progress in our evening groups and learning how to live life in what may be termed as 'the normal lifestyle.' Normal was described as getting up in the morning, remembering what happened the night before, eating breakfast, and going to work. And doing the normal thing at the end of the day meant eating dinner and then learning to relax without the use of drugs and alcohol. As I practiced 'the normal lifestyle,' I realized that after ten plus years of drugging myself, I actually had no clue how to just relax. It was almost like what I would describe as meditating. I had no clue how to do it, and I didn't see any benefit in it either.

After practicing relaxation every night after dinner, I was ready for some type of fun and if not with drugs, then what? Well, one thing that I and a few of the friends I made at this place had in common was desire for women. We talked about women daily in our conversations, in our groups, and almost every night before heading to sleep.

As our discussions of chasing women became more frequent in our groups, one of the staff members who ran the evening group mentioned that she thought a few of us may be ready to branch out to carefully test our social skills. The staff gave three of us the green light to plan an evening out on the town, possibly at a bar that had dancing. One of the provisions we had to follow was that we stick together and watch each other's back as far as abstaining from drinking alcohol.

We were all to be responsible for the others' mistakes and would be held accountable for any one of our possible mistakes, period. None of the three of us had a problem with that at all. We were all very confident that alcohol and drugs would be a non-issue. Looking back, I believe that I then saw women as a new outlet for my addictive personality. "What healthy young man wouldn't want this?" I thought.

Three of us—me, my old friend Jerry, and an guy named Mike—decided to go to a bar on the east side of Milwaukee that had a dance floor. We were three guys from three very different backgrounds which I was sure would make for a very interesting night. Here I was, the olive-skinned Dego from the northwest side of Milwaukee, and Jerry who was as black as night from the inner city of Milwaukee, and then there was Mike, a blond, blue-eyed guy from the old south side of Milwaukee. What a crew we had!

When we left for the night, we headed to the bus stop. That was just the way we had to do it, unless we were to walk. The whole bus experience and the fact of being free for the first time in over a year felt very strange but good. Though we were headed for a bar, I really felt that I was reaping the benefits of all of the hard work I had put into myself, both emotionally and physically. I felt like how I imagined a normal human being would feel.

We laughed all the way down on the bus. One of the jokes was about what the hell we would do if we actually met a woman who would want to leave with us. "What will we do?" I said. "Do we tell them that we have to leave on the bus to make curfew?" There were all types of scenarios we discussed, but the bottom line was, let's just worry about that if we even get that far. Jerry told Mike and me that we white boys didn't have game enough to get that far, and Mike said that Jerry wouldn't have a chance after dark, because he was too black.

When we arrived at the bar, we ordered three sodas and stood by the dance floor, people watching and laughing. It seemed like a whole different lifetime for me. I hadn't been in that type of bar, or any bar for that matter, in years.

As we hung out for a while, we met three women who were together celebrating a birthday. We all seemed to hit it off right way, and we laughed and danced together. Time seemed to get away quickly and before we knew it, it was the last call for alcohol. For us it was just a clock telling us our fun was over. But, none of us drank or drugged. It seemed that all three of us had a great time.

As we were leaving the bar, one of the girls asked if we cared to have breakfast with them. There was a twenty-hour-hour breakfast place called Fishers that was known for getting a rush of business when bars closed. It was hard to get a seat by three o'clock in the morning, most every day.

When we finally got seated for breakfast, we were all starving. As we waited for our food and talked, one of the girls asked how we knew each other. All three of us were caught off guard, and we just looked at each other like deer in headlights. Then Mike let out a nervous laugh and said, "In the timeout corner." That comment gave us just enough time to respond that we worked together over the years. Well, we weren't lying; we did do a hell of a lot of work in that place we lived.

When my question to the girls asking what they did was answered, it also brought a nervous laugh from all three of us. The answer they gave was that they worked for the FBI. Mike said, "OK, what do you really do?" One responded again, "Pam and I work for the FBI, and Susie works at XYZ. Truly we do." At this, I felt like my gut took a 180. I went from feeling so good and relaxed for the first time in probably ten years to suddenly feeling sick to my stomach. It was as if I invited that dark corner of my mind to remind me of who I really was, a no-good crook. It was a shame because I felt like I connected with these women until that very moment of that disclosure. Still, when we finished breakfast and said our good-byes, we got their phone numbers.

We decided to walk back to the facility since the weather was nice, and we had some fun conversation on the way. It was at least fifteen miles, so we had plenty of time to talk. I expressed my feelings about where the women worked, and all three of us laughed. Jerry just said, "Yeah, but they had some nice butt." He was right. Truth be told, the fact that they worked for the FBI was really not such a big deal. After all, if there was anything in my past that was FBI-worthy, I would have heard from them long ago.

As time passed with our daily grind of living life on life's terms, and having our fun and laughs, Jerry, Mike, and I became closer. We worked hard and planned our every bit of free time to spend it with women. We had been in touch with the girls we met at the bar and began to visit their apartment on the east side of Milwaukee. Eventually all of our free time went to visiting these particular girls. The staff didn't discourage what we were doing since it didn't include drugs, alcohol, or crime. We were beginning to learn how to live without all of the dirt in our lives, and we discussed our leisure time activities with the staff in our group therapy sessions.

In between work and play, I began to draft my exit plan from the final phase of the program. I had to lay out my goals, both short-term and long-term. I needed to include my ongoing support mechanisms, such as my twelve-step meetings and friendship network with other sober men and women, along with a long-term goal of where I could see myself in the distant future. The staffed helped us explore our aspirations so we could develop our long-term goals, which included things like becoming a husband and father, going to school, having a career, and making time for clean and sober hobbies.

For me, I had always coveted the thought of having a loving wife and children. My thoughts about my long-term goals also included raising healthy kids, with beautiful grandchildren at the end of the rainbow. My ultimate goal was enjoying fun and laughter with my children and grandchildren and being a strong and wise sounding board in times of their trying moments of life.

My long-term goals were my dreams of how I would like to see myself in the future. Planning my mid-range goals, however, was a very difficult task. When a staff member and I explored the steps I would need to take to achieve my dreams, it was like being doused with a bucket of cold water. I had no f***ing clue what my mid-range goals would look like. I had no real skills other than manipulation and scheming in doing my self-serving fund-raising for my selfish ends. And though I thought these skills would make for a successful politician, I didn't have a college degree, and I was now a convicted felon.

When I shared this thought with my career counselor, she looked at me and said, "It's never too late to start a career by going to college or taking up some type of apprenticeship." As far as being a convicted felon she said, "Tony, I think you will find out in the normal world, so to speak, that there are convicted felons, and there are non-convicted felons." She went on to say that no person that walks this earth is without misdeed. And though this made me want to look away from my past and into the future, the fact remained I was on public record as a criminal. But, she told me, with a fresh outlook and a promise to myself that I would do the right things on my new journey, I could succeed in accomplishing the goals I mentioned. Now the hard work would begin by taking the necessary steps to succeed.

Branching Out

The summer was winding down and I would soon be released from the long-term treatment program I had been in for over a year. Seeing this new version of my life before me, I had some real reservations on how I would succeed in the outside world. I would be walking out into the same cold world that was there before I was locked up. And I wouldn't have the luxury of the structure that I had become accustomed to over the past year or so. Years before I would have seen structure as a punishment, but I had become very comfortable with it. Nonetheless, I knew that I could set up my own structure and support system necessary to succeed and live happily. The only real obstacle before me was that committee inside that dark corner of my mind. It was still there to remind me that I was the same old loser that I was before.

I sat down and wrote a short list for myself on an old piece of paper that I would carry in my pocket day and night. It was a list of the crucial pieces of the puzzle I would need to succeed: Job, School, Meetings, and Pastor George. It was a short and sweet list, but for me it was a mission. It seemed to give me a bit of direction toward where I needed to aim in order to stay focused. Making lists was an old habit my mother once taught me. She told me in no uncertain terms that I had a severe attention deficit. That term wasn't around back then, so she just told me that I was too darn scattered.

So, with my list before me, I went right over to the University of Wisconsin Milwaukee, on the east side of Milwaukee. (Of course, I started with the second bullet point on my list. I never did do things in order.) When I went to register for what would be my first time in college, I found out what was needed to get accepted: a copy of my G.E.D. and a copy of my high school transcripts.

When I went to my old high school to gather my transcripts, I saw my old assistant principal whom I had many run-ins with. He remembered me very well. I stopped in his office for a visit while the office staff gathered my transcripts. He had a big grin on his face and asked how life had been treating me. I immediately told him the truth. I said that life treated me as it always had, which was the same as it treated anyone else. I told him that the key was how I treated life, and I hadn't been fair to life.

I said I was planning to attend college with the goal of becoming a drug and alcohol counselor in an attempt to help other troubled kids. I also told him that I wanted to apologize to him for the type of kid I had been while I was at his school. I told him that making amends was part of my new program that I was involved in, and I just simply said that I was sorry for all of my ill behavior. And in particular I apologized for the most notable moment when I threw a full can of Pabst Blue Ribbon beer which hit him on the side of the head.

He just grinned and said, "Was it Pabst? I thought it was just a Red White & Blue beer. I guess you really meant business, huh?" We both laughed and he told me that he would certainly forgive me, and he wished me luck in my journey. With my transcripts in hand, I headed right back to UWM to register. I now knew that my intentions were golden and I would succeed.

After I completed my registration, I went to a nearby temporary help service to apply for some part-time work. I explained my situation with school, and I gave them my history of work back at the prior temp service I had worked for while I was back at the treatment program. My history at that temp service was great. They knew I was reliable and worked hard while I was with them, and they gave me a glowing review. I was accepted that day, and they told me to call in each morning I was available at 6:00 am.

Next, I jumped on the bus and headed over to the old facility I was in for a group meeting. I felt grounded when I was at that place, and at that time, even though I had made some real progress with my list, I was uncomfortable. The outside world seemed a bit fast for me, and I had been feeling somewhat lonely. I felt that I didn't have anyone to share my successes with, and I didn't get any accolades. The bottom line was that I was doing what normal people do on a daily basis, but I was looking for a pat on the back for doing the routine and expected things. I realized that it's just what people do in life to succeed and grow. When the person actually completes something successfully, then the accolades come. I had thought registering was completion. Shit, I hadn't completed much of anything in my life, except when I was forced to, like completing a jail term. So, WTF did I expect, a certificate for registering for school?

When I went to the evening group, I talked about my fears of being back out on the street and the loneliness I felt. After the group, my old staff person took me aside and told me I was doing what I needed to do. She said that it was all positive stuff and that I just needed to know and trust it would turn out the way it was meant to, as long as I put in the work. She said that I needed to take a good look at my fears and face them head on. She reminded me of the old term we used in defining fear, which was False Evidence Appearing Real. She was right, and I think my whole life was pretty much based on my reaction to fear. I had always seemed to be afraid of most everything in life. And that dark corner of my mind always seemed to blurt out "What if?!" If only I could shut the door on that f***ing useless part of my brain.

When I was leaving the facility my old buddy Jerry was also heading over to the bus stop. He had been working at a local restaurant as a short-order cook. He seemed to be doing great. He told me the only thing he wasn't happy about was the fact that he was staying at his mother's house. Jerry loved his mother to death! She was a wonderful woman. When Jerry and I stopped over periodically, she always treated me as family. I was kind of like the Italian son she never had. Momma was a real down to earth country woman with a heart of gold. And she always let Jerry and me know how proud she was that we were clean and sober.

I clearly remember a day Jerry and I stopped to visit Momma after we had both graduated from the final phase of the treatment program. After visiting for a bit we told her we were heading out to meet up with some girls. She said in her southern drawl, "Before y'all catch the bus, y'all need to go talk some sense into that sister of yours! She in a bad way with those drugs, and messing up with them kids too!" She said it with a look on her face that was pleading with us to go help her daughter, Jerry's sister.

Well, we agreed to give it a shot. We went over and talked with Debra, to no avail. Shit, Jerry and I both knew when we stepped foot in that apartment of hers that things were not good. There were kids running around in their dirty diapers, almost no furniture, and no food. All her money was going to the dope man. She was an absolute mess. Jerry and I said our piece about getting sober, and we got the hell out. It still played on our heads too, so we just couldn't stay there long. As messed up as things were at her house, and as depressing as it seemed, we were still dope fiends.

We just seemed to be wired differently. I would think that any normal person, seeing what we saw in her house, would most certainly get sick and run. We, too, were ill from seeing how she was living, but it seemed our minds still gravitated toward entertaining the thought of using again. It didn't seem to matter how much pain and agony heroin may have caused me in the past, all of that goes out the window once you have a syringe full staring you in the mind. It's the devil, I'm telling you.

We got on that bus as fast as we could just to escape the temptation. Luckily we had each other on that day. We both knew that this was no place to be for guys like us. We agreed to call Momma another day to talk about Debra.

New Horizons

Jerry and I were down on the east side visiting the FBI girls we had met out in the bar a couple months earlier. We had been visiting with them periodically since we had met, and things were getting pretty intimate. While we were sitting around the girls' apartment that night, I shared that I was going to give college a shot at UW Milwaukee. And Jerry mentioned his job as a cook at a place called Coco's Restaurant.

The girls then shared some news of their own. They told us that they were looking at renting a large four-bedroom flat, which was one block away from UW Milwaukee. They mentioned that they would entertain the thought of having one or both of us move in to help with the rent, if we were interested.

The woman I had been involved with took me aside and told me that she was moving out of the apartment mainly because of her ex-boyfriend. She told me that he was an agent, and he had been pleading with her to take him back. She showed me a few notes that he had left on her car at night and at work.

As we sat and talked for a while, there were various thoughts going through my head. One of my thoughts was about her insinuation that she was interested in me for more than just an intimate evening here and there. I also obsessed about the fact that she would even consider someone like me. How would some woman dump an apparently successful FBI agent for me, a convicted felon and an ex-junkie with almost no relationship aptitude?

Then after viewing a few of the notes her ex had written, I had a revaluation of sorts that slapped me in the face. I realized the truth of a statement that my old counselor had once mentioned to me. It was a statement she made in response to what I shared as my view of my self-worth, when I explained how I saw the comparison of myself to men who had noteworthy success. This counselor told me that career success should not be equated with interpersonal success. She said that some of the most successful career professionals she knew had no more people skills than me. "In fact," she said, "you will probably find that you possess an abundance of interpersonal skills in comparison." She went on to warn me that I should never mistake 'book smarts' for 'intuitive savvy.'

That whole night of personal reflection that went through my head reminded me that we as people are all subject to the 'Human Condition.' A person's upbringing dictates some of these skills, while one's own personal experience into adulthood and the work put into becoming a better person along the way are crucial for success and harmony. Eventually I thought, "Enough with my interpretation of successful relationships. After all, if I am so successful, why do I need an on-call therapist twenty-four-seven?

As the month of August was quickly passing, the girls made arrangements to get the lease signed and secure a move in date. They were able to get early occupancy for us to move in and get the living arrangements set up. We each had our own rooms, given there were four bedrooms, and a study which we made into a bedroom, but the sleeping habits varied. There was a girl named Susie who also moved in with us, and she and Jerry began to flip flop rooms. That made for some interesting stories and laughs between Pam and me, behind closed doors. The first month seemed to go very well.

As the month of September was zipping by, the girls informed us that they were planning a house warming party. They mentioned that all of the FBI agents and other employees at the bureau were invited. Jerry and I laughed about the fact that this would probably make for an interesting evening. A few friends, the FBI, and then there was us. We both knew that we would be quite a contrast from the other company that would be attending.

When the night of the party came, which I had been agonizing about for days, I was very uneasy to say the least. As the company arrived I remember shaking hands and greeting them at the door. I also remember thinking that with my luck I would see a familiar face that probably wouldn't be a face of good memories. But, this was the girls' party and the girls' coworkers. And, as long as I was living my life as I had been over the past year and a half, I knew I should not spend any time feeling guilty. This was a new day and a new life.

After the party had been going for a few hours with food and drinks, a guy brought out some marijuana. I remember about four people gathering in an empty bedroom, and I was one of them. Here I had been completely clean and sober for almost two years, but for some reason I made an ill-advised decision to join in. I thought if someone brought pot to a party with FBI agents in the house, it was probably safe. Or, maybe I was just that f***ed up to think that was OK. Another thought looking back, maybe I felt it was exhilarating and daring to do something like that.

The reality of it was that the whole thing was insane and offensive. It's not that for the fact that an FBI agent wouldn't pull a badge, because I'm sure they couldn't care less about someone smoking pot. But, I'm sure it offended them, and it ultimately offended Pam. I am still baffled about why I would pick a time like that to relapse after almost two years of being drug free. To throw it all away by smoking pot? I never even found pot to be a pleasant high for me. It was definitely not my drug of choice.

I didn't wake up the next morning thinking I needed more pot. And I didn't entertain the thought of going on a run for some heroin. But, I did feel sick about offending Pam, and I felt very guilty about crossing the line of my sobriety. That dark corner of my mind not only gave me constant reminders of the fact I was no good; it also helped me find a way to prove to myself that I was indeed a loser. Then it would follow up with the excuse of saying to me "Well, maybe I'm just one of those unfortunates. I was born that way."

The reality of the past twenty-four hours proved that I was just plain defiant in accepting that I was powerless. It seemed that out of that corner of my mind I would create some delusional thought that I had it all under control. But, if history should have taught me anything, it's the fact that me being in control of the direction in my life proved time and time again to be futile. Needless to say, my days were once again numbered in the realm of living life on life's terms. I was once again in the driver's seat, and with me steering? Forget about it!

Though I didn't go out and begin to use drugs again, I also didn't have the guts to face my demons. I simply lodged them into that dark corner of my mind. There was a lot of room in there, but it wasn't because it was empty but rather for the fact that over the years I must have stretched it enough to become a black hole. My problem was that I would invite its poison to come out like a venomous snake bite. And in doing that, it never failed, or rather I never failed, to hurt the people in my life as well as myself.

Even without using drugs now, I had now begun to destroy any and all progress with school, and I succeeded in alienating every healthy relationship that I had been cultivating in the previous couple years. It couldn't have been more than a month after that ill-advised night of insanity that I found myself looking for a new place to live.

CHAPTER FOURTEEN

An Old Friend

I was evicted from my apartment with the FBI girls for nonpayment, but probably violating my relationships with the girls was the main reason. I had begun to cultivate somewhat healthy relationships, until my relapse. I then had to contemplate my next move. I knew that going back to my group therapy sessions or some twelve-step program wasn't the answer to my problems.

The bottom line was that I was a coward. I didn't want to face the fact in front of others that I was weak, even though that is exactly where a person like me needed to be. But, I wasn't through with myself destructive ways. Though I really did want to be a normal person, I somehow thought that it meant moderation, and not abstinence, from drugs and alcohol.

My first order of business was to visit my mother and father. Once again, they welcomed me with open arms. How these people did it, I'm still not sure. There weren't any "I told you, Son's" or "This time you'd better Yadda, Yadda, Yadda. . . ." It was just a loving welcome and a sandwich. My father was still the same guy he had been since I was a kid. And my mother sat across from me at the same old kitchen table and asked how I was doing with school. I gave her the news that I may not be cut out for college.

What I didn't tell her were the reasons why, which was that I just didn't put in the work that it took and I surely didn't tell her that I had relapsed. I only told them that I had found a new apartment on the east side, and I asked for a place to stay for one week. I hadn't really secured the place I was looking at, but it was a building that always had vacancies for studio apartments. They were fine with me staying at their house for the week before I could get into the apartment.

While I stayed at my parents' house, my father asked me to go to a twelve-step meeting with him. I couldn't very well say no, because it would have broken his heart. He hated watching people fall off the wagon, and I surely didn't want to disappoint him, so we went. It was a very strange meeting, I thought. Out of about forty people at this meeting, it seemed the youngest guy was about sixty years old. I didn't feel like I could relate, and I certainly was not going to discuss the fact that I had recently relapsed, given that my father was there.

While we were at the meeting, my father introduced me to his close friend, Gerry, and his wife Dorothy. My father mentioned to the couple that I had been sober for about two years. Dorothy asked if I was employed. I told her that I had recently been attending UW Milwaukee and working as a laborer part time, but that I was always looking for work. Dorothy went on to say that she was always looking for good employees at the company she managed. As my father and I were leaving the meeting, Dorothy mentioned to me that she may be in touch with me about a job.

On our ride back home, my father explained that he and Gerry had been very close over the past twenty-five years or so. And he said that Dorothy was a wonderful person with a heart of gold. My father jokingly mentioned that anyone who could put up with Gerry for all those years would no doubt be canonized a saint. It was funny, but I have to say that my impression of Dorothy was a bit scary. She was very kind, but she seemed to be someone you wouldn't want to mess with. She had a very tough demeanor, and the thought of approaching her for a job seemed to be treacherous territory—if I were to be offered the job, I would have to be on my A game, with no screwing up. That would require a commitment to staying on the straight and sober road.

Sure enough, I received a call at my parents' house about a week later from Dorothy who asked me to come to her office the next week.

On the meeting day, I left a couple hours early to view apartments close by the building, in case I did get a full time job with her. I knew that I needed to be out of my parents' house soon, for their sake and mine. I scoured the area for "for rent" signs and found one directly across the street from Dorothy's building. I took the number down just in case I did get the opportunity to work with her.

Dorothy's office was in a very large condominium complex directly across the street from Lake Michigan. I was astounded by the look of this complex. I noted that the cars that pulled up to the building were all BMW's, Mercedes, and Cadillacs. And at the front door, there was a doorman dressed in a suit and tie who greeted each resident by "Mr." or "Mrs. So-and-so." The residents were dressed to the nines and looked like people I had only seen in the movies. It had the Hollywood look as far as I could see. After all, I was just a poor boy from a very modest upbringing.

During my formal interview with Dorothy, she asked a variety of questions about my work history. Although my resume showed quite a few years of good, stable work from ages fourteen through twenty-one, when I had worked pretty steadily at restaurants and then the City of Milwaukee, it was after I was twenty-one that my resume was spotty, to say the least. The benefit of Dorothy knowing I had been in recovery for a few years on and off was very fortunate for me. With my work history, I don't think any other employer would have even taken the time to meet with m

As my interview came to a close, Dorothy told me that if I were willing to work hard right off the bat, she would want me to report to her office the next morning at seven sharp.

The next morning, I reported at 6:45 am, and I was ready for work. My first three days were sweeping the underground parking garage from the third level sub-basement up to the ground level of the garage. With a push broom I swept my way up, covering every inch of the garage. It may not sound like a big job, but believe me, it was work—and dirty work at that. But I did it, and I did it well. After three days, Dorothy came down to inspect my work and gave me the thumbs up for a job well done. She then asked me to show up at 6:30 am the following day and report to the parking garage manager.

The next day I reported at 6:30am, and I was greeted by Gary, the parking garage manager. He was a very friendly guy, who seemed to have just one thing in mind while on the job: He was there to please the residents of the building, and give them assurance that their cars were in good hands and safe. It was a simple task.

In teaching me my duties, he showed me a map of the three floors of the parking garage and the numbered spaces designated for each resident. He told me that it would soon become second nature to me to know the names of the residents and the spaces for their cars.

I was amazed by the cars that came in, and I took notice of what type of person was driving what kind of car. I seemed to see a fit for the car matching the driver's personality. An example was Herb Kohl, the owner of the Milwaukee Bucks basketball team and a US Senator. He would pull in with his little two door Mercedes Benz convertible, and he would park it himself right along the wall just inside the garage. His spot was premium. After all, he was Herb Kohl.

Then there was a very attractive, professional woman who drove a beautiful little two door BMW. I envisioned her as a successful attorney. There was an elderly woman in her early eighties, and I saw her as most likely a widowed millionaire. In time I saw that my presumptions about these people were pretty accurate. The attractive young professional woman was an attorney, Herb Kohl was who he was, and the elderly woman was a widowed millionaire.

I really began to enjoy parking these cars. I had a chance to envision what type of car would be my dream car. And I liked learning how to treat each person as they pulled up. Some of them just parked and walked into the building. Others enjoyed some small talk, seeming to take an interest in who I was as a person. It was a great learning experience for me. There were some people I loved seeing pull in, and others whom I came to dislike.

This whole experience led me to look at myself and wonder who the hell I really was, and it gave me some valuable insight as to who I wanted to be. Well, I knew replacing Herb Kohl was probably not in the cards. And I knew being an attorney too was not a realistic goal, given my academic skills. But, I did realize that I could use some of the people skills I saw in these individuals whom I had come to admire. I also realized that it wasn't about the money, though I won't deny that's definitely a big plus.

I just realized that I could begin by practicing to be the best person I could be. I learned to treat everyone with the utmost courtesy and respect, in the same way that I picked up from the people I had come to admire. I wanted to emulate the same type of demeanor that I observed in them. They were the people in this place who were successful, wealthy, and seemingly always happy, but most importantly, they were people who treated me as an equal, regardless of their wealth and stature.

After about a month of working at my new job, I moved into my new apartment directly across the street. It wasn't nearly as luxurious as the place where I worked, but it was better than anyplace I had ever lived. It was on the eighth floor with a view of downtown Milwaukee and the Lake Michigan shoreline. I furnished the apartment little by little with some of the best furniture I ever dreamed of owning. For a guy who had slept under bridges, in abandoned homes, and in damp cold basements, I was feeling like a king.

A few months into my employment, Dorothy offered me yet another position at the complex with the building maintenance crew. There were two other guys on the staff—one was my new supervisor, and one had the same position as me. I started on-the-job training with a plumber who was under contract with the building, who Dorothy asked to train me on basic plumbing jobs. It was a crash course on plumbing, heating, and air conditioning. This was a huge building, heated by city steam. I was amazed at how much I learned over the first thirty days of working with these people. I began to see that Dorothy believed in me, and that she was really trying to do anything she could to see me succeed. I couldn't remember anyone ever believing in me the way she did.

I began to perform my daily duties at work as if they were second nature to me. I seemed to excel in maintaining the building. My immediate supervisor was also very pleased with my work, and he began to push quite a bit of the workload my way. Though I very much enjoyed the work, I could see that he too had his own demons he was battling. For him, it was alcohol, and I could tell he had been drinking on the job almost every day. He would page me to meet him on the roof of the building where no one but us went. When I'd respond to his pages, I would find him on the rooftop having a few cans of beer. He'd ask me to join him, telling me that I deserved it for working so hard. I never indulged in drinking with him. I just told him I didn't like the taste of alcohol. I also told him that I wouldn't repeat what I saw on the roof, so not to worry about me snitching.

I wasn't sure that this guy knew what I knew about Dorothy. She seemed to despise alcohol, probably because of her experience with her husband's drinking problem. Sure enough, Dorothy had already suspected that this guy had issues with alcohol abuse. She called me in the office one morning and asked if I suspected that my boss had been coming to work intoxicated, or if I saw him drinking on the job. At this question, I just sat silent for what seemed a very long minute. Dorothy just shook her head and said, "I suspected so." I really didn't know how to respond to the question, as it caught me completely off guard. About a week later, Dorothy found this guy's stash of booze.

When we arrived at work at 6:00 am one Friday, he was confronted with the evidence. For the first time I saw Dorothy in her confrontation mode. Shit, it was ugly! It taught me not to mess with her. She was tough as nails. I don't think he knew what to say, so he reacted with a childish rant. He told Dorothy to go f*** herself. Well, needless to say, he was escorted out of the building with his termination letter.

I remember thinking how insane it was for someone to jeopardize their career because they couldn't wait to drink after punching the clock. This guy had a wife and three kids. I realized how cunning and baffling this disease of drugs and alcohol really was. This was my first experience of seeing it from the sidelines.

A week later Dorothy asked me if I was up to the task of becoming the supervisor, and I told her I would give it my best shot. So, I moved up, and I was ready for the position. I handled scheduling for my three employees, filling out reports, and coordinating the contractors for the building. And I was involved in the weekly meeting with the office staff and Dorothy.

In my newfound success, I was beginning to feel that I had finally made some real strides in becoming a normal person with a normal lifestyle. Though this was very foreign to me, it began to feel exhilarating. I felt that I had begun to dispel that dark corner of my mind where my disease resided telling me that I was no good.

While I was making decent money, staying clean, and becoming physically healthier by the day, I began to venture out. I started to explore the upper class bars looking for women. Within a week or two, I had a few different women stopping over at my new apartment—they were nurses, lawyers, and even a DEA agent. With the agent woman, I wondered if I was being set up for info on something from my past or if she really found me appealing.

I thought this woman was amazing. She was drop-dead gorgeous, and she seemed to bring the best out of me. But, one night while we were out, something happened that was a deal breaker. I remember the conversation we had that night like it was yesterday. We had met out at a bar on the east side of Milwaukee, not far from my apartment. We eventually took a walk to the fountain, which was across the street from Lake Michigan and next to the hospital where I was born.

While we were walking and holding hands, I felt like 'this could be the one' and I was exhilarated. When we finally arrived at the fountain, we sat and began passionately kissing in a moment's time. And as crazy as I always was, I needed to dispel my worry about being set up for an info purge. Even as I had intimacy foremost in my mind, I still had that dark corner of my mind coaxing me to see if she were wearing a wire. As I caressed her, I reached inside her blouse and began to explore. Shit, if there was no wire, at least I could have fun while I was check-ing. She did stop me shortly into my exploration, and after kissing awhile, we began talking.

Our conversation developed from small talk into a deeper explora-tion of one another. She asked me if I was romantically involved with anyone, to which I said "No." Then she divulged that she had been recently involved with her field partner who was married. I saw a proverbial red flag go up in my mind. And then she answered a question I asked, with the response that I didn't expect to hear.

We were discussing her role with the DEA, and I mentioned the crazy world of cocaine, which she had earlier told me was the main focus of her job. My simple question to her was, "Wouldn't you just love to make a major bust to rid our country of cocaine?" I shouldn't have been shocked by her answer, but I was. She said, "No! Then I wouldn't have a job! I hope it keeps flowing in!" When I heard that response, I felt taken aback and kind of heartbroken. I think I now can understand what she was trying to convey. I may not agree with the moral logic, but I do better understand the view she had, from the perspective of her career.

That evening sent me into a mild depression. I felt very torn in my life's direction. I think it was due to the fact that I pretty much sheltered myself in the heroin bubble for so long, that I didn't see life for what it is in a broader sense. I had impulsively jumped to the conclusion that since this woman was gorgeous, came from a good family, and did not, herself, do drugs, that she was 'the one.' That was just who the f*** I was back then. I never seemed to look at the big picture.

I treated my relationships with women as another one of life's pleasures, the same way I treated opiates. It was almost like, hurry up and get what you want and worry about the specifics later. I don't think I was superficial in my love of people, but it was just that I seemed to jump now and think later. I didn't take in account the work of a true relationship, beyond the initial infatuation. It's like there was no tomorrow. I want what I want when I want it, and we can worry about the aftermath later.

She called me about two days later and asked if I wanted to go to a party which was going to include people from her office, and some Milwaukee Police Department detectives and higher-ups attending. While I entertained the thought of going to the party, I also feared the thought of running into some detective who would recognize me. It was then, for reasons unknown to me, I felt the need to have an unsolicited storytelling day, like a little kid in kindergarten.

I decided to spill my guts to this woman. I told her just how bad of a past I had and what a terrible person I was. I wasn't all that unique among drug addicts or alcoholics. Our need for distance from people can easily be accomplished by telling them just how bad we are. Because when we scare them off, there's little chance of having to work at a relationship.

And my guess is that addicts share one common denominator, which is fear. It seems that I had based so many of my life's decisions on fear.

Well, it seemed that I was successful in portraying who I was, because I didn't hear from this woman for the next few weeks. Then she called me one evening to tell me her job was reassigned to Miami. She said her good-byes and wished me good luck. The End. . . of that.

New Contacts

Back at my job working with Dorothy and her daughter Debbie, who was being groomed to succeed Dorothy in her position, things for me were going well. I began to have more and more responsibilities within the complex, which was great for me because when left idle, my mind was one hell of a treacherous place to be. There was that committee in my head that seemed to make some crazy decisions for me, and when I allowed them a chance to dictate my actions, I was in for a dangerous ride, to put it lightly. It was like 'letting the inmates run the asylum.' There's no doubt that this head of mine housed some pretty scary characters! And when they got to talking. . . forget about it!

I was branching out in my daily duties, doing repairs in some of the units—changing faucets, fixing leaks, and responding to other requests made by the residents. There were very few repairs that I couldn't do myself, but if I couldn't, I knew which contractor to call to get things done. As I made my daily rounds, I became very familiar with many of the residents. There were the very wealthy elderly widows who seemed to enjoy a social visit while I performed minor repairs. There were some very successful physicians who just didn't have time to do their own repairs. And there were some of the actual rich and well-known residents who always wanted things perfect.

One day I was asked to assist an elderly woman who had been diagnosed with brain cancer and was in her final days of life. When Dorothy and I visited the woman one morning at the request of her family, who were in a different part of the country, I noticed a prescription bottle by her kitchen sink. My eyes were fixed on the "May Be Habit Forming" label on the bottle. That stuck in my head the rest of the day. It was that dark corner of my mind that seemed to fixate on it like a dog with a sock, and it wouldn't let go.

Later that day after work, I called my old friend Mike to catch up on old times. In reality I wanted my conversation with Mike to help me justify the thought that I had earned a long awaited reward for all of my hard work over the past couple of years. I had proved that I could control this beast, and I proved it to myself months before when I smoked pot at the FBI party. I did it once, and I let it go, so I thought. The thing I didn't do was go to one of my meetings to admit my mistake and confront my vulnerability. I felt that admitting my secret would only expose my weakness and take away my control. I figured that I just needed to exercise self-control and use my will power.

Mike and I reflected on the glorious moments of our using days. And the glory of those days seemed to drown out any reminder of the price I had paid for those moments. My disease was no doubt running the show in my head during this conversation. Because after hanging up the phone with Mike, I found myself asking a woman I had been seeing in my apartment building if I could borrow her car. She agreed, and I was off to the races.

I met up with Mike that evening and bought some heroin. It only took about ten dollars' worth of heroin to get me back to that ultimate euphoric feeling I had missed so much. I hadn't been working the steps that originally brought me out of hell and into the life I had coveted for so long. Here I was, throwing it all away for one night of euphoria. Unfortunately, that one night took my head back to the place I never ever wanted to be again.

After that night, the committee in that dark corner of my mind voted to make my decisions for me. They knew how to get what we needed to feed that black hole of my disease. The committee convinced me that this so called 'disease' thing was just a big myth.

For the next few months I seized every opportunity I could by discreetly manipulating every physician I knew who lived at the building where I worked. I would wait for the right moment, guided by my sharply honed intuition, to ask for a one-time prescription of pain pills. I convinced them that it was just until I could get in to see my regular doctor, which I never even had.

It was amazing how this network grew so rapidly. I was very careful not to pick a doctor who might know another doctor I had been approaching. A few of the doctors I encountered seemed to know what my game was, but they also had their own stake in the game. One physician gave me a number of prescriptions for Percodan and eventually asked me to join him for dinner at his place one evening, at which time he would give me another script. I knew he probably wanted a romantic involvement, which wasn't going to happen, and I also knew I would need to tread very carefully, so as not to cause him to get angry or become retaliatory. I knew to expect some possible fallout by denying any advance on his part, and I knew leading him on might cause even more strife between us.

That evening as I contemplated stopping up to his condo, I knew that if I didn't show there would surely be no more prescriptions of Percodan coming from him. I talked to Mike before making my decision, and we laughed about the possible scenarios that could come about. Mike just said, "WTF, go see what happens. The worst that can happen is that he doesn't give you one." So, as I headed across the street to the physician's place, I decided I would tell him that I couldn't stay long due to a prior commitment.

When I arrived, I saw that he had dinner on the table with two place settings, a bottle of wine, and two wine glasses all set up along with lighted candles. What the f*** was I doing, I wondered. He gave me a quick tour of his place, and he stalled while showing me his bedroom and shower area. His voice seemed even softer and more feminine than usual. It was then that I just told him I couldn't stay long because I had prior plans with my girlfriend.

At that, he gave me a disappointed and somewhat angry look, pulled out his prescription pad and quickly wrote me a script for sixty Percodan. He looked me in the eyes and said, "Here's what you came for. Have a nice date." As I walked out, I thanked him and apologized for having to leave so fast. So I got the script, though it was surely the last from him. About a week later I was on the elevator, and he stepped into the elevator from the parking garage with a young boy in his late teens—my earlier suspicions about him were seemingly confirmed. I never saw much of him after that.

As time flew past during my crazy binge, I had a similar type relationship with a female dentist, probably in her sixties. She was very accommodating filling my Percodan and Dilaudid needs, and she stated one day that she knew I had been abusing this stuff. She pointed out that I had needle marks on my hands, and she asked to see my arms—I had begun to wear long sleeve shirts every day. She asked me to stop up to her condo after work one evening.

When I arrived I noticed she had a pharmaceutical bottle with about 200 Percodan in her hand. She asked me to sit down beside her while she laid her arm over my back, pulled me closer and said, "We're going to get you off this stuff once and for all." It was only a matter of minutes before she had her head in my lap, while saying that I just needed some good attention. About a half hour later, she gave me ten Percodan and told me that I needed to stop up to see her every evening after six. At that I asked if I could just take the remaining Percs with me, stating that I would still come to visit her. She just laughed and told me that was out of the question. She said, "Come and see me tomorrow."

As I went to visit her nightly, we got into some bizarre conversations. She told me she was a pagan and went on to tell me that I was also. She said that she and the Percodan were my gods. I knew this whole thing was getting very crazy, but I wanted to drain her of every pill in that bottle, and further, I hoped to get a steady supply.

One day Dorothy paged me to come to meet her by the elevators. She told me that the woman with brain cancer had just died, and Dorothy wanted me to accompany her up to the woman's condo to be sure the condo was secured. On our way up in the elevator, I was picking up on a vibe from Dorothy she sensed I had been slipping from my sobriety. It was unspoken, but it was there just the same.

When we went into the condo to check everything, I had an eerie feeling in my gut—surely the death thing in this lady's place. I saw her multiple bottles of medications, and my eyes quickly fixated on a bottle of Dilaudid and a bottle of morphine sulfate. I knew I couldn't take them with Dorothy by my side, but I also couldn't get that sight of the pills off my mind either.

That night after leaving work, I obsessed for hours about how I could get my hands on those pills. After all, the dead lady wasn't going to need them anymore, and I couldn't bear the thought of them being flushed or tossed out. But, there was almost no possible way to get back up in that condo. It bounced around in my head for a while before I decided to visit the doorman at the building. I told him that I needed to go check to be sure that nothing was left 'on' such as an iron, an alarm clock, or anything else. I just knew I had to get in there. At this stage of my addiction, I was extremely desperate. I would have broken the lock to get those pills, but I needed to exhaust all other options before doing that. I did not think of tomorrow. To me, at that point, tomorrow didn't exist.

The doorman on duty that evening was a guy I knew pretty well. When I asked for his assistance in getting me in the condo, he was adamant that he couldn't do it without risking his job. So, what that told me was that he did have a key somewhere. I pleaded with him to the point of exhausting his patience. He finally said OK, but pointed out that if anyone at all found out, we'd both be fired. I just told him that it would be our secret. I had quite a few secrets so what the hell was another one?

He agreed to let me in, but he insisted that he come up with me to unlock the door and wait until I was done so he could lock it back up and accompany me back out of the building. Once I was in, I immediately went for the pill bottles. It was like a rush in itself to get them in my possession. There were a couple hundred pills in all. These were some premium pain pills almost exclusively given to people with terminal cancer, and toward the end stage of their lives. And for me, it seemed I was at that stage every single night.

After returning to my apartment, I immediately indulged in the drugs by cooking them down and shooting them into my veins. It was a Friday evening, so I knew staying up late wouldn't pose a problem with work the next day. On Saturday mornings all I needed to do was to check the building's heating or air conditioning functionality and see if there were any urgent service calls.

That evening I sat at my dining room table shooting dope and nodding off into my own secret dream world. It was hours later that I awoke on Saturday morning to the sun shining in through the window and the sounds of the birds chirping. I was still numb to the outside world; however, my brain kicked in, and my conscience woke up. It was if that dark corner of my mind was saying, "I told you that you're no good." It was an emotional hangover—one of the worse I had felt in years. It wasn't only the fact that my arms and hands were riddled with battle scars from the night of insanity. It was mostly the thought of what I did to get the drugs in the first place. I had violated this dead woman's space. And whether she was gone or not, it was a horribly offensive act of selfishness, not to mention that I conned that innocent doorman into doing something outright criminal.

When I went to work that Saturday morning to check everything, I was very careful to avoid people. I was like a sleuth finding my way throughout the building to check everything out. When I was done, I carefully found my way out of the building and back to my apartment.

There I sat down and did some soul searching. This old soul was as dirty as it had ever been. The overwhelming feeling of guilt came over me like a dark cloud—so dark that I couldn't see another day before me. I knew this insanity had to stop. And the way I would stop was to shoot up the rest of the drugs. After all, I couldn't very well waste the stuff that I had gone to such lengths to obtain.

I barely made it through my work day on Monday, trying to have as little contact with Dorothy as possible. But, when I did see Dorothy briefly that dark day, and our eyes met, I could tell she knew that I had fallen off the wagon. As soon as I returned home, I called the dentist I had been seeing at the building. I told her that I needed her help badly. I was already feeling some withdrawal from my weekend binge, and she was my safety net in coming off slowly. She asked me to come over to her place to talk.

When I arrived, she told me to sit at the dining room table while she examined my arms and hands. With a look of pity, she went to her medicine cabinet and brought some type of salve in a little tin. She opened it up and rubbed it onto my hands. And, she told me that I needed to get into a rehab facility fast. She then made a call to a friend at De Paul Rehabilitation Hospital, the same place I had already been a few times in prior years. She told me to grab some belongings from my apartment, lock up, and meet her at her car outside. I complied, and off we went to the hospital.

When we arrived, she told me that she was going to call Dorothy to let her know where I was. I hesitantly agreed, because what else could I do? I was a mess. After her call to Dorothy, she told me that Dorothy sent her best wishes and said I should focus on getting better. My job would be waiting. I suddenly felt worse. I had not only let myself down, but I had let Dorothy down, too.

After I was admitted into the hospital, the medical staff tended to my hands, treating them with some topical antibiotics and wrapping them in gauze. The dentist said her good-byes, wished me well, and told me that she'd be in touch daily.

This was, I believe, the fourth time I had gone through the entire process of being admitted to this place. This time I wasn't as physically sick, as far as withdrawals were concerned, but I was spiritually and emotionally ripped apart inside. Everything seemed to happen so fast, and while I sat looking outside reflecting on what had transpired over the past couple months, I remembered something I heard numerous times while I was in rehab, and at my meetings. It was that at the onset of a relapse, people quickly find themselves right back at the point they left off in their prior relapse. And, once you take that first drink or drug, everything snowballs very quickly.

I was beating myself up over and over about how stupid I was to ruin the great strides I had made and the wonderful opportunities that had come my way. When I made a decision to take that first shot of dope, it changed my whole course of life in what seemed like a split second. And now here I was, torn and broken down once again, and it affected so many more people this time.

During the next thirty days, which seemed to last forever, I knew I needed to do some deep soul searching. I needed to become completely honest with myself and other people without attempting to make excuses or to minimize what I had done. And last but not least, I needed to give the healing process time to run its course by attending those meetings regularly, even if I didn't like the idea of sitting in church basements with a bunch of drunks and drug addicts. To be honest, I had to admit to myself that something about these seemingly useless meetings did work for some people. The same old people kept coming back to the same old meetings and for them it worked, even though it sounded pretty stupid to me.

Stupid or not, I knew that I would need to attend these meetings regularly if I was going to keep my job, appease my parents, and make amends with the people who were close to me. I knew all eyes would be on me as I left the hospital this time. I also knew that it wouldn't be easy to convince people that this time was different, since this was the sixth or seventh time I had been in such a place.

CHAPTER FIFTEEN

Did I Offend You?

I was released from the hospital on a Friday morning, and I started trying to clean up the mess I had created with my latest binge. It seemed as though I had burned more bridges in two months than I had in my previous relapse that lasted years. What a mess! But I left myself with no other choice—other than taking the coward's way out and committing a quick suicide leap. I opted out of that since I knew that deep down I didn't want to die before giving this thing one more try. After all, I had living proof of what I had accomplished in the prior two years before I relapsed.

That evening when I returned to my apartment, I cleaned out all of the dirty spoons, all of the syringes, and anything that had to do with my relapse. There was a note under the door of my apartment that said I was two months delinquent in my rent. I knew that I would probably have to bite the bullet and search for a less expensive place to live. I had spent almost everything I had on drugs, above and beyond all of the drugs I stole or had been given. There wasn't anyone I could expect to bail me out. All bridges had been burned.

I went back to work at the condo association on Monday morning with anxiety and embarrassment coming out of my pores. It was like waking up from a bad nightmare, but unfortunately in this case, it was like my nightmare was televised for public viewing. This reminded me of the time in when I was in my second day of first grade and I had to pee really badly. But looking at this stern nun at the front of the classroom, I just didn't have the nerve to ask to go. I ended up pissing my new corduroy pants, and when the nun saw this, she sent me to the office. I felt like she made a spectacle of me in front of the entire class. After something like this, you're pretty much known as the guy who pissed his pants. And I remember having to face the next day after pissing myself.

Well, I had sure pissed myself again, only this time I also pissed on a number of other people in the process. And I would now have to face the class again as an adult. I knew that I would need to mend some fences and man up in order to get things right in my life. I knew that I would first need to prove myself worthy of the second chance Dorothy had given me—by showing up every day, doing my job well, and keeping my chin up.

It was difficult that I couldn't immediately make amends to the people I had harmed during my recent binge. I had promised myself that I would take the advice of my new sponsor at these stupid ass meetings, to practice patience to prove I was worthy to even be heard by the people I had harmed. He told me that I would first need to show up consistently, and when the right time came to make the amends, I would intuitively know it. Well, that dark corner of my mind would always seem to chime in when I was given advice I didn't like hearing. It would secretly say to me, "F*** him! You're in the driver's seat!" As this battle in my mind continued, I tried my best to follow the sponsor's advice. I told myself not to deviate from his directions regardless of what the committee in my head commanded.

As the days back at work turned into weeks, and the weeks into months, I began to gain some self-confidence and more importantly, the piss stains seemed to fade. I was still the guy who pissed himself, but it seemed to me that people began to trust that it was a onetime deal. Thank God they didn't know the rest of my storied past.

The day came when I went into Dorothy's office to make amends. She was definitely the number one on my list. She had trusted and believed in me and had given me a chance that probably no one else would have. Dorothy was very good in hearing my apologies, and she seemed to have confidence in me without hesitation. She simply told me to continue as I had been doing, go to meetings, and things will be fine.

I continued down the list of people I had harmed in my last tirade and did my best in being honest and forthright. I tried not to make excuses during my apology by saying things such as, "I didn't know what I was doing, I was on drugs." Well, f*** the drugs; I knew exactly what I was doing before and during the time of my insanity. Truth be told, when I was doing drugs, I didn't give a f*** about anyone or anything as long as I got what I wanted. It's as sick and simple as that.

Casualties of Life

As time went by, I made a transition to a new apartment which was in the same area of town near the condominium complex, so it was still only a five minute walk to work. It was a small studio apartment with a foldout bed, a small kitchenette, and a small breakfast counter. It wasn't nearly as luxurious as the place I had previously. However, it sure beat the hell out of sleeping under a bridge.

I began to get back to a somewhat normal pace back at work, and I wasn't feeling as apprehensive when I faced my coworkers and the residents. I attended my meetings as I promised myself and Dorothy. There was a sobriety club for recovering alcoholics and drug addicts a half a block from my new place. It was housed in a very large historic mansion. It had a bar area which served burgers, coffee, and soda, and it was staffed by volunteers. There were numerous meeting rooms on the second floor and a large meeting room on the third floor which also served as a hall for occasional dances and parties—drug and alcohol free, of course. When I went to my meetings there, I never stayed long enough to socialize. I just had way too much going on in my head to add more confusion and complicate things with new relationships.

In looking for things to occupy my free time, I considered some local night clubs even though I had been told that if I wanted to stay clean and dry I would probably need to avoid bars. But, where else was I going to meet women? Yes, relationships were hard work, but I guess I either enjoyed the challenge, or I had just become addicted to the drama that I always dragged into them. After getting clean I had been feeling much better physically and looking healthier than I had in quite a while. So, when I was looking to fill the void in my life left by the constant obsession with drugs, I knew it was imperative to acquire a new obsession. For a guy like me, there had to be some type of obsession, and back then the only viable option I thought existed was chasing women.

After being in my new apartment for a few weeks, I went out one Friday evening and met an attractive and very outgoing Korean woman, Celeste, who seemed to be as sweet as they come. She and a friend had been out listening to bands when I met her, and she asked about going out the next evening, so I, of course, immediately pictured what she was going to look like in my bed. I seemed to treat my new obsession the same way I did drugs—from the initial thought, the anticipation, and then the fantasy about the pursuit.

That next evening Celeste and I went out for dinner, and sure enough, we did end up at my place within about two hours. She turned out to be an extremely wild woman. It seemed she had been lacking romance in her life and was trying to make it up all in one night. When she left that night I felt great, but as usual I wanted more. When something quenched my thirst for passion and exhilaration, more was always better. After she left, I could still smell the scent of her perfume on my pillow, and I craved more.

It was about noon the following day Celeste stopped by my apartment and wanted more herself. She stayed for a couple hours and then told me that we needed to shower up and go out again because she wanted me to come to her house. At her house were her three young children sitting with her friend that I met when we initially hooked up. She explained that these were her children and that she had recently been separated. She was apologetic about not mentioning the kids earlier. I didn't see it as a problem; however, it was all quite foreign to me. She and I sat with the kids while her friend made lunch for everyone. It was like instant family-hood.

Later in the evening, Celeste asked that I stay the night, and said she would get up early to make breakfast and drive me to work. At about one o'clock in the morning the phone rang, and when she answered, I could hear a man's voice ranting and raving on the other end of the phone. When she hung up, she told me it was her husband. I asked her just how long ago she had been separated, for him to be so upset. From the sound of things when we'd met it was years but come to find she had left him two weeks earlier. About an hour later, he was pounding on the apartment door threatening to kill her. We didn't open the door. A neighbor called the police so he left.

I was beginning to think that once again my decision making may just need a bit of fine tuning. I somehow always impulsively jumped at the sight of excitement, and by the time I realized the pitfalls that accompanied the fun, I would see logic in the rear view mirror. I would be in damage control mode by then.

Even after Celeste's husband went ballistic outside her door, and with her three kids sleeping in the other room, this woman kept me up all night. She was really trying to make up for lost passion—she was treating me like a new toy out of a Cracker Jack box.

That next morning she was up early, made breakfast, and took me to work at seven while her friend across the hall watched the kids. Even as she dropped me off, she again mauled me in the car. I didn't complain, but I wasn't sure I would live long being around this woman. It seemed if her husband didn't kill me, she might very well f*** me to death.

A couple hours into my day at work, Celeste paged me to call her as soon as I could. When I returned her call, she told me that her husband had just died. The police told her that he had fallen off a sixty-foot scaffold while working on a church. She sounded emotionally shaken, but I wasn't real sure that I was the person she should be turning to in this instance. After all, forty-eight hours before this, I didn't even know she was married, and if I had, I wouldn't have been involved with her.

The past few days had been like a blur to me. Now, I was trying to evaluate where I was going with the decisions I had been making in my personal life. I also realized that people, in general, were all vulnerable to the human condition. In past years I had been so wrapped up in my own crazy head that my thinking was that if a person didn't use drugs and didn't abuse alcohol, everything else in their lives was fine. Well, I was learning that there may be some real validity to the meaning of original sin, where we as people are all subject to some defects of character, some inherent and some learned.

On the day of Celeste's husband's funeral, she showed up at my work asking the doorman to tell me that my ride was there. When I saw who it was, I felt very strange. She was all dressed up, and she asked if I would accompany her to the funeral home for her husband's wake. I was almost numb at this request and just told her that I wasn't comfortable with that. I said that I thought we should take a break from each other for a while. She pleaded with me to at least drive to the funeral home with her, drop her off, and take her car for a few days. She said it would help her get things straightened out, and she also had her husband's car to drive. Since I hadn't had a car of my own for some years, I agreed. It was again my self-serving needs that took precedence over doing what I felt was right. What I thought was right was for me to just cut things off with her right there and then. But of course I didn't because I saw this new Pontiac Trans Am in front of me for the taking.

While I had a car at my disposal for a few days, I could go about the town to visit some old friends. When Friday came along, I called my old friend Terry, whom I hadn't seen in a couple years. I had wondered how he was doing in his struggles with life. I told him I would pick him up and we could go out to chat and catch up on old times.

Terry and I went to an old bar we had frequented years before, and we sat and talked. He had a tall glass of beer and I had a coke. I told him that had been clean for a couple years, and though I had slipped up in between, I was now back on track with sober living. Terry disclosed to me that he had begun the methadone program in an attempt to get away from heroin. And he said that he was also taking a new prescription drug called Xanax and an anti anxiety medication given to him by the doctor who ran the methadone clinic. At that time, I actually saw this as progress for someone who had been so heavily involved in heroin and morphine.

As the evening came to a close for Terry and me, we agreed to stay in touch. He said he thought it would be good to stick around people who were clean and sober, and I agreed. After dropping Terry off, I went to see Celeste to return her car. I asked her take me to my apartment so she could drive her car back home. When we arrived at my place, she asked to come up for a bit to talk. Well of course, talking was only part of what we both seemed to have in mind, and it led to her calling her neighbor to watch her kids for the night.

She made some comments about the funeral though very few. I had thought she may want to discuss it. Maybe she just wanted to move on. Or maybe I wasn't the one she wanted to discuss it with, so I just let it go. I had to keep from judging what I knew very little about.

The next morning we were awaken by my phone ringing. Celeste answered. She nudged me with this very strange look on her face and said it was some hysterical woman. I took the phone and heard Terry's frightened mother blurt out that she just found Terry in his bed, and she thought he was dead. She said, "His lips are blue and he's not breathing! Can you please come over here?" I quickly responded by telling her to call an ambulance, and I'd be right over.

We immediately threw on some clothes and headed over to Terry's house. Without cell phones in those days, the ride seemed like an hour but in reality was about fifteen minutes. The ambulance was already there. The paramedics had just covered Terry's still body. This was the guy who just the previous night had been telling me his hopes and dreams of cleaning up his life. He had sounded so hopeful. Now here sat his poor mother who had just lost her only son, and who had lost her husband just a year earlier. We sat with her and consoled her as best we could before leaving.

This had certainly been a whirlwind of events over that three-day period. I was feeling like I had dreamed it all. When Celeste dropped me off at my apartment, I told her that I thought we should take a break from seeing each other, and she seemed to understand. She just told me to call if I needed to talk. We had both experienced a very trying week and needed time to reflect.

Back at work, the whole previous week still seemed like a dream to me. But I was able to function well as I was feeling more grounded in life. The thought of my friend Terry lying in the morgue seemed almost unreal. At Terry's wake I found out that the night he and I had gone out, he later went to a corner bar by his house, and he had apparently mixed too much alcohol with his meds, and that caused his death.

At the funeral home that night, I saw all of the familiar faces from the old neighborhood. There were people I had longed to see for years in an attempt to make amends of sorts, along with some faces that I had hoped I'd never see again. As I walked through the door of the funeral home with Mike, here in the hallway was our old buddy Paddlehead asking if we wanted to buy any Percodan. Only Paddlehead would have the balls to do something like that. I remember feeling just plain violated and disgusted, even though I wasn't exactly surprised. This guy never really had any scruples to speak of. I felt like Mike and I had just crossed the path of Satan once again. And he even looked like the pictures of the devil you'd see in Bible stories, dressed in black pants, a black shirt, and a long black leather coat.

When we stopped by the casket for our last good-byes to Terry, his mother pulled me aside to tell me that Terry had been telling her days before he died that I had been doing good, and she thanked me for being a good friend to her only son. It broke my f***ing heart!

After I returned to my apartment that evening, I did some real deep soul searching. I saw the pain in Terry's mother's eyes that night which made me think of my mother, and how the things I had done over the years must have made her feel. Losing a loved one has to be the most anguishing feeling there is in life. But, if there is any feeling through that process that could possibly be of benefit, it is to see a loved one who had seemed to be so troubled with no end in sight, come to rest.

Devil in the Detail

By November of 1982, I had been attending my meetings regularly and working steadily, without issue over the previous six months or so. And I began to feel alive and well. I had let go of some unhealthy relationships, and had gone through a mourning phase over lost friends, an ugly past, and some bad habits. I seemed to have come to grips with the old self-pity habit that I carried around as a reason to continually relapse.

But, there was one bad habit that I didn't acknowledge was harmful, and that one was that I didn't see going to bars seeking female companionship as a detriment to my sobriety. Where else were you going to find a healthy woman that probably doesn't use drugs? It certainly wasn't at some meeting full of drunks and drug addicts. And I didn't feel real comfortable prowling for women at church services. So,

I felt that I just needed to go to more reputable bars to look for good female companions.

One evening I was out at the same bar where Terry and I had met the night before he died. I played pool and surveyed the women in the bar who seemed to take care of themselves physically and didn't look like druggies. While I was at the bar ordering a coke, a woman approached me and introduced herself as Mary, and she mentioned that we had attended high school together and had mutual friends from years past. I remembered the face, but I never was good with names.

Later she introduced me to a couple of her friends, and we reminisced about years past and mutual acquaintances. By the end of the night our conversation was flowing well, and she offered to drive me home. Well, since we knew each other previously, it seemed acceptable to invite her up to my apartment, and we ended up in bed. As we were on our moment-after cigarette, she disclosed that she was living with a boyfriend with whom she had a three-year-old child. She went on to tell me that he was abusive, and she had been trying to break free from him.

As soon as I heard her story, I flashed back to my last episode with the woman who was married with three kids and whose husband had died. I knew this just wasn't good and felt I needed to run quick. I felt that I needed to let go slowly to avoid any hurt feelings. When she left that night, she told me that she would call me soon. All I could get myself to say was, "OK," while in my mind I was thinking that I needed to avoid her at all cost.

A few days later, she showed up at my door. When she came in, I saw a different side of her. I realized that the night she initially came over and had sex with me, I just didn't think of anything but the sex. And now I saw a woman trying to escape a bad relationship by rebounding, and I was the target for her safety net. That evening she disclosed quite a bit about her boyfriend's abuse patterns and also described her sweet three-year-old son whom she loved dearly. As the night went on, we each talked about our demons, hers being that she wanted badly to get away from her boyfriend, and mine being my horrid past that she already knew much of. I felt that I was doing my best to let her know that I was no good for any relationship and certainly not a good candidate for a parent.

I spent the following evening with her, even after promising myself that I was going to run for the hills. This time, she said something that was very detrimental to my health and wellbeing. She told me she had some Percodan in her purse. She said that she only took a couple once in a while, and I then realized that this woman really knew nothing about me or about real addiction. She was the type of person who used drugs as recreational fun and drank alcohol occasionally in social settings. She seemed to enjoy being around the bad boys, so to speak, the guys that got into trouble.

The thought of the Percodan sitting in her purse nagged at me for all of about ten minutes before I asked for a few. I told her it usually took at least five to get me high. When she handed me the Percodan, I swallowed them down before I could let any logic set in. And, for the next fifteen minutes, I did my best to convince myself that this would just be a recreational moment of drug use. And since I didn't take the time to soak them down and inject them, that was further proof that I was different now.

As that night went on, she shared a secret. She told me that she and her boyfriend had been selling cocaine for some guy who used them as the 'middle' for dealing ounces of the stuff. She said that they knew people who were in the market for ounces of cocaine, while their friend had pounds of it but didn't want to risk selling to anyone other than her and the boyfriend. Now the real secret was that they eventually scammed the guy out of $87,000 by telling him that they had been ripped off. She told me that she and her boyfriend buried the money out in a field miles north of Milwaukee.

Hearing that story made me leery of being with this woman, in the event the dealer came to collect while I happened to be around. I wanted to avoid that. This whole story made me think I may be better off running from this woman, and quick.

Geographic Escape

The next day I went to my parents' house for a visit. I didn't have any needle marks on my arms or hands since I took the Percodan orally the night before. And I always felt less guilt when I wasn't using my extremities as a pin cushion. I felt more like a recreational user, except for the fact that I could feel that monkey pulling at my coat sleeves.

When I arrived at my parents' house, I saw my old childhood friend Dennis in front of his parents' house across the street. Dennis was my older brother's friend while we were growing up. He had spent time in Vietnam which I am quite sure affected his psychological health. As I visited with my mother and father, they were in their same positions at the kitchen table, with my father insisting on making me a sandwich as usual, and my mother telling me to sit with them to talk. I couldn't get myself to let on that I had relapsed yet again, nor did I think there would be any benefit in disappointing them yet again either. So, we sat and talked about the rest of the family as well as how I had been doing.

My mother asked the same old questions about the possibility of me settling down with a woman in the near future. My same old answer was that I settled down quite often. I'm not sure my mother knew that I was not only a drug addict, but a cheap whore as well.

After I sat with my parents for a while, I went across the street to visit Dennis and Billy. Billy was Dennis's younger brother and my best friend, next to Stevie, while I was in my grade school years. Billy was always kind of a loner, a kid with very low self-esteem, and in his school years he was labeled a 'Special C' which nowadays means 'learning disability.' He was always picked on and teased and called a

'Dummy.' When we were kids, I always felt like I needed to protect him from the ruthless ridicule of the insensitive kids in the neighborhood.

On this visit, I found out that Billy had just joined the Army, and he was set to leave for boot camp in two weeks. As for Dennis, he had just been laid off from the factory job he had since returning from Vietnam. Dennis mentioned that he was going to drive down to Houston to look for work and start a new life. He said that he and Mike, another mutual friend from childhood who had spent time in Vietnam, were planning to leave in a week. He told me that I should consider going with them as there were a lot of construction jobs there.

As I rode back to my apartment on the city bus, the thought of going to Houston was feeling right for me. I was thinking that the geographical escape may just do me good. I wasn't big on the winters in the Midwest, and I didn't see any light at the end of the tunnel for me in this place. I seemed to continually spin my wheels and go nowhere but down.

The next morning when I went to work at the condo association, I purposely admitted to Dorothy that I had once again relapsed. I knew that she would probably feel the need to relieve me from my job, and she did. I felt absolutely horrible about letting her down after all she had done for me, and she was still very pleasant when she let me go. She was a very caring and dynamic woman, to put it lightly.

The truth of the matter is that, after fantasizing about the idea of going to Houston and starting new, free of the chains of heroin, I was on a mission. I remember going home and calling Dennis to ask if he would still consider having me join him and Mike on their journey to Houston. When Dennis gave me the green light, I immediately began calling people I knew to sell my few belongings, which amounted to a couch and a mattress. The rest of my apartment furniture was the property of the apartment building. The next day I packed my clothes and headed over to Dennis's house. Within a couple hours, we said our good-byes and headed for Houston.

When we finally arrived in Houston, we grabbed the first cheap motel we could find. Dennis and Mike had all the tools we would need to get work with a construction company loaded in the trunk, and we planned to head out to find work early the next morning. We settled in to the two-bedroom motel suite, which actually wasn't 'sweet' in appearance, but it would serve its purpose.

At the time my sleep was still very light due to a slight withdrawal and all of the guilt stuck in that dark corner of my mind. And to make matters worse, this place was crawling with huge cockroaches. I remember feeling those nasty things crawling over me as I was trying to sleep, and I could hear Mike and Dennis laughing about how many of them there were. They told me to do what they were doing, which was to shake out the sleeping bag, climb in right away, and zip it up all the way over your head. Even at that, I could feel those f***ing things crawling on me even though some of them may have been phantom roaches at that point. It was certainly not a good sleeping environment for me.

We started working at least ten hours a day, roofing houses in ninety degree heat with ninety percent humidity. We were spent by the end of each work day. When we got through the first full work week, we found a new temporary apartment. It was an upgrade from the cockroach motel, though it seemed every house down there had at least a few roaches.

As the weeks went by working on construction crews all day and playing basketball every night until dark, we were getting acclimated to our new life in Houston. I began to feel very physically healthy once again, and it seemed all the anxiety and obsession about heroin was lifted. My thoughts were centered on a more normal lifestyle, if there is a 'normal' style that registers in my brain. What I can say is that I was now working hard, eating well, and sleeping through the night, which for me was true progress.

In June of 1983 a few months after getting settled in to a normal routine of life, I received a message from my mother to call home. Worried that something bad may have happened, I immediately returned the call. My mother told me that a girl named Mary had called them trying to reach me and saying that I needed to call her. My mother told her she couldn't give out my number, but would relay the message.

When I returned the call, it was the Mary I had last been seeing before heading to Houston. She informed me that she was pregnant with my child. Now I knew she told me that she was on birth control while I was seeing her, and the fact that she had been living with the boyfriend, made me question whether I should just hang up the phone. I listened to her explanation which was that she had missed a couple days of taking her pills and that she hadn't been sexually active with her boyfriend for almost six months. At the end of our conversation, I told her I needed to think things through and would get back to her.

At work the next day all I could think of was the possibility of being a father. I knew I wasn't fit for fatherhood in the psychological condition I was in and the phase of life I was at now. Truth be told I was feeling great physically though I had quite a bit of work to do in getting my head in a healthy and stable condition. But, my second thought was that maybe it was time for me to settle down. I had always loved kids and dreamed of having them someday. But I wasn't sold on the fact of having kids now, and probably not with her, seeing that she was more of a one night stand. And more importantly, she already had a son with the guy she was currently living with.

The very next day she called me back and told me that she had moved out to a new apartment with her son living back and forth between her and her now ex-boyfriend. She went on about how nice it would be to settle down and build a family with me. Well, in my mind I had already folded, though I hadn't let on to her. After hanging up the phone, I spoke to Mike and Dennis about the situation, and they just said, "Good luck with whatever you decide," and they told me that I'd make a good dad as long as I could keep myself clean.

Well, the next day I packed up what little belongings I had and grabbed a Greyhound bus back to Milwaukee. As soon as I arrived at the Milwaukee Bus station, I called Mary to pick me up, and within an hour she drove in with her son and dropped me at my parents' house.

When I discussed my dilemma with my mother, she seemed conflicted. On one hand, she said that missing birth control was the oldest trick in the book, but she reminded me that I always wanted to settle down and have kids. Her suggestion was to think it through very carefully before jumping, though she was of the belief that I probably needed to do the right thing and do my best to be a father to the child. So, what I ultimately decided was to have a shotgun marriage and give it my best without looking in the rear view mirror. Mary was already planning a wedding for us, as she was pretty much a take charge woman. The child was due at the beginning of August, and it was already coming close to July.

I called my old minister friend George to see if he would do the honors of the wedding, which he happily accepted. George didn't know the extent of my recent drug escapades since I had last met with him at the county jail, but I don't think he would've cared even if he did know. This man was always a positive, move forward, and leave-mistakes-behind kind of guy. That's just who he was. It seemed that every time George and I had discussions, I always left with the feeling that the future would be bright and that I was truly absolved of whatever baggage the prior day was holding. The discussion George and I had this day was no different. In fact, he assured me that I would be a great father, and he promised me that he'd always be a phone call away. So, by late July, I was suddenly married with a three-year-old son and another child on the way.

CHAPTER SIXTEEN

The Monkey's Claw

A week after being married, I found myself looking for a job to help in supporting our new family. Mary was always very crafty at finding ways of making money doing side jobs and such. Well, the 'such' was that she still had her connections with her old acquaintances for getting Percodan, and that was one thing I didn't argue with. Since I had been clean for a while and never really had a honeymoon, I decided this would be a one-time deal.

I got ahold of some Percodan and some new syringes, and I found a little hideout in the basement of our new apartment. I would head downstairs to do laundry, and I would make shooting Percodan a part of the laundry ritual. Before I knew it, that monkey had his claws dug so deep under my skin, I wouldn't leave our apartment unless I needed more Percodan or syringes.

Mary had been busy doing her cocaine deals and playing pool. She loved her billiards and participated in a number of pool leagues at her favorite bar where we met up. As for her three-year-old son, he went between his dad's house and ours. When he was with us, I was, not surprisingly, a useless parental figure. Mary loved her son, though she never really had that maternal thing that I saw in other women with their children. She seemed to lack something that I could never really put my finger on.

I was told by a few people who knew her, including her sister, that there was something missing from her emotional attachment to people. Mary and her sister had been adopted by an older couple who had no children of their own. They were wonderful people, but they also seemed to have a cold demeanor about them.

As far as my attachments were concerned, there was only one—my addiction. I was surely the most selfish, self-serving person there was, with my wants being the only important things in my life. It seemed everything else was just formality and thoughtless motions on my path to the next fix.

By the time my wife was a couple days from her due date, I decided to go back to the methadone program at the Milwaukee Methadone Clinic. I could not afford the drugs and, in all honesty, I was sick and tired of being sick and tired. But I was also convinced that I was just one of those unfortunate souls who would never grasp the true meaning of sobriety. The sobriety that I speak of is what I had heard of and had seen in some people at those twelve-step meetings I previously went to. It just never worked for me.

On the due date of our child to be, I took my wife and her son to a Milwaukee Brewers game. If anything were to get this kid to come into the world, we figured it might be the roar of the crowd that would give it that extra push. Sure enough, the next day her water broke, and we knew it was time.

Well, we made it to the hospital a few hours before she finally gave birth to our eight-pound, twelve-ounce boy. I sat in the delivery room and observed the birth which actually made me light-headed. I really couldn't explain what the feelings were exactly—just being witness to a human being born into the world was an amazing thing.

I had absolutely no clue what to expect as far as caring for a newborn, and even less idea how to go about raising children in the years ahead of us. At the time, I really wasn't ready to learn, as I couldn't even take of myself. But, when I looked at this little guy who just came home from the hospital and my new three-year-old stepson, I felt that I was ready to give parenthood a good try. And to do this parenting thing successfully, I knew I would probably need to stay on the methadone program. I figured that it would keep me away from heroin and another stint in jail.

During this time I felt I was becoming more stable as I was always at home with the two kids. Mary always seemed to have something going on at some local tavern with pool tournaments and such. She also always had some deal going on to make some extra money, too. More times than not it was a cocaine deal. She never really seemed to do any of the stuff herself; she just made a sale for one of the bigger cocaine dealers she seemed to know.

As the months went by, I began to get restless. I decided to contact an old friend with whom I had previously pulled a few pharmacy thefts. As long as I brought home some money from doing one of these scams, Mary was fine with the idea. She herself came up with an idea of how we could pull off a theft. But she insisted that she would want to hold onto the drugs so I wouldn't do them all so quickly. I never saw the point in letting these things sit collecting dust, and the idea of selling them was pointless in my mind. But Mary was smarter than I, and she actually thought ahead enough to buy diapers, food, and other necessities.

Mary was on a medicine for epileptic seizures she told me occurred, though I never saw one of them happen. Mary's idea was that she would fake a seizure in the front of a drugstore to draw the pharmacist away from the back, and I could run back and grab the pills. It was ingenious. She was no dummy, and she could also be very convincing.

We found what we thought was the right drugstore and parked our car around the block. Mary and a friend named Steve walked in the front door, and I walked in the back. About thirty seconds later, I heard some commotion in the front of the store and a woman yell out frantically for the pharmacist. She said someone was having a seizure, and the guy immediately dropped what he was doing and ran up to the front of the store. I quickly ran behind the counter, grabbed about two thousand Percodan, and I was out the side door in no time at all.

As I ran to the car and started it up, I could see Steve and Mary walking down the block at a swift pace. They jumped in and off we went. They explained that the pharmacist told the cashier to call an ambulance while he tried to comfort Mary. As we were driving off, we could hear sirens, and I felt sick to my stomach. It wasn't the fear of getting caught as much as it was feeling horrible for those two people in the pharmacy. I could almost feel the fear that they probably had seeing this woman seizing on the floor, and then to walk back to find they had been scammed? This was some sick shit, but it served as the means to an end for us.

After this escapade the insanity of my addiction began to snowball very quickly. I was again at the point where I left off from my previous relapse. The difference with this relapse was that I was a married man, a father, and supposedly a man who was making an attempt to change. Well, nothing about me had changed except for the fact that my actions not only affected my life, but they were now altering the lives of two innocent children.

Yet I somehow managed to justify to myself that what I was doing was just a passing relapse. I was attempting to fool myself into thinking that I could somehow right the ship. Well, this time I would not only need to right my ship, but all of the involuntary and innocent passengers I dragged along with me would now bear the stain of my insanity.

That monkey had its claws so deep into my flesh that I continued to make its needs the number one priority in my life. And as far as I was concerned, my wife and the two boys were just an afterthought. They would just need to wait while daddy took care of his monkey. I continued to get worse by the moment. Though my wife was not completely innocent in the scope of things, the cold hard fact was that she had no clue of this monster I had become. Whether it was in the kitchen, the family room, or in our bed, I carried this thing of mine, and I blatantly ignored what should have been important, which was my family.

I thought I was doing my duty as a husband and a father by being at home with these two little boys while my wife went out in the evenings. The fact probably was that she needed to escape the asylum I made of our home. When she went out, I spent my time in the basement laundry room where I had my stash of drugs, my silver spoon, and syringes, hidden above the heating ducts. My two boys would be with me, and when I needed to cook up some dope and shoot up, I just told them it was time for hide and seek. I would tell them to go hide while I did my thing, and I kept them from peeking by counting out loud indicating to them that I'd soon begin looking for them. It was some of the most selfish f***ed up stuff that one could imagine.

Though I knew deep inside that I was not fit to be a parent, I still held on to the intention that I was going to change, and that if I could just put my family on hold while I completed this one last binge, everything would be fine. The reality of it was that even if I were to quit, I would still have been an extremely dysfunctional person with absolutely no parenting skills. To add insult to an already maladjusted family, my wife told me that she was again pregnant.

Cocaine Blues

One morning as I was driving into the county methadone program to get my daily dose, I saw an old friend I hadn't seen in quite a few months. He had allowed me to live in his basement a couple years previously. I'm sure it was no surprise to him to see that I was back on the methadone program, but for me to see him there was somewhat of a surprise. He had been a moderate drug user for years, the type that kept a steady job and just chipped periodically. He regularly spent time with his wife and children.

Well, seeing him was both good and bad. The good was that I always appreciated him as a friend, and the bad was that he ended up on methadone. He was another one of the guys like me that seemed to catch the drug bug that infected many in our generation. It was also a proven fact that when my friend and I hooked up, a certain synthesis seemed to occur that equaled trouble with the capital 'T.'

The whole point of getting on this methadone program was to eliminate the physical withdrawal, to keep us away from needles and street drugs, and to stabilize our lives by eliminating the criminal element most every addict seems to carry along the path. This methadone program obviously wasn't working for me, and I began to see that my monkey was not only demanding fulfillment of the physical pleasure, but it had also instilled the need for the excitement that went along with it.

The fact that reared its ugly head was that even when I eliminated the physical dependence, I was still absolutely insane. I found that I was so wrapped up in the activities that went along with the physical addiction that feeling 'normal' was nowhere near enough for me. I had this black hole in me, and I realized that this monkey was just an errand boy sent to feed the bottomless pit. I now completely agreed with the saying that one was too many and a thousand never enough. Whenever I felt good, I was convinced that more would be better.

Soon enough I decided to hunt down some cocaine to go along with the methadone. It made much more sense to me, since it is in a very different drug category and would be like the old speedball, which was what we called it when we mixed heroin and cocaine up in a spoon and shot it. The rush I got from it was great, because I had never really liked cocaine by itself. To me it was just too stimulating, made me paranoid, and I found myself thinking too much.

Later that evening I headed down to the inner city area of Milwaukee to visit my friend Jerry at his apartment. There was a dope house across the street from where he was staying, and he knew the people running the place. When we went to the door, I noticed the intercom and security camera. When Jerry rang upstairs some guy came down and unlocked the door. It was a big solid door with a slide bar across the inside and three separate deadbolt locks. This place was as secure as I'd seen.

When we went upstairs there were at least ten people spread out through the rooms of the upper flat apartment shooting dope. Now that was a shooting gallery. It was very bizarre to look around at all of the people there shooting. There seemed to be people from all walks of life. Some of the people were doing cocaine and some heroin, and I chose both. As soon as we got ours, we left right away. We didn't want to be around if the police decided to ram the door down and raid the place.

Eventually I found myself counter hopping at local drugstores and trading the Percodan, Dilaudid, Valium, and whatever else for cocaine. My cocaine binges began to escalate at a very fast pace, and I found myself going out to my garage and sitting in my car to shoot it. I was hitting bottom very quickly, but it didn't deter me from doing it more and more. I remembered sitting with my old friend Willy in that locked and barricaded room while he did cocaine nonstop until the break of dawn, only to stop because his stash was depleted.

I sold anything of value to get more cocaine. I had the luxury of being able to lean on my methadone to deter my opiate withdrawals, so I only had to worry about my cocaine supply. It seemed that food, water, and the essentials were just hideous distractions. As long as my kids were asleep, I was good to go.

One cold winter evening I was out walking the street, while my wife was resting before she was to have a late night out. I had a couple grams of cocaine, a spoon, and a syringe in my coat as I walked for miles with light snow falling. I made stops at every gas station I passed to use the bathroom as my temporary shooting gallery. I'd walk out with that hyped up paranoid feeling but still wanting more. My last stop was a local hospital. I went in to use the bathroom right across from the emergency department. I had about a gram of cocaine left, and I wanted to up the dose as high as I could before passing out. Taking it to the very limit seemed to be the way to go, and what better place to be than about twenty feet from an emergency room?

Well, I did every bit I had left and even licked every remaining flake off the inside of the packet, and I didn't pass out. I left the hospital while blocking out every single logical thought that attempted to make way into my brain. I needed to wait until I was finished with my binge, which I swore was the final one, before the committee in my mind would even consider hearing the thoughts of logic. And I just needed to block those thoughts for just a bit longer, because the committee had decided that we needed to get more cocaine to do while my wife was out the rest of the evening.

I stopped at the hospital pay phone and called the guy I had been getting my cocaine from. He agreed to drive over to a corner gas station near the hospital and bring me a quarter-ounce. I swore I would have his money along with some Percodan as interest on the deal, by noon the next day. He was under the impression that I was going to sell it, which just wasn't going to happen.

When I returned home in time for my wife to leave for her night out, I was pretty wired to say the least. She said she was late for meeting a friend, said good-bye, and headed out for the night. Once she was gone, I called the neighbor who would babysit the kids occasionally and told her I may be going out for a while. She said that she could watch the kids for the night if I needed, as her niece always liked to hang out with the boys.

I brought the boys next door for the evening, then I went back home and pulled out the cocaine. I was shooting up within minutes, and less than thirty minutes later, I was to the point of high alert paranoia. I could have sworn that I heard the police outside my bedroom window and saw flashlights crossing by the window shades. I found myself crawling down along the wall making my way to the back sunporch. I quietly opened the door, crawled out the back, and peeked out to find there was no one in the front or back. It seemed all so real.

I locked and barricaded both doors and covered the windows with bedsheets. Then I went right back to the needle and spoon. After the first shot I began to think that this was the way I might leave this world. I went to the phone and put the hospital emergency room number on speed dial. My thought was that I would do bigger and bigger amounts that would take me right to the limit between the plane of life and death.

My stash quickly diminished. I was down to about a half of a gram left in the packet and decided I would do one big shot sitting next to the phone. I injected it and I felt so good though deathly afraid because I could feel my blood pressure go through the roof. I hit the speed dial and within a couple of rings, a woman answered. I asked to speak with a doctor as it was an emergency. She said she was a nurse and asked what my concern was about. I told her that I thought I may be dying because I was feeling my heart racing and I was beginning to feel cold. She asked where I was so that she could send an ambulance immediately. At that, I just said that I was sorry and hung up the phone. I used a slow deep breathing pattern while caressing my carotid artery, and I slowly but surely felt some relief from my symptoms.

My stash was completely gone, but that f***ing committee in my head was giving me ideas on how to get more. I rapidly began to crash back to earth with extreme anxiety and depression setting in. I was so conflicted on what to do that I just sat listlessly and felt that my world was collapsing in on me. Then I thought of my boys only about fifty feet away in the neighbor's house. I began feeling remorseful and very sorry for those poor kids. They had a caring, though maternally absent mother and me, a degenerate drug addict with absolutely nothing to offer in the way of parental presence.

Feeling the cocaine blues fast setting in to every fiber of my being, I felt I needed to hug my boys. I called my neighbor and asked if she could bring them back to the house. A few minutes later she arrived with the boys in their pajamas looking at me with big smiles. My heart warmed in a way that was comforting to the soul, but I also felt so damn guilty. My neighbor asked if I was going to be OK and commented on how I looked very sick. I responded that I just woke up. I'm sure she knew something was out of order and that it was more than just fatigue, but she just smiled and said good-night. She was a gem of a neighbor and always took good care of the boys; she probably knew our home was not an ideal place for kids.

I took the boys to our room and all three of us climbed into the king -size bed. With one boy on each side of me, I clenched onto them as though they were my emotional blanket. Though I was distraught and depressed, the feeling of their warm little bodies next to mine was the most comforting feeling I'd had in a long time. They were actually being the parental presence for me that night.

When my wife returned home from a night out playing in her pool league, she told me that her contractions were getting closer together, and it was almost time to give birth to our little girl. She had called the doctor's office and spoke with the nurses. They had instructed her to come to the hospital when the contractions reached certain intervals. According to the nurse, it would probably be within the next twenty-four hours. This would give me time to go to the methadone clinic, get one small amount of cocaine to do, and then call it quits. I had to celebrate a little bit given this was a special day.

That day, January 19 of 1985, I called my parents to let them know that Mary, the boys, and I were coming to dinner. I couldn't be the one to transport my wife and kids to the hospital because my old Fiat didn't have brakes.

It was right during dinner with my parents that my wife's contractions told us it was time. My father said he'd drive, given the condition of my brakes, and I followed to meet them there.

When my wife was admitted, they said it would probably only be a couple of hours before it was time to deliver. This gave me time to head out to my car where I always had a spoon and syringe under my floor mats, just in case. After I did a few shots in the car, I went up to the delivery room. A few minutes after midnight, our baby girl came into the world. She was a healthy little girl with black hair so long it had a ducktail. She was beautiful! Unfortunately for her, she had been born into a very dysfunctional mess.

Family Ties

My wife and little girl were released from the hospital a few days later. This was a time I needed to be around the house to help out with the boys while my wife was recuperating. I'd take the boys with me when I went out to the methadone clinic, and I'd even stop to pick up whatever cocaine I could afford on our way back home. When we were home, I found that I was spending a lot of time in the basement doing laundry (and shooting cocaine). We played a lot of hide and seek during this time period.

I knew this was some sick shit, but I did it just the same. The fact that I had a wife, two children, and a newborn baby girl should definitely have been a deterrent, but it seemed to have the opposite effect for me. I seemed to want to do more and more to escape life on life's terms. This stuff brought me to my knees faster than I ever could have imagined. I was no doubt in a worse physical condition than ever before, and I could see that I was progressively getting worse by the day. Given the fact that my family was a distant second to my drug use, I knew in the back of my mind that this insanity needed to end soon.

My methadone dose had been raised to the maximum limit allowed at that time; it was enough to kill an elephant, but the effect on me was just enough to get by. While I was at the clinic one morning, I heard of an old friend of mine who had been rooming with his brother. Apparently my friend stole some pot from his brother, and in retaliation, his brother waited until my friend fell asleep and then took his thirty milligram bottle of methadone from the refrigerator. The next morning my friend woke up and found his brother dead.

The next day I received a call from another friend who informed me that his brother had hung himself in his basement with a garden hose. What desperation must have been going through his mind to commit suicide, but on top of it, with a garden hose? He had been on a marathon cocaine binge and ended up selling his wife's jewelry and all of his kid's electronics. He even sold the microwave, television set, stereo, and anything else of value.

What a crazy few days. And though I saw all the red flags that should have set off an alarm in my head for what I had been doing, I just buried it as deep as I could.

One Friday afternoon about a week later, I was feeling very desperate. I decided I would write a prescription for sixty Percodan and have it filled at a nearby pharmacy. Two days earlier I had stopped by a doctor that would occasionally give me a prescription for sixty Percodan, and while I was in his office I stole some blank scripts. That way, if the pharmacist didn't call the doctor when I filled the legitimate prescription, I knew I could write one out identical to the original without a hitch. So, I checked the prescription over to be sure it looked legitimate, and I took it in to be filled. Apparently, this wasn't a good day to fill scripts. No more than five minutes after stepping into the pharmacy, I heard a police walkie-talkie go off behind me and before I even turned to look back, I was on the floor being handcuffed.

Well, I was yet again on my way to the Milwaukee County jail. When I was brought in and booked, I was told by some guy in the bullpen holding cell that the jail was overcrowded. He said they had been shipping people out to the House of Correction instead. After a few hours of sitting in the bullpen, I was called out by a jailer. He told me that I would be going to night court for my initial appearance, and bail would be set.

I was then taken to another holding cell near the outside of the courtroom. When I was called up to visit the judge, and he asked how I pled, I just said, "Not Guilty" and sat down. The prosecuting attorney suggested that a $7,000 bail be set. Though the judge agreed on the bail amount, he requested that I be released on my own recognizance, which meant I would have to sign off that I agreed to show up for court. His reasoning was probably due to the jail overcrowding.

But the fact that I was already currently on probation for a similar crime meant that I would still be sent to the House of Correction until my probation officer lifted the hold (which wasn't going to happen). I could have been immediately shipped off to serve a few years in prison as part of the previous sentence.

Meanwhile, Mary had apparently been contacting the court to check my disposition, and she came down to visit me with the kids. After my hearing, I had been put back into a bullpen holding cell. But then, a jailer called me out and told me I was being released. I thought, "What the f***? I'm being released?"

Sure enough, I was taken to the property room where I was given the court paper to sign for my release. And since my wife was already at the jail, she waited until I was cut loose, and we headed home. Later on, I found out that the courthouse computer system—which contained the information that I was on a probation hold and should not be released—had been down. So as fate and dumb luck would have it, I got out.

Then I returned home, I was a complete train wreck. I was exhausted from all of the drama and insanity I endured the night before. I lay down in bed next to my boys and held them for dear life until I nodded off into a deep sleep. I woke up the next morning with the sunlight creeping its way between the window shades.

With my court date set for the following week, I knew I needed to come up with a plan as far as contacting an attorney. The only options I saw were to somehow find a public defender to take my case or to call my relative who was an attorney. I really didn't like the latter option, mainly because of embarrassment and the probability of my mother and father hearing of it. But, with not a lot of other options at my disposal, I called in the favor, and my relative came through. I hadn't really taken the time to get to know him because of my embarrassing lifestyle and the fact that I was a loser. When I called him, however, he was very pleasant with me and told me to come on down to his office.

When I met with him and explained my dilemma regarding the charge, which was in legal terms 'Attempting to Obtain Controlled Substance by Misrepresentation,' and the fact that I was on probation for the same offense, he actually laughed. He told me that it was almost a miracle that I wasn't still in custody. As we discussed the court hearing, just a few days away, he looked at the case file to see which judge I was going to appear in front of. He seemed to know most of the judges quite well.

I knew that I was living on borrowed time. Whether it was for violating my parole, the new charges, or both, I knew I was going to be locked up in less than a week. What bothered me the most, after the fact that I wouldn't see my children grow up, was that I let my probation officer down. I had violated the trust he had that I would change, now that I had a family. Even though he would be considered the enemy in most criminal minds, I saw him as a guy who truly did care about people. He seemed to be all about family, and with the fact that he was Italian, I almost viewed him as an older brother. He wasn't aware of my arrest due to the computer system outage. But I knew I would need to contact him eventually, and my anxiety grew as the anticipation of facing him loomed in my mind.

As I tried to get up the nerve to face the music and pay for my sins, the committee in that very dark corner of my mind seemed to convene and come up with a solution for all of my problems. I figured that if I committed suicide my children could ultimately have the benefit of collecting social security on behalf of losing a parent. They certainly were not reaping any benefits from having me around as the pathetic and detrimental father I was now. I thought that with me out of the picture, they may just have a chance at a better life ahead. This was not about self-pity and not a 'Poor me, I'll just kill myself' ploy that I may have toyed with in my teen years. This was a reality check of the monster I had become and what I saw as a hopeless future. After a clandestine meeting with the committee in my head, I had a plan in place.

The next morning I picked out a drugstore in the inner city of Milwaukee that I knew probably had a pretty hefty stock of Percodan. I called my friend Jerry to see if he would be game to my plan, and he reluctantly agreed, though he told me I was one crazy mother f***er! My friend Mark was also interested in joining us by driving the getaway car for a piece of the action. I really didn't care how the split was done, provided my share would suffice for executing my ultimate plan. I needed enough that would kill me, or preferably, enough that would allow me to buy a sufficient amount of heroin that would put me out with no chance of survival. When the three of us met up, we decided that Jerry and I would go into the drugstore, and Mark would sit with the car running and wait until we came back, no matter what. As Jerry and I entered the store, I noticed it was quite busy for the time of day it was. There were three people in the pharmacy area: the pharmacist, who looked to be in his mid- to late-thirties, and two young female pharmacy techs. I quickly spotted the bottles of Percodan on the back shelf. Those bottles just seemed to be magnets for my trained eyes.

So, as Jerry and I browsed the store shelves to feel things out for the right moment to make our move, he gave me a look that said, "Let's do it." Jerry's part of the plan was just to assist me if anyone interfered with me. I made my way back to the pharmacy area and saw that there was a metal security door as opposed to the typical swinging gates that most every other pharmacy had. I numbed myself so as to block any signals of fear from my mind. I walked back by the door, and as carefully as I could, I turned the doorknob without being noticed. The door wasn't locked, and I knew this was it.

I opened the door and walked back to the shelf where there were four large 1,000-count bottles of Percodan. As I pulled them off the shelf and began to stuff them under my coat, the pharmacist excitedly said "Hey, what are you doing?!" I just told him I had a pickup, and I quickly began my exit from the pharmacy area, out the big door, and toward the front entrance. The pharmacist yelled out to the cashier at the front of the store to lock the door.

Just as I hit the front door to exit the main entrance, I heard a buzzing noise—they had an electronic door lock. I pushed with my shoulder and it didn't budge. I stepped back and solidly kicked it a couple times with no luck, as it was Plexiglass. And just as I was turning to see if there was another door in back, I saw the pharmacist pulling a thirty-eight caliber revolver out of a shoulder holster he was wearing under his smock. Holding the gun with both hands, he pointed it directly at my head and yelled for me to lie down on the ground. With the end of the cold barrel touching my head, I figured I'd lie down and do what he said. I did want to die, but I didn't want to go out this way.

It was only a matter of seconds after I was lying face down on the floor with the barrel of his gun against my head that I heard a number of sirens right outside the store and what sounded like more coming. The pharmacist yelled out to the cashier to make sure nobody else left the store. The cashier said that I hadn't come in alone, and he pointed at

Jerry, who was standing near the front of the store waiting for the door to be unlocked. Jerry looked at the pharmacist and said, "I came in alone to buy some aspirin."

Just then I heard the police rushing in the door with their guns drawn. One of the officers told the pharmacist to put the gun down on the floor and move away. While the pharmacist did as the officer said, another officer handcuffed me. They pulled me up to my feet and directed me to be still.

As the police were trying to sort out what exactly happened, they took me to the back of the store. Another two officers questioned a few of the other patrons still in the store and then allowed them to leave. When they came to Jerry, the cashier blurted out that he had come in the store with me. The police took Jerry to the front of the store to question him, and shortly after speaking with him for a few minutes, a detective came to the back to speak with me. The detective looked at me directly in the eyes and said, "Your friend is denying he even knows you. Are you going to go down alone on this?" I just said that I came in alone.

The detective then told me that the cashier said he saw us come in together and that we had been talking while in the store. I looked the detective and said, "To be honest, I don't hang out with niggers. I don't know him." At that, he proceeded to walk back up to the front of the store. Minutes later, the front door opened and Jerry walked out.

There was one thing I remembered from when I was very young, and it was that being a rat was a definite 'no.' There were no benefits of being a rat. I'd many times been offered leniency if I could give helpful information, but I had never, ever, seen anyone get the better end of things by being a rat. You might see a rat avoid jail or get less time, but they still ended up doing time whether it was in jail or out on the street. Either way, it got into their head, and they did time in fear and guilt. It's just what a rat's life is like.

As I was put in the police wagon, I was just completely numb. My body was numb, my head was numb, and my spirit was broken. What I saw as the most depressing thing was that I had no backup plan. I always seemed to block out the possibility of being caught, probably because it would allow my nerves to keep me from doing what I did. I guess my flaw was what could be called 'a rational disconnect.'

I was now back in a cell block at the Milwaukee County jail, a place that I was unfortunately so familiar with. With a sense of impending doom, I anticipated the end of my life on the streets. I was being extracted like a rotten tooth from the very streets I had brutalized for so long. The anxiety of facing my parole officer was paramount on my mind. I felt so guilty about all of the lies I had been telling him over the months of supposedly being a changed man, a family man who had righted the ship. He would soon know that I was a big fake and a monumental selfish f*** up.

Well, a couple days later my PO did stop in to visit me. He simply said that I had put him in a bad position and myself in a worse situation. He asked me if I had thought about how this was going to affect my newfound family. He went on to tell me that I would need to face the new charges in front of the judge. And he said that after I was sentenced for these current crimes, he would visit me when I was transferred to the House of Correction to begin the revocation process, which could result in me serving another four years of prison time.

Meanwhile, my wife had called the attorney relative of mine, who I've previously turned to and explained my predicament, and he agreed to stop out to see me. When we met, he said that there was nothing he could do to get me released. He said that he would be at my court hearing to do what he could for my current charges but that the revocation process was a whole different matter.

On my court date, we met at the courthouse. My special relative told me that he was now my lawyer, not family. "Remember that," he said. He instructed me on what answers to give and told me to be sure that I presented myself as most remorseful.

When we entered the courtroom, my lawyer spoke with the district attorney and then approached the bench for a lengthy visit with the judge. Then, I was called to the front, and I faced the judge and gave him eye contact and my complete attention. The judge gave his usual statement where he mentioned that regardless of what was discussed or agreed upon between the prosecutor and my lawyer as far as a plea deal, that he was not bound to abide by the agreement.

When the prosecutor and my lawyer approached the judge at his bench once again, they seemed to be having a heated discussion. After they returned to their respective seats, the judge called me up front again. He proceeded to ask me how I pled, and I responded with an adamant "Guilty, your Honor."

The judge said "very well" and then went on with the normal run down of the court finding me guilty, and he then handed down my sentence. He gave me four years in the state prison, but stayed the sentence. That meant that if my probation was revoked for any reason, I would need to fulfill the sentence. The prosecutor was not happy with this decision, and he made mention of the fact that it was my fourth conviction on the same charge, and that there had been well over 400 such illegal prescriptions uncovered.

The legal fact of the matter was that these prescriptions had been read into the previous convictions which made them a non-issue.

I guess it didn't hurt knowing the right people. I had a lucky star of sorts.

CHAPTER SEVENTEEN

Leap of Faith

It was on March 29, 1985 that I was informed by the jailer that my doses of methadone were being halted. Apparently my last drug test had come back positive for cocaine, and the medical director at the clinic had instructed that I be removed from the program. It was abrupt. I had been on this stuff for over a couple years at the maximum dose, and now it was to be stopped immediately. This was not good! I knew that I would be sick as a dog very soon.

I was being transferred to the House of Correction when I began to feel the withdrawal slowly hit me. After I was processed, they put me in the infirmary lockup because they knew the methadone had been abruptly stopped, and I was showing signs of acute withdrawal. I was in a solitary cell which was about seven feet wide and ten feet long, with just a metal table bed with a thin mattress, a commode, and a sink. I felt physically sick with the chills, stomach cramps, a low grade fever, and every bone in my body aching. My anxiety was growing by the minute, and I was vomiting up every bit of food and drink I had forced down. This was a condition I was, unfortunately, very familiar with—opiate withdrawal symptoms. The thing that was different this time was that I had been on the maximum dose of methadone for years, along with my extracurricular activity with heroin, morphine, and cocaine. The toll it would take on me would surely be traumatic.

Another factor that made this time around different was that I was securely locked up. There were no more of the options before me. I couldn't run into a drugstore and help myself to some Percodan. I couldn't beg some heroin dealer for a bump to hold me over. And I couldn't ask to have a prescription filled, for old times' sake. This was it, an iron clad cell with nowhere to run and nowhere to hide. I had to face my demons head on.

After the first forty-eight hours, I began to feel what I thought was the peak of my withdrawal, which in reality was just the tip of the iceberg. I did get about an hour of rest, and I was hoping I could sleep this off slowly and get back to feeling somewhat normal. I was so wrong. I began to run a fever, I was vomiting up the lining of my stomach, and I was ringing wet with sweat over my entire body. I had intense chills that came and went continuously, and my muscles began to cramp to the point of intense pain throughout my entire body. I cried profusely and begged God to take it away, or take me away.

I had periods where I had been vomiting to the point of exhaustion, during which my stomach muscles became so tight that I felt I couldn't breathe. I almost felt some relief after I had gagged what felt like my last breath. I thought to myself, "Now maybe I can rest," but then I began to shake violently, with my legs kicking like a fish out of water. I screamed out for help and pounded on the iron cell door with what little strength I had left, but no one came. The only time anyone came by was to slide meals through the slot in the door. And when they came, I pleaded with them to send a nurse.

About four days in, which literally felt like months, a hard-boiled nurse came by my cell. She told me she could order some Tylenol for me and said, "You're not going to die, but you just might feel like it." Then she left.

After the fifth day, I was completely exhausted from the constant gagging, crying, and tremors. I felt so cold even though I had been sweating profusely. I literally hadn't slept in five days. My bedsheets had been removed as a precautionary measure, due to my being on suicide watch. So here I was, lying on a thin plastic covered pad that they called a mattress. All I could do was lie there and pray while I shook from a worn and torn nervous system, with my cold sweaty body sticking to the plastic mattress.

As the eighth day came with absolutely no sleep, my mind started to drift. The next thing I heard was a young child crying. It was my one-and-a-half year old son. I clearly remember getting up to go in his room, and on my way to his room, I noticed a Kit Kat bar sitting on the table. I picked it up, removed the wrapper, and began to chew it. I then immediately woke up with a disgusting taste in my mouth to find that what I thought was a Kit Kat was, in reality, bar of Ivory soap, and I just began to cry. It was one of the most disappointing experiences I can ever remember. And that disgusting taste made me begin to gag once again, as I attempted to flush it out. I began to lick my arms to get rid of the taste. I pounded on the big iron cell door, screaming for help until my hands were bloodied and swollen, but no one ever came.

I lay back down on my mattress in complete exhaustion, and again I heard the cries of my little boy in the other room. I got up again and began to quickly walk toward his room when I was awakened by a horrible throbbing in my head. I had walked right into the iron cell door head first; I could feel a bump on my head with intense pain. The last thing I remember was standing by the door when I began to feel very lightheaded.

The next thing I remember was being lifted off the floor by a jailer and the county nurse. I had apparently had a seizure, according to the nurse. I was transported to County Hospital to get checked out, and a few hours later they sent me back with some Dilantin, which was for seizures.

Back at the jail, I was put in another part of the infirmary, a big room with four beds for inmates with medical issues. There was an old black minister, an old white man with crutches who appeared to have a bad hip, and a little old black guy who was deaf. The deaf guy got up early and mopped the floor daily, and I would tease him. I'd show him where he had missed a spot, and he would flip me his middle finger, and in sign language, which I remembered from high school, he would tell me I was the devil. This deaf man and I eventually enjoyed teasing each other, while the old minister just seemed to lie back and observe with an occasional smile.

While I had begun to feel better physically, I still got very little sleep, so I was continually exhausted and depressed. I still had aching muscles and bones, and the restless leg thing, along with the depression.

It was about three o'clock in the morning, after another restless day during which I had been feeling there was no way out of the madness of my life. As I was lying in my bed with these crazy thoughts, the one thing that kept rearing its ugly head in my mind was suicide. I had been thinking very hard and very long, and always came up with the same solution.

Now, with the decision made in my mind, I needed to find a quick way out. It would need to be a way that couldn't be thwarted by some prison guard, and a way that would be as fast and painless as possible. With few options before me, my bed sheets seemed like the only way. There were some plumbing pipes near the ceiling. With three other guys sleeping in this infirmary room, I would need to be sure I had this thing planned right. I couldn't risk waking someone before I made the leap. So, I would need to have the bed sheets tied to the pipes, and the makeshift noose tightly secured around my neck, within about three minutes flat, according to my calculations.

Once I had the plan in place, I needed to drown out any logic and any emotions, and just do it. I likened it to taking a horrible tasting spoonful of medicine as a kid—I would try to deaden my taste buds and just swallow the shit. Flashing back to when I was hit by the big Cadillac when I was six years old, it wasn't the impact or pain I remembered when I was hit by that car. It was the split second between knowing I was going to take a hit and the initial impact. In some f***ed up way, it was almost to say, "Bring it, I can take it!"

At this point, God knows I deserved any and all pain I was dealt. I looked up at the ceiling above in the infirmary and contemplated when to make my move. There was a very dim light shining into the room through the wired safety glass window. As I looked around the room and heard the faint sound of snoring from the other men, I heard a soft voice saying, "It's not worth it, Anthony."

On the right side of my bed stood the older black gentleman who was a minister in the outside world. All I could make out was the outline of his face and his glasses reflecting the dim light from the hallway. He said, "Anthony, I can see and feel your suffering, but there's nothing God can't help you overcome." I thought, "What freaking luck! It's 3:30 in the morning, and this guy's awake." I had procrastinated as usual, and now I would have to sit in this shithole and wait who knows how long to get another chance to bail out of this miserable life! I just said, "Thank you sir, I'm sorry if I woke you." I rolled over and eventually fell asleep.

The next morning, I could see that the minister didn't forget the incident. He gave me a half-grin and said, "Let's talk after breakfast." Great! This is all I needed, to hear some minister preach 'The Word.' But, I had no place to hide. Knowing I probably had to listen to at least some of his sermon, I finished breakfast and looked over at him. He was clenching his little Bible and watching me out the corner of his eye. He sat up, looked at me and said, "You ready to talk, Anthony?" I just glanced at him and thought, "What the f*** mister, do I have a choice?" The truth is that there also was a part of me that was very curious about what he had to say.

I pulled up a chair alongside his bed, and he began talking with me. He said he could see my anguish by the look on my face that I looked very distraught and lost. He went on to say that he was only trying to give me a little advice from his experiences in life, that I could do what I wanted with his advice, but that he needed to say his piece. He read a few passages from his Bible I don't even remember which passages he read, but something about what he read, the way he read it, or both, stuck with me.

He told me that whatever trouble I was having in my life was only temporary. He went on to say that his approach to trouble was to make things right with his God, with himself, and with anyone he may have harmed. He had found that any problems he encountered in his life always passed, with him growing in character as a result of making amends for his wrongs. He always felt a closer and stronger relationship with his God, after making things right with all parties. He said, "It's just that simple, Anthony. Our thinking is the only thing that gets in the way of righteousness."

The fact that this guy was in jail along with me surely meant he was not in line for sainthood. But, regardless of that, I thought about what he said, and I believe I better understood myself. It didn't clear up all my issues, but it did give me a new outlook. And the thought of suicide became a distant option. Even if it was just for that one day, his presence along with his words made a difference in my life.

A few days later I was going to be transferred back to the dorm—a big room with sixty other guys all cramped in together. I was not looking forward to it. As I was packing my belongings to leave the infirmary room, the pastor stopped me and handed me his little Bible. He told me that he believed in me and said that if ever I began to doubt, to just read a few passages. I still have that Bible.

I believe it was at that time that I came to realize the truth of the words that I had repeated, day in and day out, for a good period of my life. It was this:

"I am here because there is no refuge, finally from myself. Until I confront myself in the eyes and hearts if others, I am running.

"Until I suffer them to share in my secrets, I have no safety from them. Afraid to be known, I can know neither myself nor any other, I will be alone.

"Where else but in our common ground, can I find such a mirror? Here, together, I can at last appear clearly to myself, not as the giant of my dreams, nor the dwarf of my fears. But as a human being, part of a whole, with my share in its purpose.

"In this ground, I can take root and grow, not alone anymore as in death, but alive—to myself and to others."

In short, I guess I could say that I needed to come to the realization of who I was, and who I was not. I was not this 'Mighty Morphine Power Ranger' with no regard for myself or any other human being on this earth. But, who I was, who I am, and who I will always be, is a flawed human being. The fortunate thing for me is that I realized that I had an opportunity to live a somewhat normal life if I so chose. It would not be an easy path, and I may feel lost sometimes, but if I could stay the course, this path could work for me as it has for so many before me. I saw it work first-hand in my own home as a young child, and into adulthood. It had been in front of my eyes for many years and didn't even know it.

Sobering Reality

On a sunny spring day in early May of 1985, I had a visit from my probation officer, Joe. He sat down with me to explain his findings, the court's findings, and the stand his department was taking in regard to my revocation. He had looked at the history of my drug use, along with my criminal involvement. The courts had already taken their stand, which was to leave it in the hands of the Wisconsin Department of Corrections. Joe's position was that my case was unusual in that every one of my crimes was connected with my drug use. And he noted the physical harm that I had inflicted upon myself—hepatitis, numerous broken syringe needles in my body, severely damaged circulation, two incidents of bacterial infections of the heart, all due to my drug use. Sending me to prison might keep me from harming myself anymore, he said.

However, it was his decision after much thought and consideration, that I should be released. The fact that I came from a good, close knit family and the fact that I never used weapons or caused physical harm in any crimes played into his decision. He explained that his department's recommendation was that I be mandatorily placed in an in-patient rehabilitation hospital, and that I follow any recommendations they may suggest upon my release—whether that would be a halfway house or a continuation of long term treatment.

As Joe left, he told me that he was going to fill out my release papers, and I would be transported back to Milwaukee. He gave me a date and time to be at his office, at which time we would map out the plan for my in-patient hospitalization and follow-up.

The next four hours of sitting and waiting for my release felt very long. As I contemplated what I would do once I was out, I was very conflicted. In spite of all the pain and agony I had endured over the previous weeks of withdrawal, I still considered the possibility of going back to the methadone clinic to plead my case to be reinstated, even though Joe had made it very clear that methadone was absolutely off the table as an option.

While I lay on my bed among the other fifty-nine men in this facility, I thought about how my lifestyle of the past, if continued, would lead to my spending a good part of my life in these places. I remembered eating lunch one afternoon with the old black minister. He was looking around the loud cafeteria, and he reached over the table to me and said, "You see, Anthony, a whole lot of these cats here are doing life on the installment plan. They're in and out all the time. But, it ain't for you, Son." That stuck in my head, and though I couldn't comprehend a person actually liking jail, I did remember my own feeling of safety while I was locked up years earlier.

Finally I heard my name called by the dormitory guard and I knew it was time to get the f*** out of this zoo. I was taken to the property room where I put on my old street clothes. They barely fit now as I had begun to gain weight, but they were the same street clothes I had worn in battle for quite a while, with blood stains on the pant legs from shooting and wiping blood drops on them. They smelled of cigarette smoke and carried the stench of not being changed or washed.

Along with others being transported to various places, I boarded an old yellow school bus, and as we drove off, I looked out at the sunny clear sky. Although I was very nervous about returning home, I felt so free. It was almost a miracle that I was still alive, and almost more miraculous that I had been released. Down the road, I looked up and saw this big beautiful red-tailed hawk soaring in the sky, probably searching for his lunch. It was gorgeous. As I watched it, I began to think about some of my conversations with the old black minister, and in some strange way I almost felt like he was watching over me through this hawk.

When the bus stopped downtown at the Milwaukee County Jail, my wife was waiting for me in her car. I felt strange seeing her. It was almost as if I had awakened from a very long dream. I honestly felt like I really didn't know her; I felt self-conscious and almost shy like when I met someone new. From downtown, we headed over to my parents' house to get the kids and visit with my parents for a bit, before going home.

When we walked in, there were my parents sitting with all three kids in the living room. I kissed all three of the kids as well as my parents and then sat on the couch. I had a strange and new feeling. As I looked across at my wife and the three kids, I remember feeling like I honestly didn't know how this had all happened. And I felt like I didn't really know any of them. I did my best to act as if nothing was wrong.

We soon headed to our home, and even the house seemed foreign to me. This whole thing felt unreal. As we settled in for the night, we put our three-and-a-half month old daughter in her crib, and took the boys to bed with us in the big king-sized bed. We laughed and goofed around with the kids for a little while, and then everyone fell sound asleep, except me.

Here I was, lying in this big bed with a woman I felt that I barely knew, along with two innocent little boys who barely knew me. My mind raced, while my body became more and more exhausted. I had to keep the faith that this physical nightmare would eventually end. In reality, what could I expect after so many years of heavy dependence on opiates, with the past two years on methadone in combination with cocaine, heroin, morphine, Percodan, and alcohol?

That old path could not, and would not, lead to anything but death to me and destruction to any human who may be emotionally or spiritually connected to my life. I had finally come to the realization that I hadn't been hurting and affecting only myself with my lifestyle, as I had previously fooled myself into believing. And now, there were three beautiful and innocent little children who would be right in the middle of the battlefield. The battle I am referring to is the one I, myself, created with my addiction to drugs.

I could see that sobering reality, now that my mind had been clear of drugs and alcohol long enough to honestly know what I was doing. I could see that the dark corner of my mind seemed to be losing momentum. I found myself defying the committee that always used to have its way with me. This, I intuitively knew, was a war worth fighting. I had finally opened that door to the dark corner room of my mind, and I had begun to fight what I knew in my heart was a just and righteous war.

Finally, I was able to get an hour of rest. And when I opened my eyes, I could see that I hadn't been dreaming. It was true reality that I was a part of this new family. We all sat at our kitchen table eating breakfast and laughing about our cute little girl draining her baby bottle with a funny look in her eyes. When breakfast was done and the kids were watching cartoons on television, my mind began to drift back to the cold reality of what my new life was to entail. I knew that I had a monumental task before me if I were to succeed in leading a normal life and learning to be a parent.

Hospitals, Institutions, or Death

It was only one day later that I had to fulfill my commitment to rehab, as ordered by the probation and parole department upon my release. A spot had just become available at the same rehabilitation hospital I had been in four times previously. When I was admitted, I was given a daily schedule to follow, which included group therapy, individual sessions with a drug and alcohol counselor, and some other therapeutic group that consisted of crafts and recreation, which was listed as mandatory. I thought, "WTF? We gonna play hop scotch, paint by numbers, and sing Kumbaya?" Well, it sure beat the place I called home the previous week at the House of Correction.

The first night there the staff suggested I attend a twelve-step meeting like the ones I'd been to numerous times before. I knew they didn't work for me, but I figured I would attend just to take my mind off the withdrawal.

The psychological part of withdrawal was almost as big as the physical part of getting well, or maybe even bigger. The fact is that perception is reality, and when that dark corner of my mind was desperate to get what it wanted, it seemed to get more creative. That committee in my crazy head seemed to make one last attempt to convince me to feel tremendous guilt and anxiety, along with the physical aches and pains. And it was pleading for help in relieving these ills—a few Percodan or even just a half pint of booze to get by. But, during the meeting I attended that first night, I heard something that stuck with me. It was some old-timer who talked about his 'stinking thinking.' It struck a chord with me and made me question the advice of the committee that once had its way with me 100% of the time.

The next day was the first recreational therapy session. Although I went into the session with a negative attitude, I have to admit I kind of enjoyed it. The therapist was a very pleasant woman I took too immediately. I participated in pottery class, and by the end of the first week, I had made a dinner plate for each one of my kids, with each kid's name and their favorite cartoon character on the plate. It was almost like I was growing up all over again. I began to participate in all the groups I was scheduled for almost effortlessly. It seemed like it was working wonders for taking my mind off the psychological part of my withdrawals. I began to sleep a few hours a night, and I even took catnaps whenever I had free time.

But now, the reality of what was waiting for me in the outside world began to sink in, and I knew it wasn't going to be easy. I surely wasn't going to make a living and support a family by making pottery or singing Kumbaya. I knew I would soon be faced with the huge task of finding my way into some viable type of career.

After the first week of nightly twelve-step meetings, I met with John, a pediatrician I had known in the past who had agreed to be my sponsor. We met in the hospital lobby and talked about how my life had transformed since we had last talked, about twelve years ago. As we were talking, a group of about six doctors he knew walked by. One of the physicians was one that I also knew pretty well from years past. He and the other doctors sat down with John and me, and he introduced me to each one of them. He told me that a few of the docs were interested in hearing how I was doing this time around in treatment. They had heard quite a bit about me, my life on the streets, and my drug issues over the previous few years.

While I was explaining some of my war stories, so to speak, one of the doctors looked at me and said, "You know, given your past and the fact you were on methadone for so many years, what do you realistically think your chances of staying clean are?" He went on to say, "I don't remember one successful case of someone with your history actually making it. Some people I've encountered relapsed shortly after and never returned. Some ended up in prison, only to relapse as soon as they got out, and others, they just died or committed suicide." At this I just said, "Time will give you the answer." I remember feeling a heaviness in the pit of my stomach after this interaction. And I felt resentment and even anger toward this guy.

At the end of the second week in treatment, I was scheduled to see the admitting physician of record at the hospital. The doctor said he was surprised I was back in the hospital after being in remission for almost two months. We discussed my treatment progress and aftercare program. He said he was comfortable in discharging me if I agreed to the follow his recommendations. The plan included outpatient group therapy for one year, and an honest attempt to take a daily medication called Naltrexone which was new at that time. This medication that was an opioid antagonist, which was supposed to curb the urge for opiate drugs and alcohol. When I thought about the fact that I had three small children at home, I agreed to follow the plan. It was the right thing to do.

The next morning after my probation officer was notified and all my aftercare plans were written out, I was released from the hospital. My wife and kids came to pick me up. I still felt somewhat strange about this new family thing, but I just thought, "It is what it is, and I may just like it." Loving them was one thing I felt sure I already did, and, no doubt, always would. But, liking them? That remained to be seen. When we got back home, I looked around at these kids and just thought to myself, "What the f*** were you thinking?" The honest answer was, I wasn't thinking! That was the problem with most things I had done in my life.

The next day, my wife and I spent some time talking about finances, which were embarrassingly poor on my end, and only a little better on her end. She had been making things work with AFDC, which was for low income parents, and some child support. I was going to look for work that day and also make up some flyers to hand out door-to-door for handyman jobs like painting, cleaning, and such.

The following day a relative and I began to put flyers in all the doors of the surrounding neighborhoods, and soon we actually began to receive some calls for various jobs. It felt very good to receive what little money we did, mostly because we had worked hard for it. At night I went to my group therapy or one of the twelve-step meetings, and I began to feel like I might be able to do this thing.

I was beginning to sleep a bit better as a result of working hard, going to meetings, and playing with the kids. By the time the kids went to sleep, I was ready, too. I was getting about four to five hours of good sleep before waking up with my mind racing. I could still feel my bones aching from the methadone withdrawal. The doctor had told me it may take as much as six months to feel close to normal.

After about a month of doing odd jobs and bringing home some money, I thought things were getting better in our household and that this family thing might work out. But, just when I had been thinking these promising thoughts, I came home after work one afternoon to find a couple of visitors. Two guys I'd never seen before were in the kitchen with my wife, while the kids were in the living room watching cartoons. My wife had a scale on the kitchen table weighing up some cocaine for the visitors. Immediately, I got a sick stomach, and I could just smell the cocaine, which made matters worse. Not only was I shocked that it was going on in our house, but I also had a few quick thoughts of using some of the shit.

When the two guys left, I went into the kitchen with my wife and asked what the f*** she was doing. She just said that we needed the money, and she felt that she was doing what she needed to do for us to live. I told her that I couldn't live this way and that this couldn't happen again in our house. Her next response was depressing to me. She told me about a friend of hers who paid his way through medical school by selling cocaine. I said I didn't see that as something to be proud of, and I also asked her if he had a problem similar to mine. I said that if he could sell cocaine without dipping into his stash, good for him. But, I told her, I couldn't even be around the shit, and I wouldn't. From her response to what I said, it sounded like she would respect my request. We never really discussed it again.

Stark Reminder

It was the middle of May in 1985. I had just finished a painting job, and I took my kids over to my parents' house for a visit. My father mentioned he had a couple extra tickets to a Brewers game. He also said that my old childhood friend across the street, Billy, had recently stopped by to see him. He said that Billy confided in him that he had recently quit drinking, and that Billy was asking about me.

Billy was one of my closest friends while growing up. We always got along very well even though we just didn't share a lot of the same interests. I remembered Billy was always being picked on by the older kids because he had a learning disability. He took things very hard. So, when I heard from my father that Billy was struggling with alcohol, I decided to go across the street for a visit. We sat in Billy's backyard and talked. When I told him about my battles with drugs and alcohol, he too began to open up to me. He had quit drinking for a few months because it had become a problem and had destroyed his marriage.

Billy had been in the Army until a few months before this. He had married a woman who was also in the military. After a couple months of marriage, he came home after a night of heavy drinking to find her in bed with another soldier they both knew. At that point, Billy became very quiet. I could see that he was hurting, and he was hurting real bad.

In an attempt to get his mind off what was eating away at his soul, I told him that I had two tickets to the Brewers baseball game that evening. He told me he would think about it. And I came out and said, "Come on Billy, let's just go and try to enjoy a night out. I don't want to see you go back to drinking." Billy just looked at me with his depressed expression and his dark tired eyes, and said he would call me at my parents' house in an hour or so. He said that he was meeting with a minister from his church at his house shortly.

When I saw the minister leave his house, looking out from my parents living room window, I went back to see Billy. He seemed to be in better spirits. The minister had read some verses from the Bible with him, and Billy told me that he found the answers he was looking for. I said I was happy to hear he was feeling better, and I again suggested that we head out to the baseball game. He said he had promised his dad he would help him around the house, but he thanked me for asking.

I went back over to play with my kids in my parents' backyard. A couple hours later, I noticed an ambulance pulling up across the street. I led the kids to the kitchen table for lunch and went outside to see what was going on. I saw Billy's father sitting on the front steps of their porch, and when I saw the look on his face, I immediately knew it was Billy. Apparently when I left his house earlier, he told his father he was going to hang some curtains up in his room. The box he told his father contained the curtain rods, held instead a .610 rifle. He had put it in his mouth and blew his brains all over the ceiling of the very room where he and I played for so many years. I now realized what he meant about finding his answer.

I was just sick. It was a very sad and numbing day. I may always think about the 'what-if's' of that tragic day. What if I made him go with me to my parents until the game? What if I took him along with me to a meeting? But, it was what it was. May 17, 1985 will be a day that stays in my head forever.

Billy's funeral was absolutely horrible, to say the least. His mother and father asked if I would be a pallbearer, which I of course accepted. His brother Dennis and his sister Carol were both there, and understandably both were very distraught. The casket was closed due to the gunshot wound to his head. The minister who conducted the service was the one Billy had met with the day he died. At the conclusion of the service, he said how tragic it was for this big-hearted man to die so young. As we were carrying his casket from the funeral home to the hearse, his sister literally began to climb onto the casket, clawing and screaming. It was one of the most distressing scenes imaginable. The minister had to gently guide her away the best he could and almost carried her to the family car.

At the burial, there were a lot of tears and sobbing from almost everyone, including me. The thought of the pain and agony he must have been experiencing immediately before pulling the trigger kept running through my head. I just had celebrated forty-five days clean, and my nerves were still raw from withdrawals. All I could think of was the poor little lost Billy I knew as a kid. When his casket was being lowered into the vault, I took my thirty day sobriety coin and dropped it down in with his casket.

Vanishing Act

Shortly after watching Billy buried and off to wherever the heck people go when life leaves their physical remains, my mind seemed to take on a new load of questions. I saw what happened with him following his meeting with the minister, when he told me he found his answers. It made me wonder about my whole effort in life. It seemed like I was spinning my wheels just to survive, struggling to put a roof over our heads and food in our mouths, just to shit it out the next day, and needing more, while the roof over our heads continually deteriorates.

But now, regardless of what this journey holds, whether it is part of something bigger or all for naught, I had put myself in a position where it looked like it didn't matter which was true. I had a wife and three children who would be depending on me to show them what path to take on this journey. It was all due to the results of my decision making while I was wandering aimlessly through life. And I was wandering in that direction because of the previous decisions. Decisions, decisions. . . . I guess they do take some careful thought, just as my mother and father told me. I had just been flying by the seat of my pants. Well, the reality of my current situation was that I just needed to make the best of it, or jump ship and run as fast and as far as I could.

I was coming up on sixty days without a drink and completely drug free. I began to feel stronger each day, and though it seemed that more and more obstacles presented themselves, each day I felt better equipped to deal with them than the day before. I had just found a job with a commercial real estate investor, as a handyman. I felt like I was actually making progress. I knew that raising three kids working as a handyman probably wouldn't put us in the best of living conditions, but it was a start. I was looking at the reality of being a convicted felon with an extremely limited education.

One evening shortly after I returned home from a meeting with my sixty day sobriety coin, there was an obstacle that presented itself which I didn't think I could withstand. And it was one that I didn't expect. I came home to find that my wife had her scale out again, and I asked what was the story with the equipment being out. She just simply said that she was doing a favor for an old friend who didn't have a scale and had asked to borrow it. I bit my tongue, though inside I was burning up. In my usual passive aggressive demeanor, I just shut down, probably to keep from blowing a gasket.

She ended up leaving for the night while I sat home with the kids. As the evening was passing by, I had all three kids bathed, which was tedious, but I have to admit was also fun. While these little ones splashed around laughing, we sang songs that we made up as we went along. With the boys in the tub, I bathed my daughter in the kitchen sink. I sang a song that would get them to join in. It was an old diversion tactic that gave me assurance that no one had gone under water. If I didn't hear both boys joining in on the song, I knew I needed to grab my daughter and do a quick spot check on them.

When the baths were over and the kids were in their pajamas, it was time for them to go to sleep. But before going to sleep, I gave them each a big hug. And I didn't do this just for them, because I really got some comfort out of hugging these clean little kids in their warm fleece pajamas. It was a new kind of pleasure for me. There is nothing else like that feeling. I guess I would call it warm innocence. And I think I was actually beginning to like these little kids, to a point.

When the kids were all in bed off to their dream world, I got on the phone to call my sponsor, the old pediatrician who was kind of like my lifeline through all things, good, bad, or indifferent. I discussed my anger about the scale incident with him. He just listened and asked if I had been to a meeting. And he told me to get to a meeting the next free time I had. What kind of advice was this, I thought. I felt he was supposed to agree that I had justification to be angry, and possibly tell me to verbally rip this woman apart when she got home, but he didn't. I must have talked until I dozed off on him while in the middle of our conversation because I woke up with the phone to my ear and that constant beeping sound of the phone being off the hook.

It was coming up on three o'clock in the morning, with no sign of my wife, so I climbed in bed and attempted to go to sleep. It was useless as I grew angrier by the minute. A little after 7:00 am I heard the front door open, and in came my wife. I did my best to keep my cool and asked what the hell had happened. I said that I was worried sick and the baby was hungry. She was breastfeeding at the time, and she reminded me that she told me before she left that she made up a couple of bottles and they were in the refrigerator. She told me that she had been out with her newfound half-brother and some friends, and they decided to go to a restaurant for soup after the bar closed. She asked that we discuss it later so as not to wake the kids, and she went to sleep. Well, I couldn't sleep after the night's drama, and I found myself deep in thought, obsessing about what had transpired over the previous twenty-four hours.

When the kids woke up, I had an initial burst of comfort and distraction from my resentment for this woman. Looking at the kids smiles in the morning, still in those warm fleece pajamas, with their hair every which way, took me away for a short period of time. I made breakfast for them, and we went out into the living room to watch Saturday morning cartoons.

My wife woke up in the early afternoon and started preparations for our dinner that would be hours later. While she was cooking, I sat at the kitchen table and drilled her about the evening before. Even though I had told myself I wouldn't question her and give her the benefit of the doubt, I continued asking her questions. She told me it wouldn't happen again, and agreed that she should have at least called to let me know what the story was.

During all of this my mind began to turn inward to that dark corner, which I had felt I had pretty much held at bay for a while. It seemed that the committee had reconvened and were ready to give me some recommendations on how I should react to the events of the previous day. Since I had been clean for over sixty days, which felt like sixty months, I felt I had somewhat of a clear mind, so I now took what the dark corner of my mind told me with a grain of salt.

After dinner, I reluctantly went to a meeting and they were talking about resentments and how destructive they could be to people like us. I kind of felt like my sponsor had conspired with the people at this group and had given them the heads up on what to talk about in front of me. In any case, I heard some things that made sense, like the fact that I shouldn't let other people live in my head rent free. And if we forgive unequivocally, they are somehow evicted from our mind. Well, it made sense, but these people didn't know where I came from and what I was going through. I thought that some things just couldn't be overlooked.

When I returned home from the meeting, my wife was giving the kids their baths and getting them in their pajamas. She said that she was going to go out for a short while and said that she would call if she was going to be late, and that there were bottles of breast milk made up for the baby, if needed.

It was about 9:00 pm that evening, and I had the kids in bed so I decided to call my friend Paul from the outpatient group I had been attending twice a week. We talked about the dynamics of our group and some of the things Anne, the counselor, had brought up during our sessions. One thing she continually mentioned that I myself needed to focus on was being honest with myself. She said that I seemed to divert attention away from my own shortcomings, by pointing out my wife's questionable behaviors.

She asked me to speak to the issues that I played a part in, and to think about what the bond I had with my wife was based on. To be honest, from my view, the only bond I could see was the children. We were two very different people with very conflicting ideals. I began to enjoy each child and their individual personalities. And I had their best interests at heart—even though my mind was on who the hell I really was, who I wanted to be, and what steps I needed to take to make the best of a difficult situation.

I knew living the type of lifestyle we were in was detrimental to these kids, and it was not fair to my wife, knowing that I did not see a future with her. Our relationship was originally based on what seemed to be a passing nightmare for both of us. We had decided to marry based on a whim and a pregnancy. All of the things I heard myself saying in my groups and the feedback I received from the people that listened to me talk, pointed to finding an amicable split, which would have the least damaging effect on these three little children.

Well, that night ended with me falling asleep while on the phone with Paul, as I often did. My mind was so full of conflict that I seemed to purge my thoughts verbally until I fell asleep, but I never could voice these thoughts to my wife, as we never really talked.

I woke up the next morning about 7:00 am to the front door opening; it was my wife just getting home from her night out. I remember feeling sick to my stomach, and all I could say was, "If this ever happens again, I want a divorce." She told me that I had a lot of nerve since she spent nearly nine months carrying our daughter while I was either drinking, drugging, or in jail. She had a point, though getting home at 7:00 am was a bit out of line.

The following week was very difficult for me at work as I couldn't get my mind off of what had transpired the previous couple weeks at home. One day I obsessed about the situation to the point that I couldn't work. I told my boss that I felt sick and that I had to leave. When I walked into the house, I found my wife sitting with her half-brother. When I asked what was going on, he told me that I needed to back off and stop giving my wife a hard time about going out. I asked him to leave our house and stay the f*** out of our business. He looked at my wife and just said he'd call her later and left. I couldn't even get myself to talk to her, and I retreated to the bedroom to lie down and rest while my mind was racing.

That Friday night, the same week, she decided to again go out. I had been sitting with the kids as usual, but the atmosphere of the room had a very different feel. The kids acted as if they were walking on egg shells and got very quiet. I'm sure they felt the tension in the air between my wife and me. She left the house without saying a word. I bathed the kids and put them to bed by 9:30 pm. She didn't return that night.

At 10:00 am the next morning, the phone rang and it was my wife. She told me that she was going to be home in about ten minutes. She was at a phone booth and said she wanted to be sure I wasn't going to do anything stupid when her friend or half-brother dropped her home. She could hear the anger in my voice, as I asked where the f*** she had been. She told me that if I was going hurt her, she wasn't going to come home. I told her wasn't going to hurt her, but I was going to hurt him instead. And I yelled that she needed to come home, and come home now.

I then went into the kitchen, grabbed a butcher knife, and went out to the front yard beside a neighbor's tree and waited for her. As the car pulled up, her half-brother or whoever he was saw me, and hit the gas, speeding up the block. I sprinted after the car for about a half block with a butcher knife in my hand, wanting to just jab this guy with it. Well, I guess you could say I was mad. When their car was far enough down the block, he let her out of the car and sped off.

By the time my wife was walking back to the house, I began to shut down after that quick burst of rage. I was so mad I could hardly breathe. As I went back in the house after her, I began to yell, asking her where the f*** she was all night. I was yelling at the top of my lungs, telling her to answer the question of where she was. By this time, the poor kids were probably terrified. My wife just said that she needed to go in the bedroom to rest and think. I suggested that maybe she should consider packing her stuff and leaving.

About an hour later, she came out of the bedroom and told me that she wanted to go over to her sister's apartment to visit. At this point I couldn't even think, so I just said good-bye. As she drove off, I wished that she would never come back. Later that evening, she called to tell me she was going to stay with her sister for a while. When I asked what she meant by 'a while' she told me that she would call me sometime in the next few days and hung up the phone. I called back a few times continuously to get an answer from her, and she told me not to call back.

I had to work the next day, so I called my mother to see if she could sit with the kids and she agreed, though when I dropped them off, I didn't mention what was going on at home. On my way to work, I drove through the area I had frequented years before buying heroin. The thought of stopping crossed my mind for a brief moment but passed just as fast. Maybe another time, I thought.

Another week passed with my wife still missing in action. My parents, who were newly retired, watched the kids. I went to work though I found that I was exhausted from achy bones and fatigue from the slight residual withdrawal, not to mention the diaper parties with the two younger kids, cooking, and waiting on them.

When the weekend came, I had my next door neighbor watch the kids while I went out on a mission to find my wife. I had no clue what I was going to do or say if I found her, but I still obsessed on locating her. I stopped by her sister's and parked down the block for a couple hours watching the house. I grew angrier with every single moment that passed. I finally went to her sister's apartment and knocked on the door. I could see that my wife's car was in the lot.

Finally, her sister opened the door and said my wife wasn't there. She said that my wife had gone to Las Vegas and that she wouldn't be back for two more days. I left her apartment just livid, and on my drive back home, I began to obsess about who she was with. I felt if I would see her at this moment, she may not survive my rage. Well, that feeling subsided a bit when I went to a meeting the next morning on my way to work and vented almost to no end.

As another week went by without hearing a word from my wife, I continued my silence to my parents. They had been asking how things were at home, because my mother noticed that the kids were different recently when she babysat them. I just responded with silence, not knowing how to explain the situation.

During this time I was still consistently attending the drug-free groups and complying with my probation. One morning I went to a scheduled appointment with Joe, my probation officer, and while we were discussing my current activities such as living situation, job status, etc. I informed him about my current marital status changes. I explained that my wife had abruptly moved out of our home and left the children with me, and that I was unsure about her return.

Joe mentioned how unusual it was to see a mother leave the home, because it was usually the father. He was very empathetic about my situation and asked that I keep our line of communication open. He also mentioned that he thought I was doing very well in my current recovery status and he didn't want to see a situation such as this bring me down, because I now had other lives that were depending on me.

The next weekend I received a call from my wife. She said that she heard I came looking for her. She went on to tell me that she needed time and space, because she needed to find herself. Well, I hoped she could find herself because me and the kids sure the f*** couldn't find her! And when a woman tells you she needs space, that's just the f*** what they do, they disappear into space. It means they're moving on, and you're not included in their space.

As my hurt went back to anger and rage, I asked her what she planned to do about the kids and her belongings at the house. She told me that in time she'd contact me.

CHAPTER EIGHTEEN

Going Solo

As another month went by, I continued my daily work schedule, even though I had become useless at my job due to my constant obsessive thoughts and anger, along with exhaustion from the single parent thing. As each night went by without hearing a word from my wife, I began to wonder how any parent could just disconnect from her young children so easily. Her son from her ex, our four-month-old daughter, and our year-and-a-half year-old boy were all just seemingly discarded. I felt guilty, angry, and depressed. Periodically my anger turned into bouts of rage; I would have to go to the garage to vent by yelling and pounding my hammer. I was so disgusted and resentful. I wanted to wrap up a dirty, shit-filled diaper and mail it to her, just to send her a message.

Summer came, and my next door neighbor Kelly, who was on break from college, started to babysit which gave my parents a break. My baby daughter, who had been cut off from breastfeeding, would sometimes try to breast feed from me. I began to carrying a small bottle of formula and held it by my boobs and let her nurse. I thought it would give her a sense of breast-feeding as I figured she needed that kind of nurturing.

My stepson was just quiet and occasionally asked where his mother was. And the now almost two-year-old, who I believe was most affected, would wake up each morning, look at the bedroom ceiling, and say, "There's my mom. She's up there." That made me feel sick, and my hurt would once again turn to anger.

Another month passed without a visit or even a phone call, and I decided to take action. One Saturday evening I asked Kelly to sit the kids while I set out on my mission. My first stop was to the local pharmacy to get what I needed, materials for my plan. I then drove to my wife's sister's house. When I arrived, I asked her sister if I could see my wife. She said that my wife was out for the evening, and she asked how the kids were. We talked a bit about the kids, and she asked how I was doing through all of the stuff we were going through. She mentioned that she was sorry that things were going the way they were. She went on to say that she wished she could tell me more about what my wife's plan was as far as our marriage and the kids, but she said that my wife really had been close-lipped about the whole thing. She also said she could understand that my wife and I may need time away from each other, but what she couldn't understand was why she hadn't even called about the kids.

I asked to use the bathroom before I left. There, I spotted my wife's brand of shampoo. I took the bottle of Nair hair remover that I had picked up at the drugstore, and I mixed the entire bottle into her shampoo. When I said good-bye and left the house I felt somewhat vindicated.

About a week later, my kids came down with the chicken pox so I found myself cooped up around the house for a few days. Then about a week after that, my wife called to ask if she could pick up the kids for a few hours. I told her that they had just gotten over the chicken pox so it might not be a good time. She argued about it, but then said "Fine" and hung up the phone.

An hour later she showed up at the house unexpectedly and said she wanted to get some of her stuff. I told her it would be fine and allowed her to come in, while her half-brother sat out in his car two houses away. He hadn't forgotten about my butcher knife I guess. When my wife came into the house, she said "Hi" to the kids, but it was like she was a distant relative saying hello. She just seemed uninterested. She went into the kitchen cabinet and bagged up her bottles of wine and booze, then grabbed some clothes. All the while she was telling me what furniture she wanted to get at a later date. Then she told me that she was going to 'borrow' the kids for a couple of hours to go to a beach party, because a few of her new friends wanted to meet them. I told her that it wasn't going to work, because they were just getting over the chicken pox, as I told her on the phone. And I told her that the kids weren't to be used as a way to show what a good mother she was. At that statement she said she was calling the police and did.

About fifteen minutes later four police officers in two cars pulled up. They asked who called and then one police officer asked me to go outside on the porch, while two other officers spoke to my wife, and another sat with the kids. At first they were under the impression that I was the visitor and she was the custodial parent. Then the officer I was talking to said, "Hold on here, you live here with the kids?" And he then told me to come in the house with him.

He asked my wife why, exactly, she had called. And my wife told him that all she wanted was to take the kids for a few hours to a beach party. I chimed in and told them that the kids were just getting over the chicken pox, and since I had custody, I didn't think they should go. After hearing both sides, one police officer asked the kids to come by him on the sofa, and he asked if he could see their backs. My son pulled up the back of his shirt, and he still had visible little scabs from the pox. The officer said, "These kids aren't going anywhere; they need to be home." My wife then blurted out in front of everyone, "He's a drug addict and a criminal."

At that statement the eldest of the police officers looked at my wife and said, "So, why would you move out and leave your kids with a drug addict and criminal?" She didn't know how to respond to that. So, she got mad and said that she was going to see her attorney the next day, and she walked out.

For the first time in a long while I felt like I was on the right side of the law, and I felt that I saw good police work in action. The whole ordeal made me feel like the police did a great job in protecting the children. The episode, combined with the events of the prior couple of months, gave me a clear insight of what the future held for me and the kids. Because at least I could now see that she wasn't coming back.

Decision . . . Decisions

Now things seemed to be more cut and dried as far as who was who in my life, though there was still much confusion. I had to think about how I was actually going to do this single parent thing, at least for a while until I could make the right decision for these kids. There were so many things that needed to be considered in making a decision for the kids— and knowing my history of decision making, I knew I had to reach out for help.

My first reaction was to confide in my mother and father. I knew that I could depend on them for an honest opinion on how to proceed, though I also knew the advice they'd give would be an old-fashioned view. It would be: go to work, don't drink or drug, go to meetings, and raise your kids the best you can. I knew that was probably the clear cut advice most anyone would suggest, but there was also the fact of me being the one who would have to give direction and be the nurturer for these kids.

I had no clue what direction I was going myself, so how the hell was I going to show them how to live? I really had no clue. I had put myself through so much hell throughout the years and attempting to get my own head straight, how was I going to teach them how to live. I had gone in the direction of whatever made me feel good, with no thought of accountability for my actions.

When I attended my outpatient group one evening, I brought up the situation I was in, with my wife moving out and leaving the children behind. My counselor, Anne, asked quite a few questions about the children's ages, childcare arrangements, relatives in the city, and so on.

She asked how comfortable I felt about my sobriety, after only being clean since the end of March, and here it was only August; I was going on month five of being clean and sober. After it was thrown around a bit during the group, she asked me to see her individually after the group meeting that night and again the next week.

The following week before group began I stopped in early as Anne requested. She asked me how the past week had gone and what kind of things the kids and I did. I mentioned that there was still no interaction between my wife and me. After we discussed my situation for about fifteen minutes, Anne told me that I might want to consider the possibility of adoption for the kids. She told me her fear was of me relapsing which would be very traumatic for the children, and that with all of the stress of raising kids in my condition, relapse could be a real possibility. She ended our conversation with asking me just to think about it carefully, and she reiterated that she didn't mean to press me or judge what I should do.

Well, I did think about what she said. I thought about it continuously for the next week, every day. There were quite a few things to consider, regardless of what decision I did make. I understood that keeping the kids meant it would be my job, and no one else's, to commit to all aspects of child rearing—housing, clothing, feeding, teaching, counseling, disciplining, spiritual and emotional guidance, loving, and last but not least, enjoying time with them.

So the decision was mine. I must say that decision making was not my strongest suit, as I'd proven over the years. And ever since I cleaned up five months prior, my decision making went from split second and impulsive decisions in my using days, to an ambivalent mess. I had made so many bad decisions in years past that I now found myself hesitant to make any decisions at all. I guess that was the safest and surest way not to make a bad decision.

In looking for advice to make the right decision, I spoke with many people who I felt were capable of making good decisions. These were the people who seemed to have a proven track record of making prudent decisions throughout their lives. And there was my sponsor. This was a man who had made some very good decisions, such as working hard at his education, which led him to become a physician— and many other professional decisions that led to positive outcomes. He had, admittedly, made some bad decisions, too, but he was on a path out of insanity.

I went to visit him, and we discussed the dilemma I was facing. He listened carefully and then pulled out this 'Big Book.' He turned to a page, handed me the book, and asked me to read it aloud. It was a written list of promises. As I finished reading it, he said, "OK, now read number ten again." It said, "We will intuitively know how to handle situations that used to baffle us." At this, I looked at him and said that this wasn't a situation that used to baffle me; it was a new situation that I was facing for the first time, but it was now baffling me, and so was he.

Well, he just laughed. And he then told me to read it again, and again. He pointed out a part of the teaching that said that it works, sometimes quickly, sometimes slowly. He then told me to keep digging for advice from professionals who have experience with these types of situations, and that I should go to a lot of meetings. He told me not to panic, because the answer would come to me, and he said that he had a lot of confidence that I would make the right decision in time.

As I walked away from meeting with him, I thought, as I many times did when I heard something I did not want to hear, "F***him!" The reality of it was that I just wanted him to decide for me. My history had taught me that it was always better to have someone to blame for a bad decision.

I did end up reading those promises again and again, though when it was my choice to read it, it made better sense. After all, what did he know? He was just some clean and sober doctor with a successful career and a pretty normal family—that was all. However, by the time I had read the promises over and over again, my sponsor finally seemed to get smarter from my perspective. Decisions, decisions, and son of a bitch, I hate them.

After seeking as much advice as I possibly could from people who had successful track records, I decided that the decision didn't have to be quick, and it didn't have to be final. I could do my best over the next few months and then revisit the situation by weighing the pros and cons regarding the children's best interest, not mine. This was another thing that these promises said: "Self-seeking would slip away."

So with the decision to give this single parent thing an honest attempt, I knew I had a big task in front of me, and I wasn't going to be able to do it completely alone, because as the old saying goes, 'It takes a village.'

Family and Friends

It was late March 1987, and I had just celebrated two years of being clean and sober, and my life was taking on a new direction. I had successfully completed my mandatory drug free outpatient group, and I was up for being discharged from my probation obligation. While both my probation visits with Joe and my drug-free groups were simultaneously and successfully coming to an end, I felt both good and somewhat indifferent. I was relieved that these obligations were fulfilled, which was unheard of for me over the past ten or more years of insanity, but at the same time, I felt somewhat vulnerable. Though I was actually proud of what I had accomplished, I was also very aware of the fact that it was not something that one would equate with graduating from college. It was just a step back into the real world, and I knew life would hold many new challenges for me, though now I may be better equipped to handle them.

The decision to be a single parent became a bit easier when I realized that my wife was not coming back. She had already settled in with a new life for herself with a very nice man, and she was already pregnant.

I decided it was probably time to file for divorce. There was not anything much in the way of possessions to battle over, so I went Pro Se and did all of the footwork myself. I went down to a free legal service, a nonprofit agency in downtown Milwaukee. The attorney I met with at the time mentioned that since there were minor children involved I may want to consider hiring a firm for that reason alone. I decided against that route and wanted to do it myself. When my wife received the papers I filed, she apparently was appalled that I requested child support. She didn't feel it was fair. She ended up hiring an attorney that she knew as a family friend from her childhood.

When our court date came up in mid-June of 1987, her attorney asked to meet with me prior to our hearing. When I sat down with him, he laid out her demands which were some household items that were still in my possession at the house. She was requesting that child support be stricken from the divorce settlement, and she agreed to visitation with the children every other weekend. I demanded sole custody of the children with physical placement, and I stuck with my request for child support.

When our case was called before the judge, we went through the usual basic divorce proceedings, and when it came to the custody part, the judge granted me sole custody of my two children and child support, even though the amount of the support was quite low.

The day of the divorce, I had the children at my parents' house to avoid them having to endure more chaos and confusion. The plan was for my now ex-wife to come to my house after court to get her belongings. When I walked into the house after court, what had just transpired began to set in. I was now a divorcee. Divorce sounded so ugly and embarrassing to me, and I felt dirty and ashamed. I began to weep like a child. It felt so bad, yet so good, as I knew I needed to release all of the ill feelings of the past couple of years. I was as guilty in this situation as she, and I knew it.

When she arrived to get her belongings, I had as much as I could ready to go. She loaded her friend's car and came back in the house one last time to see if she had missed anything. As she was walking out the door, I stopped her and told her that I was very sorry for the way things turned out. I apologized for my part in the whole mess I helped create between us, and I again began to cry. She seemed to have no emotions in her response, but said that she, too, was sorry. Then she walked out the door never to return to this house.

When she drove off, I sat on the chair by the big picture window of our front room and gazed out at the leaves on the trees swaying in the wind. I reflected back on the previous few years and thought of what I could have done differently.

The reality of the situation was that it did happen, and there was no changing the past, but there was today in which I could work to make things better. The other truth was that here I was two years sober without even remembering how I had accomplished it. The chaos and distraction over those past two years seemed like somewhat of a blessing. I realized that those three young kids actually straightened me out for a long period of time. Then I thought of those three little faces looking to me for guidance in life, and I had no clue of what direction I was going day to day and even less idea how to show them guidance.

Bittersweet Changes

Over the next few months of my post-divorce blues, I spent as much time as I could with my kids, and I pretty much took them everywhere I went. I took them along to the step meetings I attended, and I even began to take them to work with me on side jobs, whenever possible.

My stepson had just turned six years old and began first grade at a local Catholic grade school just blocks from our house. He did well there. My parents helped tremendously with all three children, and with my stepson it was no different; they loved him as their own. However, not long after the divorce, my stepson's father moved back to Wisconsin from Colorado, and he arranged for his son, my stepson, to go live with him. That was a very sad time for all of the kids, my family, and me. Though it was heartbreaking, it was probably the best thing for my stepson and his father.

As the changes in our lives were happening plentifully and swiftly, I found that we just had to adjust, regardless of what happened. I found myself reciting the 'Serenity Prayer' to myself over and over, and many times I had to repeat it until it sunk in to the point where I was feeling it. I knew I had to keep my head about me or there would be consequences, and at this time in my life it was not only myself that was affected, but my two children as well.

I began to experience more and more signs of daily stress taking its toll on my nerves. 'Ordinary life' meant working on a daily basis, returning home to make dinner, and tending to the basic needs of my kids, and then it was was time for bed. And of course, it was only to wake up the next day and find that I had to repeat the same old shit. Even the word 'ordinary' seemed mundane and depressing.

The realization of what made me different than other people began to surface, and I could see that I had this part of me which would take a different thought process than the 'normal' person would. I noticed that when other people struggled with adversity in their lives, they could usually somehow find a path to the logical and rational part of their brain. With me the path was always somehow diverted to the dark corner of my mind. And when I opened the door to the dark corner of my mind, I found that the committee in my head, dormant to my conscious mind for so many years, was eagerly waiting to assist. I noticed that it had even gotten wiser throughout the years.

One day I was in one of those foul moods where any little hiccup would set me off almost to the point of rage. I got the crazy notion to go to one of those meetings just to vent, and I thought maybe I'd feel better. Something had to get me out of that funk I was in, and I couldn't use any drugs right yet. So, I got ahold of a neighbor who was also a single parent, and I asked her to watch the kids for an hour or so, to which she readily agreed.

As I was driving home from the meeting, something I heard someone at the meeting talk about kept popping up in my mind. An old timer mentioned that his wife would send him out to a meeting every time she saw he was getting grumpy. He said that by the time he got home from the meeting, he was in a better mood without fail, and this had been the way it had been going for over twenty-two years. I thought, "Twenty-two years, and you still come to these f****** things? I will not be going for any more than two years, if I have anything to say about it!"

When I returned from my meeting and grabbed the kids from my neighbor's house, we went home and watched RoboCop and laughed through the whole thing. As bedtime came for the kids, they went to sleep with smiles on their faces, and I went to my bedroom and lay down to relax. Then it dawned on me that nothing had changed in the events that were going on in my life except for the fact that I went to listen to a bunch of drunks and drug addicts babble. I thought back on what I heard in the meeting and realized that they weren't just babbling. They were not much different than I was—and here I thought I was so unique, and no one would ever know what I had gone through in my life, and what I was still going through after two-plus years of not drinking or drugging.

When I looked back on the last two-plus years, I could see that I may have just been white knuckling it. In other words, I felt like I may have just had so much going on with raising the kids and with my newfound conscious effort, that maybe the shame and guilt also played a big part of how I made it so long being clean. It wasn't news to me that I was clean though angry most of the time, and I started to understand what was meant by being 'just clean but not sober.' The 'Promises' part of the program said that it works sometimes quickly, and sometimes slowly, but that it WILL materialize if I work at it. "Well, let's just see," I thought. If the program does work as they say it does, and they PROMISE good things, then maybe humbling myself to be seen at one of these meetings may just be worth a few more tries.

Meanwhile, Back On the Street

One afternoon an old acquaintance from years past paid me a visit to catch up on old times. He had heard that I cleaned up and said that he just wanted to see how I was doing. Well, this was not your normal visit to just 'catch up.' It was what I would describe as an attempt to get me back in the drug game. He had a bottle of Dilaudid with him and said he saved a few just for me. There is that old saying that there is no such thing as a free lunch, and there is absolutely no drug addict without a strategy in mind when giving away free Dilaudid. It just doesn't happen without some ulterior motive, even it's just the old misery loves company thing.

I ended up declining the gift by saying that I had to take my kids to a family party, and that now wasn't the time, though I appreciated the offer. This wasn't the type of guy I could have easily thrown out of my house, so I did it as diplomatically as I could, and I told him I would call him sometime, which never happened. He died about three months later at age thirty-nine.

Without really realizing it, I had begun to think about what I had read in the 'Promises' which said, "You will intuitively know how to handle situations that used to baffle us." And I didn't know what possessed me to turn down free morphine, but it did happen.

I began to wonder if the wiring in my head was somehow channeled in a new way. Maybe I had been beaten into submission. Or maybe it was that I had been constantly reciting my daily prayers and meditation to the point that I had opened a channel to God. Either way, I made it through another day clean and sober.

Around this same time, I began to have some subtle reminders of just how deeply I had gone into the drug lifestyle I had been leading, or following, if you will. I had been occasionally running into people I knew from the streets, and some at my meetings. It always seemed like someone that I hadn't seen in years would just pop up. Within about three weeks of beginning to attend a new meeting, I would receive calls almost weekly from someone saying they heard I was around again. I made the mistake of putting my phone number on this call list and the info seemed to flow quickly and freely.

During this time I had attended three funerals in a matter of four weeks. All three were young males in their thirties, who were old friends of mine, and all three were drug overdoses. Each one of the funerals was crowded with old friends and acquaintances. At each one of them, I did my best to pay my respects to them and their immediate families, and then slip out the door. It just gave me too much chance of beginning to reminisce about old times and running the risk of gravitating back to visiting these old friends after the funerals, which wasn't good for me. And I knew it would be a trigger for me to relapse, as I proved numerous times in my past.

I remember dropping my kids off at my parents' house to finish a side job I had been doing for extra money. After a few hours I took a lunch break at a local restaurant, and while I was sitting by myself eating, I heard on the radio playing in the restaurant about a shooting that occurred on Milwaukee's north side. When they said the victim's name, I got the chills. It was my old friend Jerry. Jerry had been one of my closest friends for years, and hearing of his misfortune really hit me hard.

That same night I called the hospital to get his condition and found that he had been shot in the stomach. Instead of going to one of my meetings that evening, I went instead to visit Jerry. He was in bad shape. It sounded like this was a major life threatening situation, and his life would now be different as a result of his injuries.

It was only about a month later while I was driving in my car with the kids, I heard on the radio that law enforcement officials had been investigating the disappearance of large amounts of pharmaceutical cocaine and morphine from a major local hospital. I thought about just how crazy of a lifestyle I had been living, and even more, just how fortunate I was to have made some positive steps in the right direction.

CHAPTER NINETEEN

My Heroes and Mentors

As the days, weeks, months, and years passed in my everyday struggles with life, I began to see just how smart my mother and father had become over those years. It seemed that they had finally wised up and begun to make sense. And though it took many years and a lot of hard work for me to get them to that point, I think I succeeded. When I mentioned this little joke to my father, he just laughed and told me that I should go take a powder. That was his old response to us as kids when he thought we were full of shit.

My life had progressively become much different and better in so many ways, though I must admit it was continually difficult to raise children, work, stay clean, and learn how to live with and around other 'normal' people. This whole experience made me appreciate the many single mothers I knew, and it helped me to better understand the struggles and sacrifice that so many of these single parent homes endured. I also saw the two parent homes with many of the same struggles—not to mention the fact that they also sometimes struggle keeping a healthy marriage along with raising the children. Either way, living life on life's terms is a tall order.

For me, I had a very difficult time just keeping my head about me for a few minutes at a time, much less trying to show the children guidance on how to live. I had absolutely no clue on how to proceed other than to act as if, and to do my best to pretend that I knew where I was going in life. I also found myself using every bit of knowledge I learned from parenting books, as well as heeding the advice of the many older and wiser people I confided in. As time went on, I asked

Dark Corner of the Mind

many questions of people whom I saw as successful in their own lives—people whom I viewed as having healthy and successful families and careers. To be honest, I had nothing else to go on, since I had spent the better part of my life so wrapped up in my own selfish needs.

During this period of my life I continued to slide into church basements to steal some spiritual food from the many people who also attended the twelve-step meetings. I would take what I heard from people who had come back from slipping into drinking and drugging, so as to remember where I had been, and I stole some of the wisdom from the many longtime sober and successful members. It gave me direction on my journey ahead.

I also found myself observing the neighborhood people that stood out to me as healthy and happy families. I wanted so badly to know what went on in their lives that led to the richness and success that they seemed to have instilled in their families. It was always so promising to see the joy that seemed to exude from these people in their everyday contact with the outside world. In observing these families, I found it not only encouraging but almost contagious.

Over the years, there was one person who stood out among the many who always seemed to be at my side for moral support. This man was always a phone call away, and I relied on him for both moral support and spiritual guidance. That man was, and still is, my good friend Pastor George. He was the man who was there for me in times of uncertainty in my life, as well as in my days of joy and success. George didn't react any differently to me regardless of my situation. He never, ever turned his back on me; he just always just encouraged me to learn from my mistakes and to take pride in my success. In a sense, I virtually carry this guy with me to every challenge I face, and every success I enjoy in life.

There were many other people I looked to for guidance and who served as role models for me. Certainly, one person who came to mind for me was my good old childhood idol, 'Hammering' Hank Aaron. As a young child growing up watching Hank, he was my baseball hero, and I dreamed of having his baseball card. I am still in awe of his baseball contributions. But, later I took the time to study Henry Aaron's life outside of baseball, and I learned about his struggles with the everyday reality of life off the field.

Now, as I read the stories of Henry, the man, and watch his interviews, I am even more impressed than I was with his on-field accomplishments. This was and still is a very humble man with top notch class, who seems to carry himself as an equal to every other human being walking the earth, and not as the 'giant' of his reality. Both baseball Hank and the man Henry are still now, and always will be, my heroes. Both of them!

There were so many heroes in my life, and God knows I needed them all. It was probably my mother and father who were the ultimate heroes in my life, mainly because of the fact that they put up with me through my many years of destructive behavior. They stuck by me through it all, always with subtle hints about God or the twelve steps, and frequent mention of success stories of programs for people who were thought to be lost causes.

I can say now, with thirty years of sobriety, the most important things in my life that led to my success are my GOD, my family, and my very good friends. If not for all three of these, I surely wouldn't have found the steps to sobriety, the unadulterated way of love for other people, and the peace and serenity that cannot be measured against anything else in life.

Real or Fantasy

I discovered early in my life that I would need to decide for myself what was real and what was not. For example, I was taught at an early age that there were these two guys who would play a big part of my life. The first one was this big fat white guy with a big white beard. This guy would come to everyone's house on the night of December 24th and bring presents for everyone. But, throughout the year, he would have some guys watching your every move. And if you were naughty, he would know. Then, you were told, you wouldn't get shit. You would never really see this guy, but you were told "just believe." Then, at about the age of ten years old, you find out he was nothing but a big fake. It was just a big lie to get you to be a good kid.

Then I'm told there is this other big fat white guy, with a big white beard who is watching us. And I'm assured that this one is real. You never see him, but you're told that you have to "Just believe." This guy also has guys watching us. They were called Angels. And if you're bad, he WILL KNOW! Then you'll go to a place called hell and be punished for eternity.

Now, I do believe there is a definite power greater than myself. I know this in my heart! But, what I'm not real sure about is this: that there is this big fat white guy with a big white beard, who sits above the clouds and watches us. What I do believe is that there is a God, regardless of what one would call it, it is . . . Good Orderly Direction.

With all the different religions in the world, who is to say which is the 'One true' religion? For so long, I somehow didn't see all the insanity of my drug use as a problem, probably because I never knew how much it affected me, my mother, father, and the rest of our family—until, of course, there was a trail of destruction behind me. As I now relive this history of the human condition within me and our family, I do realize that every human being has their limitations. And the thing is, many of us 'enjoy,' if you will, beyond our limitations— without knowledge, or despite the knowledge. Either way, a person who crosses their limitations, has something that is called a flaw. That flaw can be defined in many ways. It can be sheer recklessness, due to life's overwhelming day-to-day problems. Or it can be due to enjoying too much. For some of us, enjoying too much is never enough.

But, the thing to remember is this: Life, if lived right, with God, or G.O.D.—Good Orderly Direction—IS the best feeling that can live forever. Hands down. It is a fact, it brings with it true friends, family, and love of life.

With alcohol or drugs, there are some of us that find that one is too many and thousand never enough. There doesn't seem to be anything that can fill that black hole. In my case, it may just be that alcohol, drugs, or anything that I enjoy, have not ever been enough. This flaw can simply be called an obsession. But then again, it can be called a disease.

After many years of living on the dark side, I believe my innate human instincts took over, because common sense sure as hell wasn't cutting it. And what I mean is that I needed to follow my gut, instead of letting my common everyday intellect make the decisions for me. While dealing with some very cunning and unscrupulous people (and having become one myself), and because of my extremely poor decision making, my own survival instinct as the only safe option before me, and in order to survive, I definitely needed to follow it.

It seems that the chemistry in one's self is altered by the environment it is in. I truly believe that my intuition and instinct had become the guide in my decision making. I had for years been dealing with people who were living a treacherous lifestyle of deceit, danger, and self-destructive behavior. It seems that the mind and soul gradually adapt to the survival instinct as opposed to the ordinary everyday life. In that survival mode, life becomes an everyday walk on eggshells.

Complete abstinence from all mind altering drugs is a necessity (unless of course, a physician orders otherwise) for a minimum period of at least two years, unless you're like me. If you're like me, it's a lifelong commitment, one day at a time, and sometimes it can be a moment at a time. It's a tall task, but it can be accomplished with the drive to work at it daily. Growing old is mandatory, but growing up emotionally, spiritually, and rationally, is optional. You have to decide for yourself if you really want to avoid repeating the same old mistakes over and over, with the same results, or worse. So, you can decide if you want to grow to be an old junkie, or to grow to be a stand-up person of integrity.

It's a Hard Knock Life

A few things can definitely challenge a recovering addict's moxie. When you are actually committed to getting clean, staying clean, and living clean, you may just find that the real world punches you in the nose. It may make you feel like you've been hit in the face with a big brick and your teeth have been smashed out. I don't say this as a warning, but rather as a wakeup call to expect the unexpected from other human beings. It's just the human condition.

You can be living a life of complete sobriety, living life as you may picture a person of the utmost integrity and kindness toward your fellow man. But you need to remember that perception is reality! The perception of many people out in this world may be very shallow and black and white. Some people view anyone who hasn't lived their entire life walking the straight and narrow as just plain defective. Then, the wall goes up. Just try to keep in mind that old saying "Judgment is what defeats us."

If you let yourself be judged by your past, while you are no longer living that lifestyle, then you are letting the evil of your past stay alive, and it may tear away every shred of good and decent progress you've made. We all have our skeletons, so let them lie in that graveyard of your past. When you've cleaned up your act and have been truly living a standup life, that skeleton has no part of your soul, unless you allow it. It's dead!

I have personally found that the people-pleasing part of me, which has been very prevalent throughout my life, has taken me to depths I never want to be in ever again. It does rear its ugly head from time to time, but I know I need to move beyond that graveyard. Let it rather, be a deterrent in those urges, which will come, I promise you.

For this addict, I seemed to approach recovery very much the way I pursued heroin. I would lie, cheat, and steal to get what I wanted. It required much soul searching and thorough revamping of my impulsive approach in relationships. It is uncanny that the behavior patterns I gravitated toward in my heroin pursuit carried over into my post heroin endeavors, including relationships. The target of my affection in relationships most times, has been a person who seems to possess a trait I am lacking.

If the devil were to be fishing for our lives, heroin might just be the most effective bait. It is easily the most luring to a young idle mind. It will pull you in with promises of pure gold to the soul, and it will devour you in an instant. If this stuff doesn't kill you, it will destroy your soul. It will at the very least, turn one to the criminal world. I don't care who you are. Rich and strong, or weak and poor, it doesn't discriminate, I can assure you, and you will become dishonest. You will find yourself to be as dishonest and manipulating as any person could be, bar none. It could turn a Catholic nun into a filthy whore in a matter of no time. My mother would definitely scold me for using such an analogy, however, it is to make my point that this drug is cunning and baffling.

I will never be a saint, but I refuse to beat myself up and fall into the mistake of dragging all the guilt of my past along my way into the future. This type of thought process will render you helpless and hopeless when you try to move forward into a productive lifestyle. That dark corner of your mind will remind you that you are indeed a complete loser.

There are numerous ways to recover from the wreckage of this type of past. For some there is the 'White Knuckle' process. This is where a person just says enough is enough, and elevates their life by putting on blinders, getting a job, and doing the best they can to become a productive part of society. There are some that choose the 'Bible Solution' in which they read the Bible, follow it the best they can, and try to be the best person they can be. There are some that are put into a situation beyond their control, and are locked up in prison, though these people still have options to get them through life without drugs and alcohol.

There are also others who find sobriety and sanity through twelve-step programs. I myself . . . have chosen all roads. I do my best by, first and foremost seeking the truth and guidance of my GOD, or Higher power. And I have also chosen a twelve-step program which I find to be a 'Recipe for Life.' For me, this is my recipe—for other people, there are other directions to achieve serenity and peace. And, I have many times white knuckled, which is one difficult way to live! However, if it gets me to the next day clean and sober, it worked!

I'd Love to Change the World

Looking back at my personal experience with heroin, I realize this one very crucial thing. That one thing is, that any young person, or any adult for that matter, who has troubling times with life and has any exposure to drugs, is vulnerable to heroin's trap. Heroin is a death trap. Especially in the case of a wounded soul, heroin will make itself out to be the one salvation. And in the process, it will steal your heart and your soul, and it will destroy any personal relationship in its path.

It seems many people hit their bottom with drugs or alcohol, and they quit because it's bottom. But for others the bottom may be death. For me, I just may be one of those unfortunate individuals with a bottomless addiction. Maybe I just had too thick of a skull. My father would have called it "Stunade" (pronounced stoo nod)—stupid. And maybe I also had some 'Stupid Luck.' How many people would be fortunate enough to survive hepatitis, endocarditis, and three or four broken needles floating in their extremities?

If I were able to turn back time and visit myself as the reckless teenager I was, I'd take that young boy in me, and slap the shit out of him! Believe this: if there is a youngster with self-esteem issues, lack of direction, history of family abuse, or any other troubling issues at hand, all it takes is one shot of heroin to alter his life forever. I would suggest to parents that they encourage children to keep a journal as soon as they can put words into sentences. This promotes reading, writing, and self-awareness.

Another deterrent to steer young people away from using heroin and other drugs, or any other destructive behaviors, is to keep them talking. A wise old woman once told me that if you can talk with your teenagers daily, you will intuitively know where they are in life. It's that simple, though I do know it is easy to overlook things because of the speed life moves nowadays for our youth.

I can say this: We all have a dark corner of the mind. We were just born that way. There is an old line from the movie 'Godfather' that comes to mind for me in raising teenagers. "Keep your friends close, and your enemies closer." As crazy as this sounds, what I am referring to here is that with teenagers, I see keeping the child in your loved one close, and that dark corner of their mind, closer. An intuitive bond with teenagers is a must! That bond is something that is developed over a period of time with our offspring. It requires time, patience, and much understanding of what drives them. When we understand what drives the child within them, we can more easily see pitfalls that could destroy them. There are things such as the negative inner voices that say, "I can't do it. I'm not good enough. What if I fail? I don't deserve it." And with some people, there are the overconfident voices: "I need more. I'm better than them. I'm the best, rather than I'm the best I can be."

It is true that what you are told you are, as a developing human being, is what you believe you are. The old saying I love most is one that I learned in a part of the morning prayer I was required to repeat every day while I was in the therapeutic community program. It says: "We are not the giant of our dreams, nor the dwarf of our fears, BUT. . . a human being, a part of a whole, with our share in its purpose." I'm not sure there is a better outlook to remind a person that we are all good enough, none is better, and we're all in this world together, regardless of ethnicity, religion, gender, physical makeup, or financial status.

I've personally experienced the devastating toll that heroin takes in one's life. And, probably more importantly, I have learned the toll it takes on the people in the user's life. It will steal the life out of any relationship and break down the family of anyone who uses it.

It seems the dark corner of my mind could be held at bay—cleansed and infiltrated with hope, confidence, and reassurance. It didn't become dark overnight, so patience and hard spiritual work over time are the keys to bring light to it. I make it a consistent habit to attend twelve-step meetings in church basements, and I make it another habit to remember at least one thing from each meeting that strikes a chord with me. It could come from a person who is a newcomer to these meetings with only twenty-four hours of sobriety or from another that has been sober for decades.

Whether it's a CEO of a large corporation, a doctor, lawyer or just a plain old bum off the street like myself, we are all equal in these meetings. I never come away from these gatherings without a bit of wisdom that I lacked an hour earlier. And I take this wisdom to my pillow with me every night, and God willing, I live to see another day. The great thing about it is, though it may not turn out to be a smooth and glorious day, I am, just the same, extremely grateful that I am above dirt and able to make it a day that I remember what I did.

Make no mistake about it—I still have good days, bad days, and horrible days. Just ask my kids! I have gone through periods in my life, and from time to time still do, becoming so wound up inside that I am unbearable to live with. It seems that these are the periods of my life that I am trying to white knuckle my way through. It's when I believe I can fix everything myself, I become extremely self-righteous, and I seem to find those stupid meetings an imposition on my valuable time. But, the reality of it all sets in when I find myself hearing people close to me mention that I am hard to live with. And my likely response is, "Don't live with me then." That is probably not a viable solution.

A moment of clarity and a sense of reality came to me one day when I overheard my teenage kids refer to me as the 'Christmas Prick.' Well, I guess I get a bit crabby during some holidays. The point is that during these periods when I become unraveled and unbearable to be around, it is generally a telltale sign that I need more meetings. I still don't know exactly how they work, but I do know that when I do go, I find that I can not only adjust my attitude and outlook on life, but I can laugh at myself as well. Then, the 'Christmas Prick' can go to his corner and wait for another day to make an appearance.

In reality, I probably could find a different way to abstain from drinking and using drugs. But I have found that, though my life isn't perfect, it's a whole lot better when I slide into a church basement more often. Then I seem to find I'm actually enjoying my moments in life, not trying to rush past them, plus I'm a whole lot easier to live with.

For me, the most exhilarating feeling I have nowadays is walking outside on a clear summer morning just before sunrise with the birds beginning to sing their song for the day, the thought of all of my loved ones still enjoying the breath of life while sleeping soundly, and the very thought that I have been blessed to see another day.

In closing, I must say again, using that old phrase my father used many times, live with God's guidance. Or, if you are someone who is not real sure what you believe in, G.O.D. can still be your guide. Good Orderly Direction. By taking either path, you may just end up in the same place.

Now if this story can possibly make at least one person laugh, I'm happy to have amused them. If it could help plant a seed in one parent's mind to take a second look, or pay more attention to the direction their offspring are going, I'd feel fulfilled. If this tale could deter just one youth from the hell that exists in experimenting with the garbage, I'd be so very grateful. If my story could assist in cutting short an addiction by moving someone to take heed of a twelve-step program, I would be delighted. If it could help steer a family back together by better understanding the insanity of the disease, I would feel successful. If my story made you cry, grow the f*** up. And if you just didn't care for it . . . then go f*** yourself.

Okay, I didn't really mean the last two, it's just who the f*** I am.

In all sincerity, I do know that some, or even many, people may find my story repulsive or even iniquitous. However, it is a story that was me, is for some other suffering souls, and may be in the future of someone you know and love.

And for anyone at all in this world of ours, searching for who or what GOD is while here in existence, let them find Him now!

Acknowledgments

Many thanks to Marsha and Lee Rossiter of Rossiter Editing Services for the best editing skills available. And to Kira Henschel of Henschel-HAUS Publishing, Inc. for the encouragement and guidance.

To Contact the Author

Email: Anonimo.anthony@gmail.com (Any contact is welcome)

Facebook: Anthony Anonimo

CPSIA information can be obtained
at www.ICGtesting.com
Printed in the USA
BVHW04s1456171018
530368BV00011B/258/P